AF763329

HOTEL MANAGEMENT-
PRINCIPLES AND GUIDELINES

HOTEL MANAGEMENT-
PRINCIPLES AND GUIDELINES

M. C. METTI

ANMOL PUBLICATIONS PVT. LTD.
NEW DELHI - 110 002 (INDIA)

ANMOL PUBLICATIONS PVT. LTD.

H.O.: 4374/4B, Ansari Road, Darya Ganj,
New Delhi-110 002 (India)
Ph.: 23278000, 23261597

B.O.: No. 1015, Ist Main Road, BSK IIIrd Stage
IIIrd Phase, IIIrd Block
Bangalore - 560 085 (India)
Visit us at: www.anmolpublications.com

Hotel Management- Principles and Guidelines
© 2008
ISBN 978-81-261-3230-0

PRINTED IN INDIA

Printed at Mehra Offset Press, Delhi.

Contents

	Preface	*vii*
1.	Comparative International Principles of Hospitality	1
2.	The Failure of Hotels	31
3.	Guidelines of Employment in the Hotel Sector	84
4.	Hotel Way of Life	137
5.	Compensation Trends in Hotels	181
6.	Guidelines for Foreign Investment	213
7.	Process and Personalities	248
	Index	277

Preface

There are many crucial elements involved in the successful operation of a hotel and show their interrelationships. In providing "meal experience," the hotel manager brings together three elements: customers, the operation (consisting of food and beverage items as well as the physical facility), and employees. The operator's task is to manage these elements to produce satisfied customers.

The detailed of hotel industry is being discussed inside while looking at the major factors affecting the growth of the business and considering the factors that make the difference between success and failure in running hotels. The first of the three elements of the meal experience: the customer.

The eating habits of the various segments of the market are described and the major trends in customer behaviour that affect the business are identified. How to develop a marketing plan to attract one or more of the segments is also identified. The importance of promotion as a marketing tool is recognized inside. The major sanitation problems faced by restaurant managers are identified and procedures developed for preventing foodborne diseases.

A programme to build effective employee habits is presented. The legal environment within which managers must operate is described and the steps involved in staffing the operation are noted and guidelines given on how to improve the quality of employees selected. The design of effective orientation, training, and development programmes is covered together with tips on how to develop the skills necessary to be an effective trainer.

Author

Chapter 1

Comparative International Principles of Hospitality

INTERNATIONAL THEMES

The Hospitality Compensation Exchange has been conducted in the United States since 1996, and has successfully established itself as the largest industry forum for the exchange of compensation information for the hospitality sector in the United States. In India, there are undertaking this effort for the first time. You may recall that, in last yeaı's, a study of compensation trends, but on a significantly smaller scale than the HCE Survey had started. The Survey is intended to be a one-stop reference for current and credible information on remuneration patterns, including benefits and bonuses.

Information contained will act as a useful tool, for hotel owners and operators, to assist them in attracting and retaining managerial talent through equitable compensation practices. Hospitality employment is important to very many countries across the globe. Although the influence of large MNCs is spreading, most employment is in small, independent enterprises. Much work is unpaid or low-paid. There is heavy reliance on females and young labour and, in some countries, on migrants. Most work is regarded as semi-skilled or unskilled, and there has been some deskilling. Training is often basic, with firms tending to buy in skills from the labour market. The HCTS also manifests different occupational categories compared to other private services.

Many workers engage directly with customers, while others whose work is still geared towards providing good customer service have a more indirect customer relationship, necessitating us to acknowledge that the employment relationship is triadic. Part-time and atypical employment is common, and may be increasing amid countries' desire to create more flexible labour markets.

The labour force is highly mobile, often with a short-term orientation to the HCTS, generating high labour turnover and leaver rates. Recruitment and retention is particularly problematic, particularly for managers where a lack of professionalism may impede business success in developing and transitional economies.

These characteristics, in combination with the fact that most workers are not trade union members, constitute what might be termed 'vulnerable' employment. Hence it is not surprising to find regulation of the employment relationship is of global concern in areas such as minimum wages, equal pay and working time. However, wide recognition is given to lower minimum rates for young workers, and unequal pay persists, reinforcing the importance of women and young people as cheap labour.

Different economic, social, legal and political factors create particular cultures and a variety of employment systems, even within the same region. Hence considerable variation of regulatory regimes remains within EU countries that are ostensibly subject to the same broad employment standards. Some countries have well-developed and relatively comprehensive systems of VET and collective bargaining arrangements.

Where union membership is low, more complete coverage may be secured by extending collective agreements to all workers by government decree. The drive for flexibility and the deregulation of labour markets stands at odds with increased regulation of employment. Cultural barriers may prevent the wider application of measures to combat discrimination. New work organization may be especially challenging in transitional countries in Central and Eastern Europe. Global changes have contributed to economic uncertainty and a more turbulent market, creating new sets of challenges for managers.

Management style is influenced by constraints and choices related to product and labour markets, organizational status and structure, size of workplace and culture. While managers' personal frame of reference influences choice, managers are most likely to place high priority on seeking to control labour costs, and have little incentive to take the 'high road' to employment.

Although we have been able to use data from 50 countries, a limitation is that most research is western-centric and drawn from 'Anglo' countries. This provides a clearer, if only partial, view of key employment relations issues in the US, Australia and New Zealand, which may have parallels in the UK. We have some information about the positive and negative influence of MNCs on employment practices in hotels, restaurants, fast food and contract catering in host countries, while hotels in the transitional Slovakian economy offer a corollary as they are still immune from international influence. More examples from Africa and Latin America would have been interesting and useful.

Managerial Evidence

WERS reaffirms that employment relations in the British HI are unequivocally different from AIS and the PSS across a wide range of employment practices, one explicit dimension of a psychological contract. Many features of global application also characterize the British HI as 'vulnerable' employment. More specific workplace practices of disadvantage include pay, how it is determined and conditions of employment.

HI employees have less access to family-friendly measures, comprehensive induction and training, performance appraisal and a healthy and safe environment. Disciplinary sanctions are more commonplace. On the positive side there is also less use of grievance procedures, although this could signify fear rather than contentment and more IiP accreditation. The balance of evidence overwhelmingly points to the 'bleak house' and 'black hole' scenarios.

Employment relations are an important part of managerial work, where decisions are most likely to be concentrated in the hands of one or two managers in the absence of specialist internal and external advice. The extent of unionization is marginal, and not compensated by other means of consultation. Managers probably hold negative views about unions. Even though managers would rather consult with employees than with unions, they do neither. The 'unbridled individualism' thesis developed from WIRS3 seems to be reaffirmed by the WERS management evidence. Managers transact the employment relationship from a unitary perspective.

In assessing the management evidence on its own, we must remind ourselves that three-quarters of HI workplaces are multi-site, and include some very large employers. Strong strategic integration is suggested. HI workplaces are much more cost-conscious and work on a lower wage cost: sales ratio. While a strong proprietorial and family effect is also evident, in most cases this is about control of a large organization, not a stereotypical single site family business.

Most of the very small workplaces employing 10 to 24 employees included for the first time in WERS are chain pubs. WERS is most likely to convey a big organization picture of employment relations and is less helpful in providing particular insights into the practices of small, independent operators. This form of employment relations is most likely to be discernible in small workplaces employing between 25 and 49 employees.

The clear implication is that big firms are not necessarily good firms, where employment policies and practices in HI workplaces within a cost-control framework continue to contradict the conventional notion 'good' employment relations. This is supported by the findings of most other UK studies, although some clearly provide evidence of 'better' practice that is more relational.

While WERS provides considerable support for a cost-control 'low road' and transactional approach to employment relations throughout the HI, it does not detail or explain managerial rationale or motive. It is argued that outcomes such as the lack of representation, consultation and grievances are likely to be a function of managers working in close proximity with employees with whom close personal bonds develop where customers are ever present.

This leads to a relationship of affiliation based on shared understanding of the importance of providing good customer service and 'mucking in' together. The suggestion of affiliation fraternalism) is well established within the management literature, but does not necessarily imply unitarism because 'liberal' managers may still recognize difference among employees as a whole.

Employee Evidence

The employee survey appears to throw up some contradictions. In spite of demonstrably 'poor' employment policies and practices, HI employees are remarkably positive about their work, workplace, organization and their relationship to them, more so than their counterparts in AIS and the PSS. They are more satisfied with the way they are treated by their managers. Pay is the only area of notable dissent. Employees are largely isolated from any trade union presence, contact or activity. They feel informed enough, considering themselves well able to look after themselves in transactions with their managers about employment issues.

Undoubtedly a number of these observations can be linked to employee and job characteristics, including age, part-time hours and short service. They must also link to the highly interpersonal nature of customer-service employment relationships, providing further support for affiliation. This creates a unity of understanding towards customer service if not a unity of economic interest. Employees who believe their future is in their own destiny and concur with their managers that employment relations are good cannot be said to be masochistic or powerless. There is neither a need to question their situation nor a need to resist it. These employees can be said to espouse 'enfranchised realism' built upon a trade-off between low pay and other factors. 'Resigned realism' might be more appropriate for those who are relatively powerless, while others may suffer real exploitation.

Even more striking is the finding that in a number of respects HI employees are indeed different from employees in the rest of the PSS, when characteristics including age, length of service, pay, size of workplace and type of organization are controlled for. This suggestion in a customer-service context is not new, but now more convincingly demonstrated across a larger sample of employees working in all sub-sectors of the HI. Importantly there is now more compelling evidence to suggest that trade unions face an even more daunting task in attempting to recruit members and organize HI workplaces.

Customers and Gender

Customers are an important influence on employment relations in the HI, and often interrelate with gender where the issue is women's rather than men's disadvantage. Managing and experiencing the service encounter are important facets of an employment relationship that hinges upon a socio-economic exchange, not simply an economic nexus around the price of labour.

The social composition of service work is part of the product, which managers see as a legitimate area for intervention. The locus of managerial control extends beyond workers' behaviour to include emotions, speech and appearance. Labour may be manufactured to appeal to customers, particularly males, and internalize customer prejudices. Female labour may be sexualized, requiring workers to flirt or suffer harassment to earn tips.

These are barriers to women's equality, and may reflect that social attitudes have moved more slowly than legal requirements. Workers respond by developing coping strategies. Alternatively customer-service work may also be highly rewarding and contribute to high levels of job satisfaction among some workers. To some job flirt may simply be an individual response of using one's skills to best effect and be a highly empowering experience, which stands at odds with notions of desexualized labour and equality.

Customers are also unpredictable and their unsatisfactory behaviour may impact on managers and workers. Where customers are drawn into managerial control strategies, e.g. high reliance on tips, employees will suffer stress if tips are non-existent or derisory or they have to draw upon behaviours that do not come naturally. Customer/guest information used to guide hiring, performance assessment for pay or other purposes, including training needs, promotion, discipline and dismissal, may be unreliable, including an unwillingness by customers to testify in formal proceedings, e.g. employment tribunals.

While there is evidence that HI employees are more likely to work in more gender-equal workplaces, some management practices are clearly not gender-neutral. Women's work may be defined as unskilled to keep costs low. The use of proxy measures in appraisal, e.g. 'being there', may penalize women working part time. There is also some evidence that trade unions have not always served women's interests well. Assumptions of women's lower commitment may shape the core-periphery and determine which jobs are full-time or part-time, with the latter receiving less favourable terms and conditions. Cost-cutting underpins job segregation.

The same assumptions can also be applied to young workers, affecting men and women alike. Labour markets perpetuate gender segregation where collective bargaining is more likely to benefit men, decentralized pay increases the probability of low pay and minimum wage systems treat young workers less favourably. It remains to be seen how far new legislation will enable these gaps to be closed. More studies are needed that take a perspective that embeds customers, gender and youth within the analysis of employment relations in the HI.

Continuity and Change

Continuity is provided by the bulk of managerial evidence but, importantly, change is heralded by employee evidence enabling us to reassess the state of employment relations in the HI. To do so inevitably runs the risk of oversimplification, as there are undoubtedly many types of employment relationship in many different contexts. WERS does not probe issues that have particular relevance to a triadic employment relationship based on close individual bonds between managers and workers within a customer-service ethos.

Overall management's approach is highly cost-control-driven, which inevitably results in particular outcomes, including low pay, flexible employment and hire and fire. Whether these outcomes are necessarily 'good' or 'bad' is a moot point. Not all managers deliberately set out to exploit their workers. Many are not unreasonable people, although some are bullies and exploit power unreasonably. Rather, most are faced with making difficult choices within the constraints of their own spheres of influence.

One might argue that the choices of an owner-manager of a small firm operating in a tight market are more constrained than the choices of the HR director of large, profitable chain. This might excuse relatively 'poor' policies and practices in a boarding house. The broad picture of British employment relations portrays a larger-firm view, where, arguably, more profitable employers could and should do better.

Yet most hospitality employees do not see themselves as a bunch of losers in the face of overbearing, unfair or unreasonable managers. Their work and employment expectations are not unrealistic, and are largely met where low pay is traded off against other factors in a customer-service employment relationship that can be high trust and positive.

Most believe they have control of their own destinies, and have little incentive to seek trade union protection. Others are more powerless and even though they can move on, some may become locked in a cycle of low trust exploitative employment relationships. For some customer-service work is highly rewarding. For others it is undoubtedly less so, threatening the unity of purpose where they are unable to provide good service to awkward customers.

We can now state with greater certainty that the metaphors of 'bleak house' (management evidence) and 'black hole' (employee evidence) are wanting. Both are based on only one side of a story that is much more complex employment relationship that is rather different from Edwards' employer-employee relationship mediated by trade unions or employee representatives and the state.

The locus is a function of dimensions related to three sets of actors within particular types of work, and also embodies explicit gender and implied youth perspectives. This allows for a variety of employment relationships in the HI, which are an outcome of the dimensions mediated by the state. The omission of any reference to collectivism and representation is made somewhat reluctantly, but as its possibility is so very marginal its inclusion across some dimensions would arguably detract from the reality of employment relations in the HI

Dimensions of a Socio-economic Customer-service Employment Relationship

Managem ent

- Affiliated, liberal individualism
- Unbridled individualism
- Determined opportunism
- Fair cost-control employment policies and practices
- Exploitative cost-control employment policies and practices

Workers

- Enfranchised realism
- Resigned realism
- Exploitation
- Relational psychological contract
- Transactional psychological contract

Customers

- Direct interface
- Indirect effect
- Rewarding, predictable and satisfied
- Awkward, unpredictable and dissatisfied

Work

- Gender neutral
- Gendered
- Satisfying and empowering
- Dissatisfying and exploitative
- High trust
- Low trust

Future Prospects

Relative consensus between managers and employees does not imply employment relations are not in need of reform. There are no easy solutions, particularly if we extend reform to include customers, and this requires further consideration, so we stick to conventional prescriptions for the time being. If we assume that trade unions and systems of employee representation are never to become a force in the HI, then we have to look to the state. The first possibility is alternative collective measures that will serve the interests of small firms.

One obvious route would be to reappraise the notion of legally enforceable state-sponsored collective bargaining on an industry basis. This would take account of particular industries' needs, in effect a more sophisticated and comprehensive version of the wages councils. Similar arrangements already operate outside Britain, but do not necessarily place hospitality workers at a much higher point in the earnings distribution. Such collective agreements would provide a bigger safety net than the NMW, which should be retained for its simplicity, and could create a sense of collective responsibility and awareness. The second possibility is that an extension of employment rights to workers would also provide greater protection for 'vulnerable' hospitality workers currently excluded from rights, such as unfair dismissal. In the current climate the latter option looks the most realistic, but may be slow in coming.

A New Approach

The data presented and discussed in this book offer a distinct and different perspective from the main primary analysis of WERS. Cully *et al.*(1999) discuss very small workplaces (10-24 employees) in a separate chapter, and do not integrate them within their overall analysis. Here the full data set inclusive of these workplaces is used. This gives a more comprehensive account of employment relations in AIS, the PSS and, especially, the HI, as these small workplaces comprise 61 per cent of the HI sample within WERS.

The inclusion in WERS of an employee survey for the first time is important because we gain a more balanced perspective of employment relations within the same workplaces, and can create a more detailed picture of employees' working lives. The main issues explored are what employees think about their job, about working at their workplace, and how they are represented at work. Three main sources of data have been used in preparing this:

- Specified output from the management questionnaire;
- All output from the employee questionnaire;
- Verbatim responses from the employee questionnaire.

No use could be made of the worker representative questionnaire due to the low incidence of unionization in the HI or the panel survey because of the small number of cases.

Appropriate questions in the *management questionnaire* were identified, where possible with a view to achieving consistency with WIRS3 data.

The main areas omitted were in relation to aspects of representation at work and collective bargaining, because of the marginal influence of trade unions within the HI. On the basis of the author's requirements, NIESR staff created the necessary variables and produced the statistical output. Selected frequency output is presented in this book to serve two main purposes:

- To compare and contrast the HI (N = 121) with AIS (N = 2,191) and the PSS (N = 1,218);
- To enable closer inspection of differences within the HI by size of workplace and sub-sector.

No question selection was necessary for the *employee questionnaires*, where all of the data collected in the survey proved relevant. The responses for the HI (N = 1,077), AIS (N = 28,215) and the PSS (N = 14,412) are presented in the same format as the management survey results. It should be noted that the AIS and PSS samples both include the HI.

Subsequently permission was obtained via the WERS User Sub-committee to access restricted data in the form of *employee verbatim responses* from the employee questionnaire. Question D12 asked 'Do you have any final comments you would like to make about your workplace, or about this questionnaire?'. Comments were provided voluntarily by a sub-set of respondents.

We present these qualitative responses for HI employees only (N = 338), which represent 30 per cent of all HI employees who responded to the survey. We can identify each response by workplace size, industry sub-sector, gender, age group, occupational group, contract status, weekly hours (including overtime), whether part of a larger organization, and the percentage of the workforce that are female and part-time (identifying characteristics).

Data Analysis

The relatively small sample size of the HI *management questionnaire* responses effectively rules out the use of statistical refinements beyond simple frequencies. Tests of significance (at the 5 per cent level) are restricted to a comparison of the HI with AIS and the PSS in all tables for purposes of simplicity and clarity. These tests are calculated using the unweighted bases. Simple frequencies are also presented for the *employee questionnaire*. Tests of significance (at the 5 per cent level) are made on the same basis as the management questionnaire, using the unweighted bases.

Additionally some multivariate analysis has been used to determine whether HI employees are more or less likely than employees in the rest of the PSS to demonstrate particular views or characteristics. The particular outcomes that have been tested in this way are contained in (employees' views about their job), 8.12 (employees' views about the organization), 8.17 (how good are managers), and 8.20, 8.22 and 8.26 (trade union membership and representation).

The multivariate analysis takes on a different form from all the other analysis because hospitality employees have been removed from private services, so that each of the samples tested is discrete. Regressions automatically test at all levels of statistical significance (1, 5 and 10 per cent), but we do not report the full details here. Results that are significant at the 5 per cent level are noted briefly in the text. The multivariate analysis takes the form of a series of probit regression models in which dichotomous variables representing particular outcomes are regressed upon a number of control variables. These control variables comprise:

- Each of the eight variables relating to employee characteristics contained in Tables 8.1 and 8.2;
- Six of the variables relating to job characteristics contained excluding the occupational group (personal and protective services);

- A dummy variable indicating employees working in single, independent establishments;
- Five dummy variables to control for establishment-size effects;
- A dummy variable identifying employees in the HI.

The interest is focused on the hospitality dummy, which indicates whether the specified outcome is any more or less likely among HI employees than among other PSS employees after controlling for the other characteristics included in the model.

Table: The Management Sample in Context, by size of Workplace and Sub-sector (Number of Cases)

	AIS	PSS	HI	<25 employee	25-49 employee	50-99 employee	100+ employee	Hotl.	Campsites	Restnt.	Bars	Cantn.
Weighted base	2,191	1,363	160	98	32	22	8	39	2	41	65	12
Unweighted base	2,191	1,218	121	29	27	33	32	51	4	30	23	12

Source: WERS98.

Table: The Employee Sample in Context, by size of Workplace and Sub-sector (number of cases)

	AIS	PSS	HI	<25 employee	25-49 employee	50-99 employee	100+ employee	Hotl.	Campsites	Restnt.	Bars	Cantn.
Weighted base	28,222	12,886	1,110	341	152	288	330	460	36	213	273	123
Unweighted base	28,215	14,412	1,077	165	178	318	416	524	68	215	134	127

Source: WERS98 employee survey.

The original probit coefficients have been transformed into changes in probabilities. This is achieved by evaluating the change in the probit index that arises from a unit change in each independent variable when all other variables are held at their mean value. The transformed coefficient on the hospitality dummy can then be interpreted as the change in the probability of the outcome (e.g. union membership) that is associated with working in the HI rather than the remainders of the PSS for the average employee, after the influences of the specified characteristics have been removed. If each regression model were to include only the hospitality dummy and no other control variables, the transformed coefficient on the hospitality dummy would correspond to the raw difference in probabilities obtained from the initial tabular analysis presented in particular.

The main identifying characteristics of each of the employee verbatim responses have also been subjected to simple frequency analysis to identify the parameters of the sub-sample. Then responses have been subjected to content analysis along three constructs of job satisfaction - only satisfied, only dissatisfied, and both satisfied and dissatisfied. These constructs and the identifying characteristics were subsequently analysed using the Statistical Package for the Social Sciences (SPSS).

The responses of the large majority (77 per cent) who gave comments on job satisfaction (N = 261) were not distributed normally. Hence non-parametric statistical tests were conducted: the Mann-Whitney test to compare two unrelated groups, the Median test to compare two or more unrelated groups and the Kruskal-Wallace test to compare three or more unrelated groups. These tests determine if any of the employee characteristics have a significant relationship with job (dis)satisfaction (at the 5 per cent level). The results must be treated with some caution because they are not representative of all employees surveyed. Only two employee characteristics demonstrated a significant relationship with job dissatisfaction.

This (general background), the main body of the text (specific employment relations observations) and Appendix 2 (summary employment relations practices and outcomes) contain tables that present key frequencies to illustrate some of the general differences between HI and AIS and PSS workplaces, a number of which are statistically significant. Tables are based on all weighted cases unless otherwise specified. Notes are given with each table to indicate these differences.

Tables are also the most effective way to show broad-brush patterns within the HI by size of workplace and sub-sector. However, statistically testing the intra-HI figures from the *management questionnaire* serves little purpose, because the unweighted bases are so low. Some caution needs to be exercised in drawing conclusions from the small samples, especially in the case of campsites and canteens because of the very small number of cases (both sum to fewer than 20). Hence these two sub-sectors are shown only in tables, and not included in the discussion. Although there is scope for applying statistical tests to the intra-HI figures in the *employee questionnaire* because the unweighted bases are larger numerically, we prefer to maintain consistency with the approach used elsewhere.

Nevertheless we can be less cautious about the sub-sectoral results, and include campsites and canteens in the discussion. The main general features from the management and employee questionnaires are presented separately in two subsequent sections. Some responses referred to in the discussion and tables relate to a sub-sample of all weighted cases, e.g. following a filter question. In these cases size of the sub-sample will normally be noted. Gratuitous use of figures and percentages is avoided within the discussion, particularly in the management questionnaire because of the small sample sizes. Thus the discussion focuses on general tendencies (vast majority, large minority) or more general measures such a half, two-thirds or one in ten.

Using statistical data of this kind can only establish patterns and broad trends, but it does provide a reliable and valid basis from which more focused empirical work can be undertaken. Even so, one the limitation of WERS remains the exclusion of workplaces employing fewer than ten employees, so we still have an incomplete picture of employment relations in their total context. Further, these data shed no light on the role played by customers in determining employees' experience of work, which we contend is integral to understanding customer-service work employment relationships.

Terminology

The following terms are used to describe workplace size:

- Very small workplaces (10-24 employees);
- Small workplaces (25-49 employees);
- Medium workplaces (50-99 employees);
- Large workplaces (100+ employees).

The term smaller workplaces is used to denote workplaces employing fewer than 50 employees. Where comparisons are drawn between AIS, the PSS and the HI, while these are normally referred to by their acronyms, they may also be referred to as 'all groupings' or 'on all comparisons'.

Principles Questionnaire

This section presents key workplace features of WERS. The HI contains more very small workplaces (10-24 employees) than AIS, although the only statistically significant difference is in the mean number of employees per workplace. From Table, we can see that a majority of these very small workplaces are bars, while most very large workplaces are hotels.

Table : Workplace size in Context (Percentage of Workplaces by Numbers Employed)

Number of employees	AIS	PSS	HI
10-24	50	56	61
25-49	26	25	20
50-99	13	11	13
100+	11	8	5
Total (%)	100	100	100
Mean number of employees	62	47	34**
Weighted base	2,191	1,363	160
Unweighted base	2,191	1,218	121

Notes: *Column percentages do not sum to 100 due to rounding.*

*** Significantly different at the 5% level from AIS.*

It is important to note that the characteristics of the HI sample have altered markedly between WIRS3 in 1990 and WERS in 1998, with the inclusion of very small workplaces. Even if we remove very small workplaces from the WERS sample, it is notable that bars constitute a much larger proportion of small workplaces in 1998.

However, this still does not represent the full industry picture, so other characteristics of the WERS sample, e.g. gender and age composition of the workforce, may differ from those established from sources like the LFS.

Employee Characteristics

The main characteristics of employees within HI workplaces (by gender and working hours) are shown in Tables. Full-time denotes working hours of 30 or more per week, while part-time denotes working hours below 30 per week.

Gender and Working Hours

Similar proportions of females work in HI and AIS, but their distribution differs significantly. Although half or more of the workforce is female in three-quarters of HI workplaces, there are very high concentrations of females (71 per cent+) in more AIS workplaces than in HI workplaces. Smaller HI workplaces are most likely to have a high proportion of females.

However, significantly more females in the HI work part-time than in AIS and the PSS, so there is a more substantive part-time female contingent in many workplaces. The growth of part-time employment among males means that HI workplaces are twice as likely to have part-time employees. There is a more substantive part-time female contingent in smaller workplaces, bars and restaurants.

Table: Hospitality Workplaces by Sub-sector and Number of Employees (1990) (% in brackets)

	25-49 employees	50-99 employees	100+ employees	All sub-sectors	Mean of employees
Hotels	22 (37)	14 (54)	5 (33)	41 (41)	64
Campsites and short-stay accommodation	0	b (2)	2 (13)	2 (2)	140
Restaurants	20 (34)	9 (35)	2 (13)	31 (31)	49
Bars	7 (12)	1 (4)	2 (13)	10 (10)	59
Clubs	3 (5)	b (2)	0	3 (3)	35
Canteens and catering	7 (12)	1 (4)	4 (27)	12 (12)	90
All hospitality	59 (100)	26 (100)	15 (100)	99 (100)	62

Notes: *All weighted cases. Row and column numbers and column percentages do not sum accurately due to rounding. b Fewer than 0.5.*

Table: Hospitality workplaces by sub-sector and number of employees (excluding 10-24 employees) (1998) (% in brackets)

	25-49 employees	50-99 employees	100+ employees	All sub-sectors	Range of employees	Mean of employees
Hotels	9 (28)	13 (60)	6 (66)	27 (44)	250-340	75
Campsites and short-stay accommodation	0	0	c	c	148-283	166
Restaurants	8 (26)	6 (30)	1 (10)	16 (26)	25-252	56
Bars	13 (41)	1 (6)	0	15 (24)	26-64	35
Canteens and catering	2 (5)	1 (5)	1 (14)	4 (7)	30-406	86
All hospitality	32 (100)	22 (100)	8 (100)	62 (100)	25-406	62
Range of employees	25-48	52-95	100-406	25-406		
Mean number of employees	34	67	160	62		

Notes: *All weighted cases. Row and column numbers and column percentages do not sum accurately due to rounding. c Fewer than 1%.*

Table : Hospitality Workforce Composition by Gender (%)

	Male	Female	All employees
By gender	43	57	100
Full-time	58	40	48
Part-time	42	60	52
Total	100	100	100

***Note:** All weighted cases.*

Table: Hospitality Workforce Composition by Working Hours (%)

	Full-time	Part-time	All employees
By working hours	48	52	100
Male	52	35	
Female	48	65	
Total	100	100	

***Note:** All weighted cases.*

Table: Hospitality Workforce Composition by Gender and Working Hours (%)

	Full-time	Part-time	All employees
Males	25	18	43
Females	23	34	57
Total	48	52	100

***Note:** All weighted cases.*

Table : Workforce Composition in Context and by size of Workplace (%)

	AIS	PSS	HI	<25	25-49	50-99	100+
Females (all) a	58	66	57	62	59	53	55
71%+	37	32	22**	23	28	10	12
50%+	60	60	77*	86	64	60	79
Part-time (all) a	26	33	51*	61	61	51	34
71%+	16	21	40*	46	43	23	4
50%+	32	35	72*	81	71	49	25
Male (full-time) a	45	40	25*	20	20	27	35
71%+	25	23	4*	6	0	0	2
50%+	36	35	10*	9	7	15	17

Female (part-time) a	**21**	**25**	**34****	**43**	**39**	**30**	**24**
71%+	6	7	7	6	19	0	4
50%+	23	23	39*	50	30	13	4

***Notes:** All weighted cases. a Aggregate percentage. *Significantly different at the 5% level from AIS and PSS. ** Significantly different at the 5% level from AIS.*

Table: Workforce Composition by Sub-sector (%)

	Hotels	Campsites	Restaurants	Bars	Canteens
Females (all) a	56	53	57	58	64
71%+	5	0	33	16	69
50%+	77	90	73	76	97
Part-time (all) a	37	22	59	78	38
71%+	0	0	47	65	17
50%+	44	0	77	96	26
Male (full-time) a	33	43	24	11	28
71%+	0	0	13	0	1
50%+	15	10	19	2	3
Female (part-time) a	26	18	40	47	30
71%+	0	0	6	12	12
50%+	9	0	47	55	26

***Notes:** All weighted cases. a Aggregate percentage.*

Table: Other Workforce Characteristics in Context and by size of Workplace (%)

	AIS	PSS	HI	<25	25-49	50-99	100+
Employees <21 years							
20%+	14	23	55*	54	52	64	45
None	44	35	12*	16	5	6	2
Mean (%)	8	12	24*	20	32	31	22
Employees 51+ years							
20%+	32	36	16*	22	11	0	10
None	14	17	39*	44	51	15	0
Mean (%)	15	14	8	9	7	6	10
Mean (%) of disabled employees	1	1	1	1	1	1	1
Mean (%) of ethnic minority employees	4	4	3	2	3	7	6

***Notes:** All weighted cases. *Significantly different at the 5% level from AIS and PSS. Means are rounded.*

Table: Other Workforce Characteristics by Sub-sector (%)

	Hotels	Campsites	Restaurants	Bars	Canteens
Employees <21 years					
20%+	53	0	69	56	16
None	5	82	19	9	20
Mean (%)	22	2	29	25	15
Employees 51+ years					
20%+	11	6	19	9	59
None	8	0	46	62	0
Mean (%)	10	19	8	5	17
Mean (%) of disabled employees	1	5	b	2	b
Mean (%) of ethnic minority employees	4	b	6	2	1

Notes: *All weighted cases. b Fewer than 0.5%. Means are rounded.*

The HI has a significantly lower concentration of full-time males than AIS and the PSS. Bars and very small workplaces have very low concentrations of full-time males.

Other Characteristics

The HI has significantly greater reliance on young workers aged 20 or less than AIS and the PSS. Conversely significantly more HI workplaces employ no workers aged 51 and over compared to AIS and the PSS. Differences in the age profile of employees by size of workplace and sub-sector are shown in Tables. These tables also indicate that disabled and ethnic minority employees are marginal to most workplaces.

Occupational Groups

The HI workforce comprises a large proportion of manual workers. Above average proportions of manual workers are found in medium and large workplaces, and in hotels and restaurants. Relatively few bar staff are manual workers. Almost all HI workplaces have manual workers and managers. There are significant differences in some occupational groupings in the HI compared to AIS and the PSS.

Workplace Status

Two-thirds of all HI workplaces are public limited companies (PLCs), which is significantly higher than in AIS and the PSS. The vast majority of HI workplaces are wholly or predominantly UK owned and controlled. Very few workplaces are Head Offices. Differences in workplace status are shown in Tables.

HI organizations include some very large employers. Just over one-fifth of multisite workplaces are part of a very large organization employing 100,000+ workers; these are almost always restaurants or bars. Over one-third of very small workplaces in the HI belong to these very large employers. Eighty-five per cent of HI multi-site workplaces are part of an organization employing 1,000+ workers. Hotels are most likely to be part of an organization employing fewer than 1,000 workers.

Very small workplaces are most likely to be bars that are brewery owned. Indeed within the very largest HI organizations (500+ sites), half of the workplaces are very small workplaces. Similarly, at the other end of the spectrum (2-10 sites) nearly 60 per cent of HI workplaces are very small. In other words, where very small HI workplaces are part of a larger organization, they are most likely to be part of an organization with very few or very many sites.

In the one-third of HI workplaces that are not PLCs, individual or family interest over the company is high, especially in small workplaces and restaurants. A majority of controlling owners are actively involved in the day-to-day management of these workplaces on a full-time basis, particularly in bars and large workplaces, although the likelihood of such involvement is below that in AIS and the PSS. The HI has relatively few franchises. The level of franchises is not as high as might have been expected in restaurants.

Table: Workplaces with Employees in the Specified Occupational Group in Context and by size of Workplace (%)

	AIS	PSS	HI	<25	25-49	50-99	100+
Managers and senior administrators	90	91	95	94	93	100	100
Professional	44	36	16*	13	16	21	41
Technical	31	25	7*	2	6	21	33
Clerical and secretarial	77	70	38*	28	27	80	92
Sales	36	45	49	48	43	54	57
Non-management/ non-manual	92	91	67*	60	70	85	100
Craft and skilled services	39	36	42	29	60	59	83
Personal and protective services	26	20	36***	31	28	61	63
Operative and assembly	20	16	12***	11	7	13	34
Routine unskilled	54	51	65*	60	75	69	86
Any manual workers	78	73	95	95	95	93	100
Aggregate (%)	44	40	65*	50	61	73	78
71%+	30	28	49*	41	59	61	79
50%+	44	38	62*	53	63	90	95

Notes: *All weighted cases. *Significantly different at the 5% level from AIS and the PSS. ***Significantly different at the 5% level from the PSS.*

Table : Workplaces with Employees in the Specified Occupational Group by Sub-sector (%)

	Hotels	Campsites	Restaurants	Bars	Canteens
Managers and seni or administrators	100	100	94	91	100
Professional	22	4	14	12	19
Technical	19	81	0	2	10
Clerical and secretarial	68	100	31	14	81
Sales	42	23	18	70	63

Non-management/ non-manual	73	100	41	76	90
Craft and skilled services	66	100	27	39	24
Personal and protective services		60	23	34	19 57
Operative and assembly	9	4	20	9	3
Routine unskilled	82	100	45	67	71
Any manual workers	95	100	96	97	80
Aggregate (%)	73	67	72	39	73
71%+	65	19	74	28	33
50%+	91	100	78	30	80

***Note:** All weighted cases.*

Table: Workplace Status in Context and by size of Workplace (%)

	AIS	PSS	HI	<25	25-49	50-99	100+
Multi-site	68	61	77***	79	67	89	64
Mean number of employees	69	54	33*	16	34	66	162
Single site h	30	38	23***	21	33	11	34
Mean number of employees	45	35	36	18	34	75	150
Franchise j	4	5	9	11	4	10	4
Head Office g	11	15	4***	2	0	17	8
Proprietorial/family controlled i	51	49	72*	66	95	61	66
Age of workplace							
<5 years	16	19	21	27	11	15	13
5-20 years	44	49	26*	12	42	47	53
20+years	40	31	53***	60	47	39	34

Notes: All weighted cases unless otherwise specified. *Significantly different at the 5% level from AIS and the PSS. ***Significantly different at the 5% level from the PSS. h Excludes cases of sole UK workplaces of a foreign organization. j Excludes public sector in AIS. g Where part of a larger organization. i Excludes PLCs. Means are rounded.

Table: Workplace Status by Sub-sector (%)

	Hotels	Campsites	Restaurants	Bars	Canteens
Multi-site	69	100	75	81	86
Mean number of employees	54	58	31	21	40
Single site h	30	0	25	19	14
Mean number of employees	60	0	33	16	41
Franchise	1	0	6	9	49
Head Office g	15	0	4	0	2
Proprietorial/family controlled i	77	0	87	56	73
Age of workplace					
<5 years	11	0	35	22	9
5-20 years	35	0	27	18	30
20+years	53	100	38	60	62

Notes: *All weighted cases unless otherwise specified. h Excludes cases of sole UK workplaces of a foreign organization. g Where part of a larger organization. i Excludes PLCs. Means are rounded.*

New HI workplaces (less than five years old) are most likely to be restaurants or very small workplaces. Older workplaces (more than 20 years old) are most likely to be pubs employing fewer than 25 employees. Over one-fifth of HI workplaces have seen changes in ownership over the past five years. Such change is most likely to have affected very small and large workplaces, with small workplaces largely unaffected.

Workplace Employment Change

In terms of the general economic conditions within which workplaces function, in the five-year period before WERS more HI workplaces suffered job losses than in AIS or the PSS and fewer HI workplaces experienced employment growth. Just over half of HI workplaces remained stable or expanded employment, suggesting that labour cost control was an important consideration for a sizeable minority, notably in very small workplaces and bars. However in the 12 months before WERS job losses were slightly higher in AIS and the

PSS, and HI workplaces were significantly more likely to have experienced stable employment than AIS.

The increased proportion of HI workplaces reporting no change, together with workplaces reporting employment growth (three-quarters) suggest that economic conditions had become more favourable to the HI, with hotels being most likely to sustain job growth. However, job loss, and hence labour cost control, continued to affect more very small workplaces. Employment flows in the 12-month period before WERS, which detail a significantly greater degree of movement among permanent staff in and out of HI workplaces than in AIS and the PSS, are discussed in detail below.

Workplace Performance

The nature of HI workplaces is significantly different from AIS and the PSS, with most describing themselves as producers of goods and services for consumers. AIS and PSS workplaces (one-quarter) are significantly more likely to be suppliers of goods and services to other companies.

The vast majority of HI workplaces regard themselves as having many competitors, especially bars, indicating that the HI operates in significantly more competitive domestic conditions than workplaces in AIS and the PSS. This is also related to workplace size, with almost all very small workplaces regarding themselves as being in this position. The proportions in this category fall as workplace size increases, such that just over half of large workplaces regard themselves as having many competitors.

A majority of HI workplaces believe their market is growing, but significantly fewer operate in mature markets compared to AIS and the PSS. Just over one-third of firms in all cases operate in a declining or turbulent market, with bars most likely to report their market as declining or turbulent.

Significantly more HI workplaces work on a low wage cost:sales ratio, with over half having a ratio of less than 25 per cent, and this particularly affects very small and small workplaces. In general the proportion of wage costs increases with workplace size, although significantly fewer HI workplaces have a ratio of 50 per cent or more. Bars are most likely to have the lowest ratios, while hotels are most likely to have wage cost:sales ratios of 25 per cent or more.

As noted, HI workplaces are significantly less likely to have attained BS5750 or ISO9000 than in AIS and the PSS. This is not to say that quality is unimportant. Monitoring quality is significantly more likely to be a management task in the HI. Customer surveys are of secondary importance for quality purposes and, as in AIS and the PSS, are used in around half the workplaces. Other methods, including inspection by a specialist section and individual employee monitoring of quality, are used less frequently in the HI. Medium and large workplaces and hotels deploy the widest combination of quality monitoring measures to the greatest extent, whereas very small workplaces and bars rely heavily on managerial monitoring.

HI workplaces are significantly more cost-control conscious in terms of keeping records of sales/fees/budget, costs, profits and labour costs than in AIS and the PSS. These records are kept in almost all workplaces, by size and sub-sector. However, HI workplaces are significantly less likely to keep absenteeism records. The majority of bars do not record labour turnover and absence. Other types of records (quality, labour turnover and training) are kept by a majority of workplaces. Productivity is least likely to be recorded on all comparisons, in around half of all workplaces.

Slightly more HI workplaces (over half) than in AIS and the PSS have used benchmarking over the past five years, but it is used least in hotels and restaurants.

Table does not indicate any significant differences between the HI and AIS and the PSS in terms of how they assess business performance. Very small workplaces are more circumspect about their financial performance, with a core reporting average performance. Small and medium workplaces report above-average productivity levels. There is a clear pride in the quality of product or service.

Table: Assessment of Business Performance in Context (%)

	AIS			PSS			HI		
	Above Average	Average	Below Average	Above	Average	Below Average	Above Average	Average	Below Average
Financial performance	49	32	7	51	32	6	57	24	14
Labour productivity	43	36	3	44	38	4	39	47	9
Quality of product or service	70	20	2	76	16	1	74	24	0

Table: Assessment of Business Performance by size of Workplace (%)

	<25			25-49			50-99			100+		
	Above Avg.	Average	Below Avg.	Above Avg.	Average	Below Avg.	Above Avg.	Average	Below Avg.	Above Avg.	Average	Below Avg.
Financial performance	51	28	14	70	7	23	62	29	8	65	32	0
Labour productivity	32	50	0	52	47	2	54	31	12	30	63	0
Quality of product or service	76	23	0	70	30	0	72	25	3	82	12	1

Three-quarters of AIS and PSS workplaces reported an increase in labour productivity in the previous five years compared to under two-thirds in the HI. Very small workplaces and bars were least likely to report increased productivity over this period. A good majority of workplaces across all groups reported an increase in labour costs relative to all other costs in the last five years, and this had affected proportionately more HI workplaces, especially small workplaces.

Workplace Change

Almost all workplaces in all groups reported some workplace change in the last five years, with a majority stating there had been a lot of change. Details of specific changes show a remarkable degree of consistency with one small exception. This indicates that HI workplaces have been more innovative in introducing performance-related pay to non-managerial employees. As a rule very small workplaces and bars have been less innovative, although there were differences in the types of changes made.

The most important cause of HI workplace change has been employee-related matters (e.g. changes to payments systems or working time) (43 per cent), and this was significantly greater than in AIS and the PSS. Three-quarters of bars reported this as the most important reason. Market and competitive change was the most important factor in AIS and the PSS (around 40 per cent). The next three most important factors in the HI were other market conditions (34 per cent), managerial changes (32 per cent) and customer pressure (19 per cent). The HI was especially immune to change caused by legislation/government policy, with no very small workplaces mentioning this as a cause of change. Quality issues and increases in communications and consultation were also of minor importance to the vast majority of HI workplaces.

The HI has been as active as AIS and the PSS in introducing workplaces changes in the last five years, although there are slight differences in the types of changes made. In the HI there is less use of technology and work techniques, and greater use of changes to pay, working time, and the organization of work and, particularly, the introduction of a new product or service. Where more than one change has been introduced by management (six in ten HI workplaces) new technology is the change that has had most impact on employees.

The introduction of initiatives to involve employees (one-quarter of these HI workplaces) has had a significantly more important impact on employees than in AIS and the PSS. The most important change that HI management was not able to introduce was to payment systems, and this was significant, although it affected a very small number of cases, all of which were very small restaurants.

Chapter 2

The Failure of Hotels

CHAIN AFFILIATION

Data for Hotels' 325 for 2004 was gathered through a questionnaire sent to hotel company contacts, who were asked to report the number of hotels and guestrooms as of December 31, 2003. Companies that do not respond are subject to an estimate through the use of public information, local consultancies and corporate Web sites. In some cases, rooms and hotels are counted more than once because Hotels chooses to separately report data from owners, managers and franchisors on the same list.

For example, Carlson Hospitality Worldwide's data includes properties managed or franchised by its joint-venture partner, Rezidor SAS Hospitality, which has its own listing in the ranking. Occupancy and average rate for all India and 30 important hotel markets for 2003 - 04 with comparative figures for last 5 years.

- In 2003-04, Bangalore was the market leader in terms of occupancy, registering occupancy of 78.9%. Hyderabad achieved the second-highest occupancy at 72.8%. New Delhi had the highest average room rate (ARR) among the 30 cities, with an ARR of Rs 4,247. Bangalore was the second highest, registering an ARR of Rs 4,109.
- All India average occupancy was 59.7%, an increase of 4.9% occupancy points above the previous year's

level, or 9.0% in real terms. All India ARR increased by 34.18% during the year.

- Occupancies ranged between 46.5% for heritage hotels to 68.0% for five-star deluxe hotels. Average rates showed a much greater spread, from Rs 4,447 for five-star deluxe hotels to Rs 643 for one-star hotels, an increase of Rs 627 and Rs 106 respectively, from the previous year.
- The All India average revenue per available room (RevPAR) increased substantially, from Rs 1,098 in 2002-03 to Rs 1,605 in 2003-04, reflecting an increase of 46.2%.
- Rooms revenue, generally considered to be the most important source of a hotel's overall profitability, represented 54.2% of total revenue across all hotels (an increase of 3.4% from 2002-03.) Food & Beverage (F&B) revenue represented 29.6% of total revenue across all hotels (a decrease from 31.3% last year).
- Rooms revenue was 54.7% of total revenue for five-star deluxe hotels, 57.1% of total revenue for five-star hotels and 53.1% for four-star hotels.

Expenses

- The All India average of Rooms department expense as a percentage of Rooms revenue declined from 20.7% in 2002-03 to 17.8% in 2003-04.
- The All India average Food & Beverage department expense as a percentage of Food & Beverage revenue declined from 58.7% in 2002-03 to 55.9% in 2003-04.
- Minor Operated department expense as a percentage of Minor Operated department revenue registered a marginal increase from 52.7% in 2002-03 to 53.7% in 2003-04.
- Total departmental expense as a percentage of total departmental revenue reflected a decline, from 37.4% in 2002-03 to 33.7% in 2003-04. The decline has been witnessed for the first time since 1999-2000 (35.3%).

- Food and Beverage expense, at 55.9% of total revenue, was the highest departmental expense. It must however be noted that the segment of luxury hotels, which are generally branded, did a far better job of controlling costs.
- Marketing expenses on per occupied room basis increased from Rs 126 during 2002-03 to Rs 180 during 2003-04. The increase was primarily in the five-star deluxe and three-star segments.
- Energy expenses on per occupied room basis increased from Rs 485 in 2002-03 to Rs 523 in 2003-04. The increase was concentrated in the heritage segment, with an increase of Rs 55 per occupied room, from Rs 572 in 2002-03 to Rs 627 in 2003-04.

Sales and Marketing

- While print advertising continues to be the most popular marketing medium used by hotels across India (93.0%), there has been an increase in the use of hotel websites as effective marketing media, across all segments of hotels. Direct mail is also the preferred marketing media for all categories, with an increase in utilisation to 81.4% from 78.8% in the previous year.
- Use of telemarketing as marketing media has increased, particularly in the three-star segment. Although the utilisation of loyalty card programmes has increased from 27.9% to 31.0%, there is decline in its usage by five-star deluxe and five-star hotels, possibly due to saturation in the market, with hotels targeting the same customer profile.
- Interestingly, radio advertisement and television advertisements have grown in use as marketing media during 2003-04. Five-star deluxe, five-star and four-star hotels used this mode of marketing the most, particularly for F&B promotions and weekend or holiday packages.

- Direct enquiry (55.0%) continues to be the main source of advance reservations at hotels in India, followed by travel agents and tour operators (20.9%). Interestingly, the use of online reservation system increased to 3.7% compared to 2.2% in the previous year, and CRS utilization increased to 5.2% from 4.3%. GDS utilization increased marginally to 1.5% in 2003-04, from 1.4% in the previous year. Also, the use of hotel websites as a source of advance reservations increased to 4.8% from 4.6%.

Guest Profile

- Domestic guests continue to be of importance across all hotels in India, accounting for 75.0% of all guests in 2003-04 (76.9% in 2002-03). Domestic business travellers represented the largest percentage of hotel guests (36.9%).
- The domestic tourist/leisure segment declined marginally, from 20.4% in 2002-03 to 19.6% in 2003-04. This segment has dropped 1.7% points over the past two years.
- Percentage of foreign guests increased to 25.0% in 2003-04, compared to 23.1% in 2002-03, primarily as the percentage of foreign business travellers grew. Of the foreign guests, the UK provided the largest market at 16.0%, followed by USA, at 12.7%, and Germany at 7.6%.
- The percentage of foreign business travellers increased to 9.5% of all hotel guests from 7.4% in the previous year. Foreign business travellers in the five-star deluxe market reflected an increase from 21.7% in 2002-03 to 27.0% in 2003-04.
- Foreign guests prefer luxury and heritage hotels; however, there was a decrease in foreign leisure travellers and tour groups in both these segments. The decline was more marked in the case of heritage hotels: foreign leisure travellers and tour groups

comprised 16.4% and 13.2%, respectively, of the market for heritage hotels in 2003-04, against 22.2% and 18.9% in 2002-03.

- Percentage of repeat guests (All India) declined, from 48.2% in 2002-03 to 45.5% during 2003-04. The decrease was mainly in the five-star and four-star segments. Three-star hotels reflected an increase of 3.9%, from 50.4% in 2002-03 to 54.3% in 2003-04.
- One-star hotels reflected the highest percentage of repeat guests: 59.3% during 2003-04 against 53.5% in the previous year.

Payment Mode

- Cash sales (including cheques/demand drafts), remain the most popular method of settling bills in India (accounting for 44.4% of all sales). The dependence on cash sales is declining slowly: cash sales were 48.4% of all sales in 2002-03. Correspondingly, credit card transactions increased from 27.7% to 30.4% in 2003-04. In the luxury segment of five-star deluxe, credit cards remained the most popular method at 46.4%.
- Credit sales (other than credit cards), increased from 22.5% (All India average) in 2002-03 to 24.1% in 2003-04. This increase was primarily in five-star and heritage hotels, perhaps due to travel agent and company related billings. Interestingly, leisure and group related business, both domestic and foreign, decreased in both these segments.
- Visa (41.4%) was the most widely used credit card by guests followed by Mastercard (36.0%). American Express has the highest collection charges (commission rate).

Change in Performance Ratios: 2003-04 over 2002-03

- The results of survey in 2003-04 with the previous year. In 2003-04, RevPAR increased in all categories except one-star. Heritage hotels and five-star deluxe hotels experienced the highest increase in RevPAR at 62.1% and 32.5%, respectively.

- Average occupancy per hotel increased in all hotels, with heritage hotels showing the greatest increase (9.6%).
- All India average revenue per hotel has shown a growth from Rs 5.18 crore during 2002-03 to Rs 9.15 crore during 2003-04 and is expected to see significant improvements in the next few years.
- House Profit (Gross Operating Profit after deducting franchise and management fees) as a percentage of revenue increased from 29.2% in 2002-03 to 34.8% in 2003-04. This is the second successive year that House Profit has shown upward growth.
- The All India average Net Income (Income before depreciation, interest payments and taxes) also increased, from 24.9% in 2002-03 to 30.7% in 2003-04, reflecting overall improvement in the industry.
- December, followed by November and February, was the busiest month in 2003-04. Average occupancy was at its highest in December at 67.1%, while November and February registered average occupancy of 65.9% and 63.2%, respectively. June through August was the slowest period, with August witnessing the lowest occupancy (52.1%).

Analysis by Hotel size and Brand Affiliation

- Average occupancy for hotels with more than 150 rooms was 70.0% in 2003-04; for hotels with 50 to 150 rooms it was 62.0%; and for hotels with less than 50 rooms it was 55.0%. In all three categories, average occupancy has increased over the level of the previous year.
- Chain affiliated hotels have registered occupancy of 63.0% in 2003-04, and an average room rate of Rs 3,786. In comparison, independent hotels have had

occupancy of 59.0%, with an average rate Rs 2,164. The difference in average rate is largely because of the fact that most chain hotels are in three-star and above categories.

- In 2003-04, the average rate for hotels with more than 150 rooms was Rs 3,960; 50 to 150 rooms was Rs 2,053 and less than 50 rooms was Rs 1,102. In 2002-03, the average rate was Rs 3,259, Rs 1,742 and Rs 939, respectively, for the three categories. Average rate increased in 2003-04 for all three categories of hotels.
- As indicated by the survey results, the average number of rooms per hotel in the larger properties is 262 (237 in the previous year), while hotels in the 50 to 150 rooms segment have an average of 78 (77 in the previous year) rooms per hotel. Hotels in the less than 50 rooms segment have an average of 30 rooms per hotel (same as the previous year). The average number of rooms for the chain affiliated hotels is 152, while Independent hotels have an average of 49 rooms.
- Large hotels enjoy economies of scale and thus are better positioned to earn higher profits. Net income as a percentage of total revenue was highest for hotels with more than 150 rooms at 34.5%. For hotels .with 50 to 150 rooms, it was at 25.0% and for those with less than 50 rooms, it was at 17.3%.
- The domestic business traveller comprises 37.4% of the independent hotel market. Foreign business travellers comprise 22.2% of the chain affiliated hotel market and only 8.3% of the independent hotel market.
- 11.1% of chain affiliated hotels utilise the chain CRS as compared to 4.5% of independent hotels. 9.5% of chain affiliated hotels have used online reservation systems and websites as a source of reservations, compared to 4.9% for independent hotels.

Citywise Trends

The year 2003-04 was a period of considerable buoyancy and upswing for the hotel industry in India. Most cities saw occupancy levels improve over the previous year and, for the first time in six years, both occupancy and average room rates improved. The following paragraphs detail our expectations of new supply and performance for 19 important hotel markets, based on research undertaken and forecasts made by HVS International.

New Delhi: Occupancy witnessed a growth of 10.3% in 2003-04. Average rate increased after a five-year decline, registering a growth of 45.5% from the previous year. However, the large growth may partly be attributed to increases in ARR experienced by survey respondents in the branded hotels category, and those with a larger rooms base.

The central and state governments are encouraging hotel development in all categories, and particularly in the mid-market segment, in preparation for the Commonwealth games to be held in the city in 2010. The National Capital Region is expected to see the development of approximately 17 hotels in various categories over the next three to four years, with approximately 11 new hotels to be in Gurgaon. Due to strong demand, we anticipate occupancy and average rate to grow over the next few years before this new supply comes in. This will be supported by significant infrastructure development in terms of roads and transportation and the (proposed) privatisation of the Airport. The development of new convention centre facilities in New Delhi, as and when this takes place, will further boost room night demand.

Mumbai: Citywide occupancy in Mumbai increased by 3.7%, and average rate registered an increase of 68.1% in 2003-04. This sharp rise in ARR is, as in the case of Delhi, due to the increase in the average rate of the larger hotels, which formed a higher percentage of the total respondents this year. Mumbai continues to experience a large surge in demand for hotel rooms, primarily in north Mumbai; however, south Mumbai has also seen demand growth during 2003-04. We expect room night demand to strengthen significantly in the next couple of years. Average rates will also increase, especially in the north Mumbai market.

The long-term outlook for Mumbai is positive: we estimate occupancy to grow in 2004-05 as demand continues to outpace supply, despite the opening of a new hotel by the ITC group in Parel, and the Grand Hyatt in the Bandra Kurla vicinity commencing full operations. Hotels in the luxury segment, such as the Four Seasons brand, are expected to enter the market in 2006. However, with not much other hotel construction ongoing, the market can hope to see significant gain. Infrastructure improvements are taking place in terms of roads and highway development and the Mumbai airport is also currently under renovation.

Kolkata: In 2003-04, Kolkata witnessed 1.0% increase in occupancy over the previous year, despite large increase in supply in the city. The average rate also increased during the same period. This increase in average rate was realised by hotels in all segments. We expect that room night demand in Kolkata will grow, although at a lower rate than other metro cities in the country, and that average rates will increase and stabilise in the next one year.

With no new supply expected to enter the city in 2004-05, occupancy will witness an increase and average rates will also rise over the previous year's levels. Occupancy and average rate will benefit from the rising number of units providing BPO and IT services in Salt Lake area. Infrastructure development in the Rajarhaat area, and an increase in transit business due to the development of north-east India as a leisure destination, will positively impact the Kolkata hotel market. Hotel performance in Kolkata will also benefit from the city's increased viability as a conference destination.

Pune: Occupancy and average rate in Pune registered an increase over the previous year. Citywide occupancy grew 2.2% in 2003-04 and the average rate increased by 59.5%. In

Pune as well, a larger percentage of the survey participants this year were from the luxury segment, thus contributing to the sharp rise in average rate. We expect the Pune hotel market to witness significant upward growth in 2004-05, as IT and BPO companies continue to shift base to Pune in view of the skilled manpower available, relatively lower cost of corporate office space, and the city's background as an educational centre.

Chennai: Chennai witnessed occupancy decline of 2.3%, for the second consecutive year. Average rates increased marginally by 0.6%. We expect occupancy and average rate to experience growth in 2004-05. This will be supported by improvements at the airport and in the airport's vicinity. We also believe that some of the supply, which had stalled, will get completed and new supply will enter the market in the next few months.

Bangalore: Bangalore's hotel market grew by 6.6% in terms of occupancy and 91.2% in terms of the average room rate. This high increase may also be due to more luxury hotels responding to the survey. Bangalore is, according to some industry observers, the best hotel market in Asia at present. It must, however, be noted that Bangalore's infrastructure has not been able to keep pace with the rapid growth in the city's population and in arrivals.

Infrastructure-related inadequacies may negatively affect Bangalore's growth as a hotel market. No significant new supply is likely to be added in the current year. As occupancy levels in the city range above 80% and almost all weekdays are sold out, we expect significant rise in average rates for all hotels, with no new supply expected until 2006. We expect this rise to continue, before reducing over the next three-four years, as at least nine new hotels are to enter the Bangalore market.

Goa: In Goa, overall occupancy increased by 5.1%. Average rates also registered an increase of 8.3% over the previous year. The city has seen a 23.8% growth in room supply in 2003-04 in the five-star and above hotel category. The increase in supply has been absorbed, due to strong growth in room night demand, which, in turn, has benefited from keen efforts by the Department of Tourism and the State Government to promote Goa as a destination. At present, no significant hotel development is being planned for Goa. The growth of the charter sector has and is further expected to result in positive development for Goa.

Ahmedabad: Following a decrease in 2002-03, Ahmedabad saw occupancy rise by 5.3% in 2003-04 and average rates increase by 15.2%. We anticipate the market to further recover in 2004-05, in keeping with a lessening of communal tensions. Gujarat, despite the negative publicity that it received due to riots, remains a state where business is doing well. Ahmedabad, being one of the main cities of business in the state, stands at the forefront.

Cochin: The overall occupancy in Cochin increased strongly by 11.5% in 2003-04. Average rates registered an increase of 25.6%, due to a larger number of respondents in the four-star category. The upward trend in occupancy and average rate was mainly witnessed in the domestic business traveller segment. We expect occupancy levels and average rates to improve in 2004-05 as Cochin, an important commercial city in Kerala, will benefit from increased leisure travel to the state. This is especially in view of the active efforts being made, both by the Kerala government and the union ministry of tourism, to market Kerela as a destination, particularly for Ayuerveda and for health tourism.

Jaipur: Occupancy levels increased by 5.7% in 2003-04 and average rates increased by 26.3% over the previous year. Despite new and increased supply, the market is expected to improve further in 2004-05. The 'Pink City' also attracted the largest number of foreign tour groups among all cities studied. Moreover, with tourist arrivals into India to grow over the next two to three years, demand in Jaipur is projected to increase. The state government is giving tourism top priority, and infrastructure for tourism-related activities is being improved in Rajasthan. IT related activity and conferences and conventions would also grow, along with the development of Jaipur 's airport into an international airport, thus boosting business-related room night demand.

Hyderabad: The Hyderabad hotel market continued to show improvement in 2002-03 and 2003-04. In 2003-04, average city occupancy was 72.9%, a 1.9% growth over the previous year's level. Average rates grew by 17.4%. We estimate that, with no significant new supply expected in the next few years, average rates will increase significantly. Hyderabad is also expected to see increased and sustained growth in 2004-05, particularly due to the IT industry. Interest has been shown in the city by both large multinational and domestic companies, particularly in this sector.

Bhopal: Bhopal witnessed a decline in occupancy by 2.7% and a 46.5% increase in average rate over the previous year. This increase in average rate is mainly because higher rated heritage hotels have been included in the survey group for this city.

Thiruvananthapuram: The city has witnessed a decrease in occupancy of 9.2%, and a growth in average room rates of 32.3%. The decline could also be because of difference in the mix of responding hotels. Thiruvananthapuram is expected to benefit as inbound tourism to Kerala increases over the next couple of years.

Udaipur: Citywide occupancy decreased by 0.9% in 2003-04. Average rate, on the other hand, showed a steep increase of 50.4%. We expect that, like Jaipur, Udaipur will see an increase in both occupancy and rates in 2004-05, as overall tourist arrivals in Rajasthan are expected to grow substantially in the next couple of years and the state government gives strong impetus to tourism growth.

Agra: The city saw occupancy and average rate grow in 2003-04 after a steady decline in the three previous years. The occupancy increased by 5.4% and the average rate increased by 74.4%. Increased response to the survey from five-star deluxe and five-star hotels has resulted in a strong increase in average rates. The meetings segment, particularly of groups of over 100 participants, grew from 5.3% the previous year to 21.5%, indicating Agra's growth as a conference destination.

Shimla: Shimla registered a decline of 1.7% in terms of occupancy levels in 2003-04. Average rates, however, grew from the previous year. As disposable income across India improves due to the economy, we can expect leisure markets like Shimla to see improvement in the performance.

In the automotive section of a Sunday newspaper, a journalist says of the British car manufacturer Lotus (which was recently divested by General Motors), "Free of the constraints, and resources of General Motors, Lotus soldiers on alone". That statement reflects two insights that deserve the critical attention of organization theorists. First, the statement recognizes that some large organizations encompass numerous smaller components (such as Lotus) that are themselves organizations. Second, the statement recognizes that the relationship to the large organization can mean both good and bad things to the component organization. Understanding what these pros and cons are is the focus of this.

Here we consider the implications for the fate of component organizations of affiliations to chains. The component organizations we focus on are hotels affiliated with hotel chains. While a chain affiliation may be a source of operating knowledge for a component, we also identify potential sources of strategic constraint. Further, a chain can affect the fate of its components by giving them resources, reputation, and market power.

By altering the competitive strengths of their components, chains may also influence the competitive dynamics of industries. Therefore, we also consider the implications of chain affiliations for industry evolution. We examine these effects of chain affiliation on the fates of component organizations and competitive dynamics in an analysis of organizational failure in the Manhattan hotel industry.

Chains are collections of service organizations, doing substantially the same thing (often the only differentiation is in physical space), that are linked together into a larger organization. The relationships between the components of a chain are horizontal, although typically there are centralized parts of the chain, such as a distribution facility, that have vertical relationships to the components. There a-re a number of types of linkage between component and chain, including ownership, franchise agreement, or other types of contracts or agreements. Although analogous horizontal linkages between nonservice organizations exist, these are not typically categorized as chains. The relationship between Lotus and GM is an example. Both chains and nonservice collections of horizontally linked organizations could be described by the term "superorganizations."

There are many compelling implications of the structure of interdependencies among the components of a chain, First, the components of a chain are almost always capable of operating without the chain. It is not surprising to see an independent hotel, but it is surprising to see an independent finance or marketing unit. This easy separability of chain components invites the question of what the component gets from being part of the chain, which we try to answer here. The chain presumably imposes mutualistic relationships between organizations of the same type and is therefore the source of some unique advantages, especially in twentieth-century North America, where interorganizational linkages between similar organizations are often viewed as illegitimate because they restrict competition.

Second, the chain suggests an intriguing wrinkle for interorganizational competition. It is at the level of the component that the chain meets its competitors. As the president of what was then the largest hotel chain said in a 1937 advertisement, "the success of any group enterprise in the long run, is predicated on the success of each individual unit in the group." Chains are too diverse to be seen as rivals by independent organizations in the same industry, and independent organizations are too narrow to be seen as rivals by chains, but, according to definitions of competition based on the overlap of required resources, the two organizational forms seem to compete, This tension between the competitive implications of component and chain motivated us to examine the effects of chain affiliations on the competitive dynamics of a population composed of component and independent organizations.

Third, the study of chains and other superorganizations promises to inform theories of organizational evolution and adaptation. While organizational ecology has focused on the replacement of inertial organizations as the principle mechanism by which populations respond to their environments, even casual observation indicates that organizations are sometimes able to adapt to changes in their environments. An important step in reconciling the selection and adaption perspectives may be recognizing that sometimes selection works at the suborganizational level, which allows a persisting organization or superorganization to adapt. By adding or dropping parts, organizations change. In this paper, we examine this phenomenon by studying the failure of chain components.

Finally, the study of chains is dictated by their increasing importance as an organizational form. The trend over the last century suggests that chains will eventually come to dominate every service industry that is characterized by some direct contact between customer and organization. Starting with retailing, chains have made significant advances in industries such as food service, hospitality, banking, insurance, amusements, business services and auto services.

Even the professions are not immune – accountants, lawyers, and doctors are increasingly likely to be part of a chain. According to the U.S. Census of Business, multiunit establishments (defined as a service organization operating in two or more locations) accounted for 25 percent of all service revenue in 1955. By 1987 their share was more than 40 percent, and it continues to grow. Figure 1 shows the share of the market held by multiunit firms in a selected group of services.

There is some existing research on chains or broadly applicable to them. Chandler (1977) argued that chains, like other mass marketers, produce economies of scale that advantage their components. Ingram (1996b) found support for economies of scale in the hospitality industry in the form of lower failure rates for larger and more spatially compact hotel chains. We are aware of no evidence, however, that shows that the components of chains benefit from economies of scale. Below, we examine whether Manhattan components enjoy local economies of scale and test the possibility that chains help benefit their components with nonlocal economies of scale as well.

There is also a literature in economics and marketing on franchising, one type of chain linkage. The franchising literature focuses on whether chains should own or franchise units and typically builds explanations for the decision to own or franchise using the cost of monitoring, which increases franchising because employee managers require more monitoring than franchisees, and the presence of brand-name capital and firm-specific assets (e.g., the Golden Arches), which decrease franchising because franchisees may be tempted to free-ride on these things. Since the franchising literature takes the existence of the chain as given and always considers the benefits from the position of the franchisor, rather than the component, it does not address the question of how chains affect components.

Certainly, franchising is important in the recent growth of chains and has a role in a theory of chains, but the literature on franchising says almost nothing about the issues we identify above and deals with only a subsection of chains. Interesting with respect to this study, only 3 percent of the U.S. hotel chains from 1898 to 1980 were franchisors, and franchises were rare among Manhattan hotels. Only 396 of 20,344 (2 percent) hotel-years in our data were associated with a franchisor or franchisee, and the 396 likely includes many company-owned hotels of franchisors and nonfranchised hotels of franchisees. The low occurrence of franchising in Manhattan would be predicted by the franchising literature, where authors have argued that franchising is less likely in urban areas because of lower costs of monitoring and lower economic risk.

Hotel Failure

The hospitality industry is a promising one for studying the implications of chain affiliation. As indicates, chains have quickly gained prominence in this industry and by 1987 account for more than half of its $28 billion U.S. revenue. Still, independent hotels have a strong presence in the hospitality industry and provide a comparison group to identify the implications of chain affiliation. Within hospitality, the Manhattan hotel market has features that make it appropriate for our purposes.

Chains have operated in Manhattan, almost since the first hotel chain was founded, but as a local market, Manhattan is not ideal for chains, which serve highway-oriented, small-to-medium-sized city markets most effectively, the usefulness of a chain affiliation is the applicability of the chain's experience and global strategy to the local market. Unlike some other hotel markets, in Manhattan we expect significant variance on these dimensions, allowing us to investigate both the benefits and the costs of chain affiliation.

Chain affiliation exposes the component hotel to the experience of a larger set of organizations, which affects the component hotel's operating knowledge and strategic responses to the environment. The Federation of Hotel and Restaurant Associations of India numbers the total hotel rooms at only 97,000. The association has been asking the government to aim for an annual 10 percent increase to meet tourism targets. India's Planning Commission projects that India will need 160,000 rooms to accommodate 6 million tourists by 2010, and 300,000 rooms to accommodate 9 million tourists by 2020.

The government appears fully aware of this need and has made plans for more hotel rooms a priority. Failure to reach these targets threatens to make Indian hotels costlier and of poor quality for their price, which largely compromises India's competitiveness as a tourist destination for all, including the Chinese.

This becomes a serious problem when countries like Thailand and Vietnam are aggressively pursuing Chinese tourists while countries such as France, Italy and the United States remain favorite destinations for Chinese tourists. The solution perhaps lies in both China and India exploring their own unique selling points along with their mutual attractions and interests.

China, for instance, has recently emerged as one of the top destinations for Indians with small businesses, and more than 5,000 Indian students are currently studying in Chinese universities. The total number of Indians in China has increased exponentially. Indian medical students, particularly from the province of Andhra Pradesh, seem to have redefined China-India travel.

Knowledge Transfer and Learning

Although it is widely recognized that organizations can learn from other organizations, such vicarious learning is typically seen as involving the imitation of high-profile organizations or using corporate intelligence to learn from competitors. One recent study, however, focuses on relationships with a chain as a means of inter organizational learning. Darr, Argote, and Epple (1995) studied organizational learning and the transfer of knowledge among pizza stores, some of which were parts of chains.

Their dependent variable was average production cost, and they included historical production he level of the component organization, chain, and industry as independent variables. They found that experience at the component and chain levels translated into lower production costs, but experience at the industry level did not. This finding demonstrates a transfer of knowledge among components of a service chain. In a related study, Greve (1996) examined patterns of hew market position adoption among radio broadcasters, some of which shared a common corporate owner. Greve argued that opportunities for communication and competence sharing among corporate units would result in self-imitation within the corporation. Supporting this idea, Greve found that adoption by a corporate contact (i.e., unit of the same corporation) significantly increases the chances of adoption beyond the influence of any other adopter. Thus a new market position is an innovation that spreads contagiously through corporate contacts.

The transfer of knowledge via affiliation with a chain should be important to hotels. As the president of the American Hotels Corporation said of chains: "The mistakes developing in one hotel, through cooperation can be prevented in all the others. The success achieved by one can likewise be passed on to the others". Hotels are complicated organizations to operate, as evidenced by the more than 200 four-year degree programs in hotel management in the United States. An example of the type of knowledge chains could transfer to component hotels is accounting practices.

Accounting, both for financial reporting and cost control, is complicated in hotels. There are many income producing activities, transactions often take months to complete, and there is no physical trace of productive activity. Early in this century, hotel accounting was so unsophisticated that most hotel managers could not determine if their organizations were profitable. Chains were the first organizations in the hotel industry to develop sophisticated accounting and control systems, and they continue to be the major source of innovative accounting procedures and equipment.

The value of the experience of a chain to a component probably depends on the similarity between the environment of the component and the environments in which the chain accumulated its experience. Affiliation with a chain should result in a significant and valuable transfer of knowledge to component organizations to the extent the chain has experience in the component's local environment. There should also be a dynamic relationship between chain affiliation and learning. Darr, Argote, and Epple's (1995) results suggest that hotels within a chain should learn faster than independent hotels because component hotels have ongoing exposure to the experience of the chain. Access to the local experience of the chain should also help the component over time through ongoing learning:

Hypothesis 1: Upon joining a chain, a hotel's failure rate will drop proportionate to the local experience of the chain, because of the initial knowledge transfer the chain can provide, and will fall further with additional incremental local experience of the chain during the life of the affiliation.

The Risk of Strategic Constraint

The strategy of hotel chains can be described with one word, standardization. This strategy probably generates benefits for the chain (e.g., economies of scale and reputation), but it creates a liability for component hotels. Fitting into the global strategy designed for the chain reduces the degrees of freedom that managers of component hotels have to respond to their local environments. The chain strategy may be designed to optimize the success of its components in their local environments, but because those local environments are not all the same, some components may have to do things as part of the chain that they would not do if they were independent organizations.

A rich illustration of the mismatch of a chain strategy and a local environment was provided to us by an experienced manager of chain hotels. This manager's first assignment with a large motel chain was in a unit in the downtown of a large city (not Manhattan). When the unit was established it was on the edge of the business district. But the area had changed, and when our informant arrived there, the unit was in the middle of a red-light district. Hotels can and have adjusted to changes like this, but this component organization did not have the freedom to make the necessary changes.

Its late night restaurant crowd was greeted with children's menus and bottomless cups of coffee. Prostitutes and their clients were offered a room-rate structure designed for traveling salesmen and families on holiday. Perhaps more problematic were the families on holiday who were occasionally drawn in by the colorful sign that they had learned to trust.

At best, strategic constraint may have no negative effect on a component, for example, if the chain's strategy was designed to satisfy an environment like the component's local environment. If the component's environment is different from that in which the chain is experienced and the chain's strategy is designed to satisfy, the component will suffer. Strategic constraint may also affect the prospects of a component organization as a result of organizational change imposed on it when a chain affiliation is formed.

Changes that render an organization's accumulated skills, roles, and routines obsolete or upset its exchange relationships with the environment can rob its history of survival value and reduce its reliability of performance to that of a new organization. Changing to fit a chain's strategy may produce not only a strategic gap between the component and its local competitive environment, but also a renewed liability of newness.

Since the nonlocal experience of a chain will sometimes be from similar and sometimes from dissimilar environments to the one occupied by a focal component, it is impossible to make a blanket statement about the effect of nonlocal experience. In the population we study here, however, we expect that most nonlocal chain experience will be from environments dissimilar to Manhattan and that strategic constraint will be problematic for Manhattan components. Hotel chains grew up with automotive travel in the United States. The ideal local environment for most hotel chains is a medium-sized city on a busy highway. Chains' standard products thrive in markets where consumers are highly uncertain about the quality of independent hotels' rooms and service.

The environment for Manhattan hotels is very different: The Manhattan market is large enough for independent hotels to be professionally managed; it is a sufficiently central travel destination to allow travelers to develop enduring relationships with independent hotels; and it is a stronghold of prestigious, world-class hotels. So some component hotels in Manhattan will likely be forced to follow chain strategies that do not fit the Manhattan market.

As with local experience, we predict both an immediate and an incremental effect of nonlocal experience. When an affiliation is formed, a hotel will suffer an immediate negative effect from strategic constraint, and this effect will be a function of the chain's experience in nonlocal environments. There should also be a dynamic effect of strategic constraint. The longer a hotel is part of a chain, the greater the negative effect of the chain's strategy. While a chain may choose a hotel or location initially for congruence with its strategy, the chain's strategy does not adjust as the local environment changes over time because its strategy is influenced by its nonlocal experience. Nonlocal experience may also lead the chain to impose practices learned elsewhere that are dysfunctional in the local environment.

Hypothesis 2: Upon joining a chain, a hotel's failure rate will increase proportionate to the initial nonlocal experience of the chain and increase further with subsequent incremental increases in the chain's nonlocal experience during the life of the affiliation.

Economies of Scale and Access to Resources

Although we expect the standardization strategy pursued by chains to create a strategic constraint for some component hotels, we expect that there is also a range of benefits accruing to component hotels. By standardizing services, advertising, reservations, operating procedures, equipment, and even buildings, hotel chains generate economies of scale. These advantages of scale at the chain level should translate into lower costs for component hotels. Moreover, when organizations establish ties to chains, they may enhance their access to resources as well as knowledge. Consistent with this idea, recent studies suggest that relationships to superordinate organizations may often serve as buffers that protect organizations from environmental uncertainty and competitive threats to survival.

Chains may also benefit their components by distributing risk. Chains may acquire geographically distributed units to implement a portfolio strategy. It is likely that when a component in a given market is facing a scarce environment, another component will be facing a more munificent environment. If components enjoying good times distribute resources to components experiencing hard times, the chain can act as a form of insurance against economic fluctuation. Although there are alternative ways to implement a portfolio strategy, the fact that most hotels are privately held suggests that those alternatives have not been exploited, Hypothesis 3: Ceteris paribus, failure rates of component hotels will be lower than independent hotels.

Economies of scale of potential benefit to components may increase with the size of the chain. Below, we discuss the possibility of economies of scale based on the chain's size in Manhattan. There may also be a more general benefit of economies of scale from the size of the chain outside of Manhattan. Our models include a control variable, the number of hotels in the chain outside Manhattan, to test for nonlocal economies of scale that are greater for larger chains.

Local Market Power and Power Dilution

Another feature of chain affiliation is that it associates the component hotel with other hotels in its local market. This creates the possibility of pursuing collective action. There are a number of ways a chain's component Manhattan hotels could benefit from collective action. Most importantly, large chains are more powerful in the market for inputs, and this is a local source of economies of scale. Chains with a strong presence in Manhattan should be able to buy advertising, food, subcontracted labor (e.g., security staff), and other inputs cheaper and might be able to collude successfully on prices.

No chain (or independent hotel) was ever sufficiently powerful in the Manhattan hotel industry that it could have dominated the whole market (the largest Manhattan chain controlled 8,937 hotel rooms when there were about 70,000 hotel rooms in Manhattan), but, as Jacquemin showed, groups of large firms can exercise a degree of monopolistic power, forcing smaller firms to the "competitive fringe." Components of a chain in the same city also refer patrons to each other. Additionally, powerful chains may be able to manipulate local laws. Rich hoteliers from the northeast, particularly the early chain entrepreneurs, were particularly effective at influencing laws pertaining to hospitality.

All of these advantages of market power should be a function of how many rooms a chain controls in Manhattan, but market power may be a negative function of the number of units over which the chain's rooms in Manhattan are spread. If the market power is divided among many component hotels, it will be diluted. Most obviously, a chain that gets economies of scale by purchasing in bulk will lose some of those economies if it has to distribute the purchases over many components.

Further, because component hotels are operated like independent organizations, and their managers are held accountable for the performance of their hotels, component hotels may actually compete with hotels from the same chain. When a chain has many units in one location (i.e., Manhattan), there will be many managers pursuing their own interests and therefore less likelihood of coordination. Finally, collective action is more costly when more actors have to be coordinated.

Hypothesis 4: The failure rate of a component hotel will fall as the number of rooms controlled by its chain in Manhattan increases.

Hypothesis 5: The failure rate of a component hotel will increase as the number of hotels controlled by its chain in Manhattan increases.

Reputation

Not all chains try to develop reputations, but affiliation with those that do should benefit components. Standardization should allow component hotels to benefit from the reputation of the chain they are a part of because it reduces consumers' uncertainty about the quality of a component hotel's rooms and service. This idea is consistent with Hannan and Freeman's (1984) contention that selection pressures favor organizations that are able to demonstrate their reliability and accountability. In the minds of consumers, reliability, the capacity to produce products or services of a given quality repeatedly, is more likely to characterize organizations with chain affiliations than independent organizations.

Similarly, accountability is higher for organizations with chain affiliations because the interdependence of these organizations creates pressure on each component to maintain and enhance the reputation of the chain. This reputation, in turn, enhances the survival prospects of component organizations. We can differentiate between chains that provide a reputation benefit to their Manhattan components and those that do not by looking al whether the chain gives other components names that link them with the Manhattan component, which is a necessary condition for building a reputation that benefits the Manhattan component.

Hypothesis 6: The failure rate of a component hotel will fall as the proportion of hotels in its chain with names linking them to the component increases.

Competitive Dynamics

Although an array of evidence has been assembled by organizational ecologists linking models of competition to the evolutionary trajectories of industries, past research has not examined how the presence of chains and their affiliates affects competitive dynamics. The arguments set out above suggest two possibilities. If advantages of knowledge transfer, scale economies, access to resources, market power, and reputation predominate, then component organizations should be more potent competitors than independent organizations, and their increasing prevalence will displace independent hotels. By comparison, if strategic constraint effects predominate and if the market power of chains is diluted, then the competitive capabilities of component organizations should be impaired relative to independent organizations, and chain expansion will be thwarted by competition.

We see the implications of chains for the competitive dynamics of a population as contingent on the suitability of the environment for chains (environments in which chains can apply nonlocal experience would be suitable), the structure of the chain population (the size of chains and their strategies for naming their units), and even the history of the chain population (the level of local and nonlocal experience). Our prediction on competitive dynamics is therefore specific to the Manhattan hotel market.

Because Manhattan is not the ideal environment for chain components, we expect the nonlocal experience of chains to have very little applicability in Manhattan, and the strategic constraint from fitting into the chain's global strategy should be particularly damaging to Manhattan components. Although our previous hypotheses indicate that there are a number of benefits of chain affiliation in any environment, the idiosyncrasies of the Manhattan market are sufficiently challenging to chains that we predict that independent hotels will have a stronger competitive impact on components than vice versa:

Hypothesis 7: Independent hotels are strong competitors in the Manhattan hotel market, and so their presence will raise the failure rate of component hotels more strongly than vice versa.

The data used in this study include life history information on all 558 transient hotels that operated in Manhattan at any time between 1898 and 1980. Transient hotels cater to short-term visitors and differ from residential hotels, which serve long-term or permanent guests and are excluded from the sample. Our examination of the effects of chain linkages on the failure of Manhattan hotels is theoretically different from Baum and Mezias (1992) and Baum (1995), which also examined the failure of Manhattan hotels.

In those papers, the authors were concerned with localized competition and the temporal dynamics of competition. Our focus here is on the implications for hotel failure of a type of interorganizational relationship, the chain linkage. Additionally, we have added new information on chain linkages to create a dataset that combines rich information on the Manhattan hotel industry with detailed data on interorganizational relationships over an extended period. As we discuss below, the effects of chain affiliation, localized competition, and temporal dynamics of competition are distinct influences on the failure rate of Manhattan hotels.

We used four archival sources to construct the life histories of Manhattan hotels. The Hotel Redbook, published annually since 1887, contains detailed information on the name, number of rooms, location, and room rates of hotels. It is the most comprehensive historical listing of Manhattan hotels in existence. The information contained in the Redbook was cross-referenced and supplemented using three additional archival sources:

1. The Manhattan Classified Directory/Yellow Pages, published since 1929;
2. The Annual Directory of the Hotel Association of New York City, published since 1940; and
3. The Hotel and Travel Index, published since 1951. Although a period of rapid growth in the late 1920s coincides roughly with the addition of the Yellow Pages data source, it is not attributable to the addition of this source. This growth, which accompanied the rapid expansion of Manhattan during this time, is reflected in the Redbook as well. Because detailed organizational data are missing for many hotels prior to 1898, the observation period for

this study begins in 1898, even though the archival sources begin in 1887.

During the study period, 425 transient hotels were founded in Manhattan. We recorded a hotel as founded in the year it first appeared in any archival source. Three hundred and fifteen (70 percent) of the hotels founded in Manhattan since 1898 had ceased operations by the end of 1980. We defined failure as the cessation of hotel services for short-term visitors and did not include changes in name or ownership as failures because the organization itself continued to provide transient-hotel services. The date, of failure was recorded as the year a hotel was permanently delisted from the Redbook. If Redbook listings differed from those in the other archival sources, we recorded a hotel as failed in the first year it was permanently delisted from two or more of the archival sources.

In 1898, 133 of the hotels in the sample were already in operation; thus, the life histories for these hotels were left-censored (i.e., founded before the study period). To include as much of the data on hotels from the 1898-1980 period in the study as possible, we attempted to find founding dates for hotels existing in 1898.

With available archival information, we were able to confirm founding dates for 112 (84.2 percent) of the left-censored hotels. Because their ages were not known, the 21 hotels with unknown founding dates could not be included in the analysis, although information on these hotels was included in computations for the variables described below. The final sample for the analysis included 537 hotels, of which 350 (65.2 percent) failed.

To identify all component hotels in Manhattan, we first had to identify all hotel chains in the United States and generate lists of their component hotels. We defined chains as any organization operating three or more hotels or motels, which is the standard definition the industry uses. The lower limit of three hotels represents the necessary degree of separability implied by our definition of chains — historically, many two-hotel "chains" were adjacent properties operated by a unified organization.

Of course, a chain can operate three or more hotels in different ways. Hotel chains in our data consisted of chains that owned and operated their hotels (85 percent of all U.S. chains), chains that franchised at least one of their hotels (11 percent of all chains, increasingly more common from about 1960), franchisors (less than 3 percent of all chains), and referral systems, which were coordinated marketing efforts between hotels that maintained individual ownership (about 1 percent of all chains).

These four alternatives for operating multiple components could be considered different types of chains. We expected that there would be implications for the component of the type of chain it was affiliated with, and in preliminary analysis we looked for such effects. Franchising was rare in Manhattan, however, and referral systems were almost nonexistent, and we found no effects for the type of operating arrangement. We thus treat all operating arrangements he same here.

We used two archival sources to generate data on chains. The primary source was the Directory of Hotel and Motel Systems, which has been published by the AHMA since 1931 and claims to list, all hotel chains and each chain's member hotels. There has never been a fee for inclusion in the directory. The secondary data source (and the primary source for 1898-1930) was the Hotel Redbook.

For the period from 1898 to 1930 we identified chains by reading all advertisements in the Redbook and scanning the listed owners of the hotels. After 1930 we used the Redbook to verify listings and delistings in the Directory of Hotel and Motel Systems, Left-censoring is not a problem for the hotel chain data. In 1898, one hotel chain operated a single hotel in Manhattan; the first hotel chain entered Manhattan in 1896. During the observation period, 103 different hotel chains operated one or more components in Manhattan.

Between 1898 and 1980 the Manhattan hotel industry gradually transformed from one dominated by entrepreneurial independent operators to one dominated by professionally managed hotels. After a period of slow growth in the decades preceding and following the turn of the century, the Manhattan hotel industry grew rapidly with the expansion of Manhattan during the Roaring Twenties, reaching a maximum of 353 hotels in 1931. Since then, the industry has become more concentrated, a trend that accelerated after 1960 as smaller and medium-sized hotels were replaced by fewer, larger, and – with increasing frequency – chain establishments. The numbers of independent and component hotels and hotel chains and independent and component hotel rooms in Manhattan in each year are shown in Figures 2 and 3, respectively.

A total of 189 hotels (35.2 percent of the hotels in the sample) were at one point part of a chain. Seventeen hotels had two chain affiliations over their lives, and five hotels had three affiliations, resulting in a total of 216 chain affiliations. Twenty-six of the affiliations resulted from a chain founding a hotel and 190 from a preexisting hotel joining a chain. There is substantial variance in both the duration of chain affiliations and the duration of ex-component status. Most (111) chain affiliations lasted less than 10 years, but 71 lasted 20 years, and some lasted more than 60 years. Seventy-one components failed, and there were 110 instances in which a component left a chain. Ten years after leaving the chain, 85 hotels remained in the ex-component state. One hotel persisted as an ex-component for 80 years.

Sample includes 26 hotels founded by chains and 190 independent hotels that joined chains. There were 71 failures of hotels affiliated with chains. Independent Variables

Local and nonlocal experience. To test hypotheses 1 and 2, we developed variables to capture the different operating experiences of the chains to which component hotels were affiliated. Benefits of knowledge transfer obtain when a component's environment is comparable to-the environment in which the chain is experienced and which the chain's strategy is designed to satisfy. In contrast, strategic constraint occurs when the component's environment is different from the environment in which the chain typically operates and which the chain's strategy is designed to satisfy.

To measure the initial and ongoing knowledge transfer from a chain to its components, we created variables based on chains' accumulation of operating experience in Manhattan, which corresponds to the cumulative output measure of experience used in the organizational learning literature. As in the learning curve estimation, the fact that the marginal value of experience decreases as knowledge grows (i.e., there is not as much learning in the 100th unit of experience as there was in the first) is accounted for by the exponential form of the models we estimate.

To measure the strategic constraint imposed by a chain on its components, we created variables based on chains' accumulation of operating experience outside Manhattan. Although some non-Manhattan experience may benefit a Manhattan component, for example, if it is obtained in a comparable urban setting, hypothesis 2 predicted that chains' non-Manhattan operating experience should typically result in more strategic constraint being imposed on component hotels.

We defined a hotel chain's operating experience in Manhattan to be a function of the number of component hotel-years it operated in Manhattan during its past history. Analogously, we defined a hotel chain's operating experience outside Manhattan as a function of the number of component hotel-years it operated outside Manhattan during its past history. More formally, we defined the local and nonlocal experience of chain i for its component j at time t as where it is the first year of the chain's existence, t-1 is the year before the current year, is the number of components operated in Manhattan by chain i in a year, is the number of components operated in Manhattan by chain i in a year, and discount, which we specify in detail below, is a weight that depreciates values of and as a function of their age. We discount the experience to account for possible antiquation (due to environmental change) or decay (due to forgetting) of knowledge gained from experiences in the past.

The local experience variables, initial local experience and incremental local experience, were set equal to zero until a chain affiliation was established. Thereafter, initial local experience was set, using equation 1, equal to the affiliated chain's cumulative operating experience in Manhattan at the time the relationship was established. Using equation 1, we set incremental local experience equal to the affiliated chain's cumulative operating experience in Manhattan at the start of each year minus appropriately discounted initial experience. Both variables were reset to zero if the affiliation was subsequently severed. When a component changed from affiliation with one chain to affiliation with another (this occurred 17 times), we reset both values to the experience of the new chain. Initial nonlocal experience and incremental nonlocal experience were computed in the same way using equation 2.

We computed and analyzed four sets of these variables based on different specifications of the discount factor. First, we set the discount equal to 1, which assumes no depreciation of knowledge gained from past experience. Second, we set the discount equal to the age of the experience, which assumes a linear depreciation of prior knowledge. Third, we set the discount equal to the age of the experience squared, which assumes that knowledge gained from past experience depreciates rapidly at first and more quickly with time.

Finally, we set the discount equal to the square root of the age of the experience, which assumes that depreciation of knowledge is initially slow and slows further with time. The knowledge decay implied by these different specifications of the discount factor for a hotel chain that operated three components in each year.

Chain affiliation and loss dynamics. To test hypothesis 3 and explore the dynamic implications of chain affiliation and loss on rates of Manhattan hotel failure, we followed a procedure based on Amburgey, Kelly, and Barnett (1993). First, we created two dummy variables. For each hotel, the first dummy variable, component hotel, was set equal to zero until the occurrence (if any) of a chain affiliation. Thereafter, the variable was set equal to one and reset to zero if the affiliation was subsequently lost.(1) The second dummy variable, ex-component hotel, was constructed analogously based on the occurrence of a loss of chain affiliation.

In addition, we created two time-clock variables to track the elapsed time since a hotel either last acquired or lost a chain affiliation. The time-clock variables were set equal to zero until an event of either type occurred. Following the establishment of a chain affiliation, the component time clock measured the natural logarithm of the number of years since the affiliation began. The counter was reset to zero if the affiliation was subsequently severed. The ex-component time clock was derived in the same manner based on the loss of chain affiliations. In combination, the dummy and time-clock variables capture, respectively, the main and time-varying effects of chain affiliation and loss on the risk of hotel failure, permitting the short and longer-term consequences of the affiliations to be different.

Market power and market power diffusion. To test hypotheses 4 and 5, we used, respectively, the natural logarithm of the number of Manhattan rooms a chain operated at the start of each year and the number of Manhattan hotels a chain operated at the start of each year. To test hypothesis 6, we computed the name concentration for each chain at the start of each year as the percentage of a hotel chain's components that had the same name as the focal component. This is a slight modification on the name concentration measure from Ingram (1996b), who examined the effect of name concentration on the chain and based the measure on the most common name in the chain. Here, we examine the effect of name concentration on the component, so the sharing of the component's name is more relevant than the most common name in the chain, although the results are comparable with either measure.

Competitive Dynamics

To test hypothesis 7, we operationalized both density-dependent and mass-dependent forms of competition between independent and component hotels. We first created density and mass measures separately for independent and chain hotels. We measured independent hotel density and component hotel density, respectively, as the total numbers of independent and component hotels existing in Manhattan at the start of each year. Analogously, we measured independent hotel mass and component hotel mass, respectively, as the total number of rooms in independent and component hotels (i.e., the total productive capacities of the independent and chain segments of the industry) existing in Manhattan at the start of each year.(2) Following Barnett and Amburgey (1990), we subtracted each independent or component hotel's number of rooms from the total independent or component hotel mass, so the mass variables reflected the number of rooms operated by other hotels, and we used a natural logarithm transformation of mass.

To estimate the effects of density and mass among and between independent and component hotels in a single model, we used the independent and component hotel density and mass variables to construct own-type and other-type density and mass variables. Own-type for a component is the density or mass of all component hotels and, for an independent, the density or mass of all independent hotels. Other-type for a component is the density or mass of all independent hotels and, for an independent, the density or mass of all component hotels.

Finally, to test for the predicted differences in competitive strengths of independent and component hotels, as well as permit differences in their own-type density and mass effects, we interacted the own- and other-type density and mass variables with the component dummy variable. Density-dependent competition implies positive effects of the density variables on the failure rate. Mass-dependent competition implies a positive effect of the mass variables on the failure rate. With own- and other-type density controlled, the effects of changes in the mass variables capture the effects of changes in the average size of other hotels.

Hotel Characteristics

We defined hotel age as the number of years since the date of a hotel's founding. Hotel size and hotel price were measured, respectively, as the number of rooms operated by a hotel and the average daily room rate (in constant dollars) advertised by a hotel in each year of its existence. The number of rooms a hotel operates is the standard measure of size used in the hotel industry and captures the "total productive capacity installed," which Winter suggested reflects the differential competitive strength of larger organizations. We constructed these variables from information in the archival sources described above. For a small number of hotels for which size or price data were unavailable for a given year, we used linear interpolation to determine the values.

The natural logarithms of size and price were used to reduce the variables' skewness. Founded by chain is a dichotomous variable, coded 1 for hotels that were affiliated with a chain at the time they were founded. It may be that chains help the components they found overcome the liability of newness that affects fledgling organizations. Alternatively, chains may imprint the components they found so severely with the chain strategy that the components suffer an increased level of strategic constraint. Lastly, a left-censored variable, coded 1 for hotels founded before 1898 and zero otherwise was also included to examine whether the hotels founded prior to 1898 had systematically different failure rates.

Hotel Chain Characteristics

We controlled for two additional characteristics of chains that may affect the fates of component hotels. First, we controlled for hotel chain age, measured as the age in years of the chain to which a component hotel was affiliated at the start of each year. Second, since larger chains are likely to possess greater scale advantages, as well as more slack resources, we controlled for the size of the chains to which component hotels were affiliated, which we measured as the total number of hotels the chain operated at the beginning of each year.

We used the number of hotels because the number of hotel rooms was unavailable for many hotels outside Manhattan. Because we include the number of hotels a chain operates in Manhattan in the model, we subtracted the number of Manhattan hotels from the total to compute the number of non-Manhattan hotels a chain operates, to ensure mutually exclusive variables and simplify interpretation.

Environmental Characteristics

We also controlled for several factors influencing the environmental carrying capacity for transient-hotel services in Manhattan. The potential demand for hotel services was measured as the number of visitors to New York City (divided by 1,000,000 for rescaling) in the prior year. This variable includes arrivals by sea, rail, and air. Because the hotel industry is vulnerable to the state of the American economy, annual gross national product (GNP) growth was included as a control. Because the number of hotel chains (as well as the number of component hotels they operate) may influence the fates of component and independent hotels, we included chain operator density, defined as the number of hotel chains that operated hotels in Manhattan at the start of each year, as a control variable in the analysis. To examine whether the effects of hotel chain crowding were stronger for component hotels than independent hotels, we also included a chain-operator-density x chain-member interaction. To examine whether the effects of the theoretical variables were simply the result of the passage of time, we included a time-trend variable, calendar time, in the analysis.

The highest bivariate correlation, .753, is between the component-hotel dummy variable and the In(component-hotel time clock) variable. For the ex-component-hotel dummy variable and the ex-component-hotel time clock variable, the correlation is .614. The correlations among the different functional forms of the initial and incremental experience variables are higher, but these variables are not included in the same models; thus, these correlations do not affect our estimation. Although some correlations are high, in general, correlations among our study variables are in the low to moderate range (.1 to .4).

Such levels of multicollinearity among explanatory variables can result in less precise parameter estimates (i.e., larger standard errors) for these explanatory variables but will not bias parameter estimates. While this does not pose a serious estimation problem, it can make it difficult to draw inferences about the effects of adding particular variables to our models. Therefore, when generating the results we present below, we estimate and test the significance of groups of variables in comparisons of a series of hierarchically nested regression models and examine coefficients and their standard errors for inflation to check that multicollinearity is not causing parameter estimates to be less precise.

Analysis

Parametric estimates of the hazard rate require assumptions about the effect of time (in these models, age) on failure. There is debate about the appropriate parameterizations of age dependence in organizational mortality, so we used a piecewise exponential model, which allows the rate of failure to vary in an unconstrained way over preselected age ranges.

To include time variation in the covariates, we used a multiple-spells formulation. In this formulation of the model, each hotel's history is broken down into one-year spells in which the hotel is at risk of failing. Each spell is considered right-censored unless the hotel fails. This allows the time-varying independent variables to be updated annually. We used TDA to estimate parameter estimates by the method of maximum likelihood. We tested the implication of our assumption of piecewise age dependence by estimating the semiparametric Cox model (not presented), which generated results for the covariates that were comparable to those we present from the piecewise exponential model.

Tests of significance shown in the table are one-tailed for directional predictions for the variables and two-tailed otherwise. Model 1 provides a baseline that includes hotel characteristics and the environmental control variables. Models 2-5 each add local and nonlocal experience variables based on one of the four discount factor specifications. The coefficients for each specification of the local and nonlocal experience variables are broadly comparable. Clearly, however, the specification in model 2, which assumes no depreciation of knowledge gained from past experience over time, is weakest (likelihood ratio test = 7.74, 4 d.f., n.s.).

By comparison, the specification in model 3 based on the [Square root] Age discount factor, which assumes that depreciation of knowledge is initially slow and slows further with time, is strongest, providing the largest improvement in fit over the baseline model (likelihood ratio test = 31.12, 4 d.f., p [is less than] .001). Thus our findings suggest that operating knowledge becomes antiquated and decays with time. Given these initial estimates, in the remainder of the analysis, we used variables based on the [Square root] Age discount factor. To examine the robustness of estimates for the nonlocal experience variables to the observations for six very large chains (Holiday Inn, Best Western, Ramada, Howard Johnson, Quality Inn, Travelodge), we reestimated models 2-5 after excluding 101 spells for components of these chains. The reestimation (not shown) produced coefficients for the nonlocal experience variables comparable to those in Table 3.

The estimates in model 3 support the knowledge transfer and learning hypothesis 1, but support is more mixed for hypothesis 2, on strategic constraint. As predicted by hypothesis 1, the coefficients for initial and incremental local experience are both significant and negative. These estimates indicate that greater cumulative (discounted) Manhattan operating experience by a chain at the time a component hotel joins it increases the survival advantage gained by the component. Moreover, the incremental local experience coefficient indicates that additions to a chain's Manhattan operating experience during the course of the relationship lowered failure rates of the chain's Manhattan components further.

• The coefficient for initial nonlocal experience is significant and negative. Thus, contrary to hypothesis 2, greater cumulative (discounted) non-Manhattan operating experience by a chain at the time a component hotel joins it increases the survival advantage of the component. In contrast, the positive incremental nonlocal experience coefficient indicates that increases in non-Manhattan operating experience during the life of the affiliation increased the failure rates of chains' Manhattan components, as predicted by hypothesis 2.

The implications of these opposing effects of chains' incremental experience within and outside of Manhattan on Manhattan component hotel failure are illustrated which compares the failure rate of a component of a hotel chain with no experience (i.e., both local and nonlocal experience equal zero) with the failure rates of components of more experienced hotel chains. A multiplier of greater than 1 indicates that the failure rate is increased relative to the hotel that joined the inexperienced chain by a factor equal to the multiplier; a multiplier less than 1 indicates that it decreased. As the figure shows, components of hotel chains that gain only non-manhattan operating experience have the highest failure rates, but the hazard rate drops off sharply as hotel chains increase their Manhattan operating experience. Thus components gain from their chains' incremental Manhattan operating experience and suffer from their chains' increasing experience elsewhere.

To provide more rigorous tests of hypotheses 1 and 2 and test our remaining hypotheses, we examined more fully specified models in Table 4. Model 6, which adds the component and ex-component dummy and time-clock variables, improves the fit of model 6 significantly (likelihood ratio test = 77.68, 4 d.f., p [is less than] .001). The coefficient for the component hotel dummy variable is significant and negative, and the coefficient for the component time clock is significant and positive. Combined, these coefficients indicate that immediately after becoming a component, a hotel's risk of failure dropped, as predicted by hypothesis 3, but then increased over time toward that of an independent hotel.

The coefficients for the ex-component dummy and time-clock variables are broadly similar. Together, the significant negative ex-component coefficient and the significant positive ex-component time-clock coefficient indicate that after a chain affiliation was severed, an ex-component hotel's failure rate remained lower than independent hotels — and even dropped below component hotels whose chain affiliations lasted longer than ten years-but the failure rate subsequently increased toward that of an independent hotel.

This figure compares the failure rate of an independent hotel to the failure rates of (1) a hotel that became and remained a component and (2) a hotel that became a component but subsequently became an ex-component after 20 years. A multiplier of greater than 1 indicates that the failure rate is increased relative to an independent hotel by a factor equal to the multiplier; a multiplier of less than 1 indicates that it decreased.

The multiplier for the hotel that became and remained a component shows that, immediately after becoming a component, the failure rate drops to less than one-tenth that of an independent hotel but subsequently increases over the life of the affiliation. Even after 40 years, however, the component hotel still enjoys a failure rate less than one-half that of an independent hotel. Thus, although component hotels derived a significant advantage from chain affiliation, ceteris paribus, the value of the relationship depreciates somewhat over time.

The multiplier for the hotel that acquires chain affiliation but becomes an ex-component after 20 years shows that immediately after becoming an ex-component, the hotel's failure rate drops below that of the hotel that remained a component but then increases toward that of an independent hotel more rapidly. Yet only after 20 years is the ex-component hotel's failure rate equal to that of an independent hotel. When interpreting extreme values for the component and ex-component time clocks, the temporal pattern presented in Table 1 should be kept in mind: only 10 components actually had affiliations that lasted as long as 50 years.

In model 7, we introduce the chain characteristics variables to test hypotheses 4, 5, and 6. Adding these variables improves on the fit of model 6 significantly (likelihood ratio test = 29.72, 6 d.f., p [is less than] .01). Supporting hypothesis 4, hotels that were components of chains operating a large number of rooms in Manhattan have significantly lower failure rates than comparable hotels affiliated with chains with a smaller number of rooms in Manhattan. Supporting hypothesis 5, the significant positive coefficient for the number of component hotels a chain operates in Manhattan indicates that increasing the number of units a chain operates in a market dilutes the chain's market power, reducing the advantage of the chain affiliation to the component hotel.

Not surprisingly, there is a positive correlation (.671) between the number of Manhattan rooms the chain operates and the number of Manhattan components the chain operates, so we conducted further analysis to rule out the possibility of multi-colinearity. We estimated model 7 with the Manhattan rooms and Manhattan components variables included separately (not shown) and found that the results were robust, and multicolinearity was not an issue. As predicted by hypothesis 6, the significant negative coefficient for name concentration indicates that component hotels had lower failure rates in chains in which a high proportion of components had names that linked them with the chain. Being founded by a chain significantly increased the failure rate, suggesting that components founded by chains suffered a more severe strategic constraint.

To test hypothesis 7, the hotel density and mass variables and their interactions with the component hotel dummy variable were introduced in model 8. In model 8, several of the interactions are insignificant. To ensure that this was not a result of high correlations among the interaction variables, we removed the two insignificant interactions in model 9. With these terms removed, the fit of the model is not significantly reduced (likelihood ratio test = 3.66, 2 d.f., n.s.), and the reduced model provides a significant improvement over model 7 (likelihood ratio test = 71.2, 8 d.f., p [is less than] .01). Therefore, we interpret model 9. In this fully specified model, the coefficients for our theoretical variables are substantively unchanged from the earlier estimates, providing more robust support for hypotheses 1 to 6.

In model 9, the main effect of other-type density is significant and negative, and its interaction with chain membership has no effect. This means that rather than density-dependent competition between independent and component hotels, there was density-dependent mutualism: increases in the number of either type lowered the failure rate of the other type, and the mutualistic cross-effect was of equal magnitude for independent and component hotels. The main effect of other-type mass is also significant and negative, but its interaction with chain membership is significant and positive. With other-type density controlled, this means that increasing average size of component hotels had a mutualistic effect that lowered failure rates of independent hotels.

So neither hypothesis 7 nor the alternative we considered, of component hotels generating competition for independent hotels, holds. Rather, independent and component hotels have a mainly symbiotic relationship. Large independent hotels did, however, generate significant competition for component hotels.

Several of the control variables also significantly influenced hotel failure. Larger and higher-priced hotels have significantly lower failure rates. Increases in the number of visitors to New York City and the U,S. GNP both lower the hotel failure rate. The main effect of own-type density is significant and positive, and its interaction with chain membership is significant and negative, this means that density-dependent competition was more intense among independent than component hotels. The relative magnitudes of the main effect ([Beta]=.012) and interaction ([Beta]=-.086) terms indicate that increasing hotel density had competitive effects only among independent hotels; for components, the overall effect of density increases (.012-.086=-.074) was mutualistic.

The main effect of own-type mass is significant and negative, and its interaction with chain membership is insignificant. With own-type density controlled, this means that increases in the average size of other hotels of the same type lowered failure rates, and the effect was of equal magnitude for independent and component hotels. The insignificant main effect for chain operator density and the significant positive coefficient for the chain-operator-density x chain-member interaction indicates that although component hotels affected each other's fates mutualistically, competition from crowding of hotel chains in Manhattan increased the failure rate of component hotels but did not influence the survival of independent hotels. Finally, any significant differences between the coefficients of the dummy variables for the age categories reveal the pattern of age dependence in a piecewise exponential model. In model 9 there are no such differences, indicating that the failure rate for Manhattan hotels does not vary with age.

We performed additional analyses to determine whether or not our findings were related to other variables known to affect the failure rate of Manhattan hotels but not included in our models. In particular, Baum and Mezias (1992) found that the failure rate of Manhattan hotels was affected by size-, price-, and geographically localized competition, and Baum (1995) found that the failure rate was affected by interactions between industry age and various measures of competition (i.e., density, mass, industry concentration, size-localized competition). We reestimated our models after including the variables from these two papers, and the results reported above are robust. Further, the findings from Baum and Mezias (1992) and Baum (1995) hold up in the models that include the chain-affiliation variables. Thus the results we focus on in this paper are empirically distinct from those considered in earlier papers. We will provide tables showing the results of these additional analyses on request.

Given trends over the last century suggesting that chains will eventually come to dominate most service industries, understanding how chains affect the evolution of industries over time is an extremely important topic for organization theorists. This research was motivated in part by the scarcity of research examining the implications of chains. We began to address the role of chains by modeling the influences of chain affiliation for the fates of component organizations and competitive dynamics in the Manhattan hotel industry. The findings reveal that the effects of chain affiliation are both substantive and complex.

Consistent with claims of the advantages of the chain form and arguments about the implications of interorganizational relations as resource buffers, in Manhattan, chain affiliation, under most circumstances, improves the survival chances of component hotels. All chain memberships are not equal, however, and the survival benefits to components vary systematically with the operating experience and the number and distribution of components of hotel chains.

Manhattan component hotels derive the greatest benefit when the chains to which they belong (1) provide a large initial transfer of knowledge based on past accumulated operating experience both in and outside Manhattan, and (2) the chain continues to accumulate operating knowledge in Manhattan that can be transferred to its components. Since we control separately for the potential resource implications of being a component by including contemporaneous measures of the chain's size, we interpret this as evidence of a less tangible benefit from chain affiliation, in the form of transferred knowledge. That components have lower failure rates even after the chain affiliation is severed also indicates that the chain affiliation provides more than just material resources. Chain affiliation, however, is not an unmixed blessing. Hotels founded by chains have higher rates of failure, and the rate of component failure increases with the accumulation of non-manhattan operating experience during the affiliation.

These effects of strategic constraint are the costs of being an instrumental part of a strategy designed to derive maximum benefit for the collective, without special regard to any particular component. We were surprised by the finding that non-Manhattan operating experience at the time the chain affiliation was created decreased the mortality rate. We had predicted that such experience would be a source of strategic constraint. Two things may explain the finding. First, there are some elements of non-manhattan experience that are applicable to the Manhattan market. For example, the chain-wide level of experience would contribute to the ability to operate a reservation system, which would benefit a Manhattan component of the chain.

Second, there is probably a self-selection by chains that enter the Manhattan market. If their past experience was such that they were ignorant about operating a hotel in Manhattan, they were probably less likely to start or acquire a Manhattan component. Therefore, the chains that entered the Manhattan market were likely those with past non-manhattan experience most applicable there. After the Manhattan component joins the chain, however, the chain may "drift." There is no guarantee that a group of organizations in similar environments at one time will still be in similar environments at a later time. If a chain with a history of non-Manhattan experience useful in Manhattan "drifted" after acquiring a Manhattan component, we would expect the observed result that preaffiliation non-Manhattan experience helps the component, while postaffiliation non-Manhattan experience harms the component.

It may seem that the advantages and disadvantages of chain affiliation are separable. What about a hotel that joined a chain and then quickly severed the relationship, perhaps to join another chain? Wouldn't such a hotel reap the advantage of transferred knowledge without the disadvantage of strategic constraint? Our results suggest that it might, but unfortunately, such a "promiscuous" strategy is impossible. The owners and managers of a hotel can be strategic about the decision to join a chain, but once they join, it is the chain that decides whether or not they will stay. This is the duality of component organizations. To the people within them they may seem like any other organization, yet ultimately their fate is not their own. Component organizations are like independent organizations in routine operations but essentially different, in that authority for all of the important decisions concerning a component rests at the chain level.

The dynamic effects of chain affiliation are also informative. The effect for ex-component hotel and ex-component time clock seem easy to interpret. When a component leaves a chain, it has a lower failure rate than independent hotels, but over time this advantage disappears. This is consistent with what we would expect given the arguments we have made about chain affiliation being a source of operating knowledge. When the affiliation is severed, the ex-component is still left with some of the knowledge it acquired from the chain, but over time that knowledge or its usefulness decays. The significant negative coefficient for component hotel is as we predicted and can be explained by the resource and operating implications of chain affiliation not captured by the other variables.

The positive coefficient for the component time clock (which was not significant in models 8 and 9) suggests that the advantage of a chain affiliation decreases with its duration. This could be explained by the fact that, since capital budgeting decisions are usually made at the chain level, needed maintenance is delayed for components, causing them over time to fall into disrepair. It may also be that the chain is a source of inertia. Operating within the chain, with its standardization and decision-making authority, may inhibit the component's capacity to respond to its local environment.

An alternative explanation for the negative coefficient for component is that chains select the best components for chain membership. The negative coefficient may represent the fact that components are simply better than independents in some unobserved way, rather than that the residual benefits of chain membership are not captured by our other variables. It is credible that chains select high-performing hotels, but we have attempted to control for as much hotel-level variance as possible by including the size and price variables, which do significantly influence the hotel's failure rate. Future research on which independent organizations are likely to be chosen by chains would be useful in identifying the importance of selection in explaining differential outcomes for components and independents.

Reputation also appears to be a significant advantage for some component hotels. According to model 9, a component of a large chain that pursues a reputation strategy (a chain that names all of its units the same way) would have a failure rate about 0.016 times that of a component in a chain that does not pursue a reputation strategy or an independent hotel. This is evidence at the component level for the advantage of common names that Ingram (1996b) found at the chain level. Clearly, reputation is important in the hospitality industry because often customers must interact with unfamiliar hotels. Reputation as a means of generating credible commitment is also important in hospitality and other industries in which chains thrive.

Because of the interdependence of components in a chain, they are better able than independent organizations to say "you can trust us because we have so much to lose if you are dissatisfied with our behavior." As an illustration, consider the recent scandal over the cheating of customers at Sears' Automotive Centers. Cheating in the automobile service industry is nothing new. Why then were we shocked to hear that Sears also cheats? It is because Sears has a national network of interdependent operations, and we expect that the cost of scandal, and therefore the incentive to resist malfeasance, would be so much higher for Sears than for independents.

Another result of the relationships between components of the same chain is the advantage of the chain's market power. Consistent with this, we found that component hotels that are part of chains that control more rooms in Manhattan have lower rates of failure. But the failure rate increases with the number of Manhattan hotels that are part of a component's chain, again demonstrating the tension between the component and the collective. It is advantageous to be part of a chain that has a high degree of market power, but disadvantageous to have to share that power with other components.

The implications of chains for the competitive dynamics of the Manhattan hotel industry are fascinating when we consider the relationship between independent and component organizations of all types over the last century. In industries such as retailing there was an explicit battle between chains and independent establishments that resulted in most states passing legislation to inhibit the growth of chains. In hospitality there was resistance from old-style "hotelmen" to the chain form of organization. The resistance expressed itself in public statements and in the politics of the industry's trade associations.

Yet we found that the relationships between component and independent hotels were generally mutualistic. Component hotels competed only with large independent hotels. This suggests that there are two niches in the hospitality industry and that component hotels and smaller independent hotels can peacefully coexist. The public conflict between the two organizational forms is not inconsistent with this explanation, because it was generally the owners of large independent hotels, which do compete with chains, that had the time and resources to be active in the arena of public opinion.

An interesting non-result concerns economies of scale, which were the basis for the economic explanation for the success of chains. We hypothesized and found evidence of local economies of scale in the form of a lower failure rate for components of chains with more Manhattan rooms. The size of the chain outside Manhattan, however, had no effect on the component's likelihood of failure.

This finding is compelling in light of findings elsewhere that larger and more geographically compact hotel chains have lower failure rates. The advantage of compactness at the chain level is consistent with the finding here of local economies of scale, but the advantage of large size at the chain level is not reflected at the component level. It may be that general economies of scale do exist for hotel chains, but they are not reflected in the Manhattan market. It could also be that existing economies of scale are exploited at the chain level and do not benefit components. In any case, our finding gives reason to reconsider the assumption that chain components benefit from economies of scale beyond those generated in their local market.

When generalizing from our result, however, it should be remembered that in industries such as retailing, economies of scale may be more important and more of a benefit to the component than in hospitality. In drawing conclusions about the success of the chain form of organization from this study, it is important to remember that Manhattan is different from many of the markets in which hotel chains thrive. The Manhattan market is large enough for independent hotels to be professionally managed; it is a sufficiently central travel destination to allow travelers to develop enduring relationships with independent hotels; and it is a stronghold of luxury hotels. These features suggest that Manhattan should be a difficult market for chains. When we interviewed Manhattan hotel managers, they voiced the same opinion. This makes our finding that chain affiliation (under most circumstances) lowers the failure rate of component hotels all the more striking.

Returning to the problem we introduced this paper with, we can now say much more about the success of the chain form. Usually, the net effect of chain affiliation is to lower the failure rate of components. Our results are compatible with what Miner, Amburgey, and Stearns (1990) referred to as partial selection resulting from organizational buffers. Rather than competing directly with independent hotels, component hotels become more numerous because, as a function of their chain affiliations, they have lower rates of failure. In this sense, our findings are broadly consistent with other research on the effect of interorganizational linkages on organizational failure.

Our detailed relational data allowed us to dimensionalize the interorganizational relationship, however, and we discovered some disadvantages, such as an increasing failure risk associated with incremental strategic constraint and a higher risk for affiliation with chains that operate many Manhattan hotels. Knowing more about when and what type of interorganizational linkages are beneficial or harmful would be valuable for managers and designers of organizations.

This paper differs in another important way from past work on interorganizational linkages and organizational failure. Past work has looked at linkages between population members and regulatory agencies, community organizations, and political parties, which are important but nondefinitive connections between organizations and their environment.(6) In contrast, the linkages between component hotels and chains create a distinct organizational form, for which we have suggested the term superorganization.

For us, the critical feature of a superorganization is that it is created by horizontal linkages between similar subunits. The superorganization is therefore commensalistic, while past analysis of multiunit organizational forms has mostly been on synergistic relations such as vertical integration. We believe that the findings here are useful for understanding the implications of the linkages to the many types of superorganizations, both chain and non-chain. For example, the sharing of certain types of experience may be an important benefit to an organization that operates similar production plants in different geographic areas.

Further, the superorganization form is representative of what Daft and Lewin (1993) called the "new" organizational forms, although it is certainly not new. Superorganizations use relatively autonomous subunits to respond to local conditions and avoid the pitfalls of hierarchy, were initially considered radical but are now familiar, and have been innovators in developing and applying technology and management techniques to operate a diffuse organization. As such, superorganizations seem like an excellent model to study the "new" organizational forms, all the better because they have been evolving for more than a century.

This research highlights a potential linkage between organizational ecology and theories of organizational learning. Many formal organizational activities are intended to acquire information or knowledge. Typically, such learning by organizations is viewed as an organization-level phenomenon. Recently, however, work by network theorists shows that learning may often be produced by interactions among organizations, rather than by isolated organizations. Consequently, learning by organizations may commonly unfold in organizational populations and communities as well as individual organizations.

Here we emphasize not learning processes present at the population level in the form of interorganizational imitative behavior but, building on Darr, Argote, and Epple (1995), those resulting from intraorganizational learning communities made up of multiunit chains. We showed that operating experience at the hotel-chain level translates into a survival advantage al the component level, contributing greatly to success of the chain form in the Manhattan hotel industry. Given the prevalence of the chain organizational form across service industries, future research combining ideas on interorganizational learning at the population level and intraorganizational learning within super organizations could provide new insights into industry dynamics and evolution.

(1) To examine whether the effect of second and third chain affiliations on component survival differed from the effect of a first affiliation, we estimated models that included a dummy variable coded 1 for components that were in a second or third affiliation and 0 otherwise. The coefficients for this variable were insignificant, and coefficients for other variables were unchanged.

(2) This is a departure from Barnett and Amburgey's (1990) measure of population mass, the total number of telephones, which, as Winter (1990) pointed out, is arguably a measure of the demand served rather than organizational size.

(3) Carroll and Hannan (1989) suggested that failure to incorporate data on the early period of a population's history may obscure the legitimacy effects of organizational density. Consequently, because data on the Manhattan hotel industry are missing prior to 1898, the competitive effects of density may be expected to dominate the estimates for independent hotels. Since component hotels were introduced to Manhattan at the start of the observation period, however, we tested for possible curvilinear effects by including both own-type density and own-type density squared in a preliminary analysis. We found no evidence of curvilinear own-type density dependence effects for either independent or component hotels. Therefore, we report only linear effects of own-type density below.

(4) These variables were constructed using information contained in the Historical Statistics of the United

States, Colonial Times to 1970, Historical Abstracts of the United States, and Port of New York and New Jersey Authority Annual Reports.

(5) The component hotel dummy variable coefficients increase markedly in size in models 8-9. This is a result of adding the component hotel interactions. Although the component hotel coefficients jump notably, the predictions do not, because the larger coefficients are counterbalanced by the interaction coefficients, which must be considered simultaneously.

(6) An exception is Freeman's (1990) analysis of subsidiary semiconductor producers.

Chapter 3

Guidelines of Employment in the Hotel Sector

NEW SUPPLY OF HOTELS

Since 1997, International Hotel has maintained its own database of new supply into important hotel markets in India. The graph below highlights the 95 hotels under active development in various cities, of which HVS International is currently aware. It is important to note that most HVS data for new supply represents branded properties. It is however quite likely that a number equal to the above may also be under some stages of planning. New economy segment hotels are being promoted by some leading hotel chains in the country, which have not been accounted for in this survey.

We are of the opinion that demand for hotels has risen across nearly all cities, in the current financial year. Leading the growth in demand are Bangalore, Delhi, Mumbai, Hyderabad, Jaipur, Goa, Pune and Chennai. At present HVS's opinion is that probably all the cities mentioned above will readily absorb all the rooms under development and there will be a major shortage of rooms over the next 3-4 years.

The current year has been a fantastic year for tourism recovery in the region. We have enjoyed the best year in terms of tourism arrivals, the economy remains relatively strong and enjoys one of the fastest growth in the world, at many forums across the globe India remains the current flavour of the day.

The year 2003-04 has been a year of consolidation and gains for the hotel industry in India, both in terms of room night demand and average rates. Taking into account the bullish trend presently witnessed in the industry, together with an overall positive outlook on the Indian economy, 2004-05 will be a record year in terms of hotel performance across nearly all cities in the country. As expected, the Indian hotel market is already generating serious interest from international operators and hotel developers. HVS International is aware that there are currently international hospitality funds and a few new operators that are exploring the Indian markets for both investment and operating opportunities.

We also feel the biggest boost to the hotel industry is going to come from the current on-going process of open sky policy and also the fact that Indian private airlines will be allowed to fly to various regions across the globe. This along with improved airports will certainly continue to benefit demand for hotel room nights. Human resources development, employment and globalization in the hotel, catering and tourism sector. Report for discussion at the Tripartite Meeting on Human Resources Development, Employment and Globalization in the Hotel, Catering and Tourism Sector, Geneva, 2001.

Sectoral Activities Programme. This seeks to illustrate how the issues of globalization, employment and human resources development in the hotel, catering and tourism sector are linked to the strategic objectives of the ILO that were decided at the International Labour Conference in June 1999: to promote and realize fundamental principles and rights at work; to create greater opportunities for women and men to secure decent employment and income; to enhance the coverage and effectiveness of social protection for all; and to strengthen tripartism and social dialogue.

The report points to recent developments in the hotel, catering and tourism sector and highlights factors driving the internationalization of tourists' travel and of tourism services, including information technologies, as welt as the internationalization or hotel and tourism enterprises. Without neglecting the huge subsector of small and medium-sized enterprises, it describes typical features related to the composition of the labour force and to working conditions. It raises questions concerning the difficulties faced by the sector in attracting and retaining skilled workers and in enhancing the skills of newcomers to the labour market in order to stabilize the sector's labour force, while increasing the productivity of enterprises and the quality of services.

Particular emphasis is put on new forms of management entailing new skills requirements, with a general tendency towards increased worker responsibility in an environment of flat hierarchies, multi-skilling and teamwork. As to social dialogue in this sector, a description is provided of certain institutions, achievements and shortcomings in this respect, but in a way that also points to opportunities for increasing its scope and effectiveness. The causal relationships between globalization, employment and human resources development are examined on the basis of the information available, and other factors such as advances in technology and training, and changes in tourism demand are also highlighted.

Hard data on the hotel, catering and tourism sector are not easy to come by as they are rarely singled out from the services sector in general. Data specifically on tourism depend on a form of accounting that covers a broad range of economic activities geared towards tourist consumption. Only a few countries can provide systematically collected data on tourism and little attention is given to labour issues.

The report draws on a wide variety of sources for information, including government institutions, intergovernmental organizations, trade unions, employers' organizations, companies, international non-governmental organizations, and individual scholars. The sources used are certainly not exhaustive but are probably fairly representative.

Job Satisfaction in Joint Venture Hotels in China

Joint ventures have become a major form of foreign investment in China since it adopted an open-door economic policy. Many studies have examined the strategic, legal and management issues involved in setting up and managing a foreign joint venture in China. However, little is known about factors that affect job attitudes of local employees in joint ventures in China. This gap in our knowledge is unsatisfactory because it is well known that staff with negative job attitudes are likely to perform poorly, cause disruptions to normal operations, and eventually jeopardize the viability of a joint venture.

The present study attempts to fill this gap by examining job satisfaction in hotel joint ventures in the Shanghai area in China. Justice theories have now been widely applied in organizational settings, and a variety of topics have been examined, such as reactions to layoffs, industrial actions, management of subsidiaries, commitment of senior managers in international joint ventures, reactions to fare increases of public transportation, employee drug testing, performance appraisal, trust in supervisors and commitment, organizational citizenship behavior, and job satisfaction. In the literature, a tripartite conceptualization of justice is widely adopted.

Distributive justice is concerned with the fairness of the allocation of a reward. The dominant theory in this tradition is equity theory, which posits that one's reward should be proportional to one's input. Procedural justice is concerned with the procedure used in allocating resources. Interactional justice is concerned with the quality of treatment received from decisionmakers and the extent to which formal decisionmaking procedures are properly enacted. These three types of justice were found to relate to job satisfaction in a number of studies in the U.S.; Moorman.

Predicting Job Satisfaction in Joint Ventures

Since previous work has shown that justice is related to job satisfaction, it would be interesting to test the generality of the justice framework in joint ventures. The first question addressed in this study is whether in joint ventures in China, the three types of justice would be related to job satisfaction as is the case in the U.S. To the best of our knowledge, the relationship between perceived justice and job satisfaction has never been tested in a Chinese context. It would be interesting to see if results obtained in the U.S. can be replicated in China.

The second question addressed is whether new constructs for the conceptualization of justice are needed to understand job satisfaction in Chinese joint ventures. Joint ventures in developing countries differ from Western organizations in an important way. The foreign partners of these joint ventures usually come from developed countries such as the U.S., Japan and European countries or more developed neighboring Pacific Rim countries.

Expatriate managers are often sent from headquarters to run these joint ventures. Gladwin and Walter [1980] have provided a detailed analysis of the problems created by this arrangement. The problem most relevant to our analysis is that these expatriate managers, as a rule, enjoy much better pay and benefits than their local counterparts who hold similar positions. This gap in compensation is often a major source of frustration and disgruntlement for the local staff, causing conflict between them and the expatriate staff.

This problem is severe in joint ventures in China because of its low per capita GDP as compared to the U.S., Japan, Hong Kong, Taiwan, and Western Europe. The GDP per capita for Japan, Western Europe, and the U.S is roughly thirty times of that of China. The salaries of managers from Japan and the West are often more than twenty times the salaries of Chinese managers. Despite this, joint ventures usually pay better than state-owned enterprises in China. If Chinese employees compare their salaries with those of expatriate staff, they are likely to be disturbed by the huge discrepancy in compensation. It is interesting to see if expatriate managers are used as a comparison group by Chinese employees in judging the fairness of their pay.

There are substantive reasons to expect that they would not be. The values of Chinese managers are much more accepting of status differentials than are those of Western managers (e.g., Smith and Wang [1995]). Chen has recently shown that Chinese managers favor greater differentiation of rewards than do U.S. managers.

The analysis above suggests that current conceptualizations of distributive justice may be too narrow in the context of a joint venture. In the literature, distributive justice is primarily concerned with performance inputs. For instance, a widely used scale to measure distributive fairness, developed by Price and Mueller [1986], asks subjects to indicate whether they are fairly paid in relation to their job responsibilities, the amount of effort they put in, the work they have done well, the amount of experience that they have, and the stresses and strains of their job.

In a joint venture, however, the scope of distributive justice has to be broadened because of the salience of social comparison processes. In fact, in Lawler's [1981] pay satisfaction model, perceived pay of referent others is hypothesized to affect pay satisfaction. Recent work on pay satisfaction also takes into account social comparison processes and the perception of other pay systems. It is interesting to note that in the Pay Satisfaction Questionnaire, a widely used instrument, items involving a comparison of the salaries of different jobs within a company are included.

However, there are no items involving comparisons with salaries in other companies. Based on the analysis above, it is proposed that in the context of a joint venture, distributive justice should be split into two subtypes. Performance-based distributive justice (PDJ) focuses on the fairness of one's reward in relation to performance inputs, whereas comparative distributive justice (CDJ) focuses on the fairness of one's reward in comparison to referent others.

Three referent groups are salient in joint ventures in China. Local staff may compare themselves with 1) overseas employees who work in the same company, 2) local employees who work in state-owned enterprises, or 3) local employees who work in other joint ventures. It is argued that because the open door policy has been adopted for a number of years, Chinese employees are well aware of the huge difference between salaries in China and in developed countries.

Thus, it is hypothesized that they would not use the expatriate group as their referent group in deciding the fairness of their salary. Comparison with expatriate employees should not affect their job satisfaction level. Instead, Chinese employees would choose local employees who work in state-owned enterprises or in other joint ventures as their referent groups because of their comparability. It is hypothesized that comparison with these referent groups would affect the job satisfaction of Chinese employees.

Chinese employees would choose local employees working in state-owned enterprises or in other joint ventures as their referent groups, rather than expatriate staff, in judging the fairness of their salary.

Perceived Justice and Rank

Whether the rank of local staff is related to perceived justice is an interesting question. Senior local staff usually have more contact with expatriate staff and are likely to be involved in decisionmaking processes with them. Thus, perceived procedural and interactional justice are likely to be affected as procedural justice is concerned with decisionmaking processes, whereas interactional justice is concerned with interpersonal treatment. It is possible that senior staff may expect a higher level of involvement in decisionmaking and more positive interpersonal treatment from expatriates.

The reasoning behind this speculation is that senior staff enjoy a higher status in an organization. Because of their higher status, they expect to be more involved in decisionmaking and receive better treatment in their interaction with other members of the organization. It is possible that because of their higher expectations, senior staff's perception of procedural and interactional justice may be less positive than the perception of low-level staff. A similar argument can be made with regard to distributive justice. Compared with low-level local staff, senior staff may expect a larger salary for the same level of performance inputs. It is possible that senior staff would report a lower level of perceived distributive justice than low-level staff. These possibilities were explored in the present study.

Many researchers have argued that when people from different cultures work together, conflicts are likely to occur because of their differences in cultural background. It is possible that if expatriate managers come from cultures similar to the host culture, job satisfaction of local employees may be higher. In joint ventures in China, most expatriate managers fall into three groups in terms of their cultural origin:

1. Overseas Chinese from Hong Kong, Taiwan and South East Asia,
2. Japanese, and
3. Westerners from the U.S. and Europe.

Obviously, Mainland Chinese are culturally more similar to overseas Chinese, and least similar to Westerners. Both Chinese and Japanese are under the influence of Confucianism, whereas Westerners are not. Chinese and Japanese are higher in collectivism and power distance than people from North America and Western Europe. Based on the cultural match hypothesis, it is predicted that Chinese employees should show a higher level of job satisfaction if the cultural background of the overseas managers is more similar to theirs.

Chinese employees, who work with overseas Chinese, should show the highest level of job satisfaction, followed by those who work with Japanese, and then by those who work with Westerners (the cultural match hypothesis).

On the other hand, it is entirely possible that job satisfaction is only remotely related to the cultural origin of expatriate employees, but is much more closely related to the perceived fairness of their managerial practices. If this, indeed, is the case, differences in job satisfaction across different groups of local employees should parallel differences in the perceived fairness of expatriate staff. In other words, according to the justice hypothesis, if perceived justice is controlled, group differences in job satisfaction should disappear.

Group differences in job satisfaction are caused by group differences in justice perception (the justice hypothesis). These two competing hypotheses were examined in the present study. Joint venture hotels in the Hangzhou and Shanghai areas in China were contacted about this research project. Almost all hotels contacted agreed to participate (42 hotels), and 137 Chinese employees from these hotels completed a battery of questionnaires for the present study.

Such a large number of hotels were included because, for many of them, only a few staff had direct contact with expatriate managers in their daily work. All of the participants were at the supervisory level, and 69.2% of the respondents were male. With regard to age distribution, 45.5% were between 20-29; 32.1% between 30-39; 11.2% between 40-49; and 11.2% at or above 50.

Most respondents (75.0%) had at least two years of college education. With regard to rank, 13.3% of the respondents were senior managers, 44.4% middle managers, and 42.2% supervisors. The majority of the respondents (81.5%) worked for hotels that employed 100 to 1,000 staff. The national origin of the foreign partners of these joint venture hotels included Hong Kong, Singapore, Taiwan, the U.S., and Japan. A team of Chinese researchers visited a number of joint venture hotels and contacted local employees of these hotels who had contact with expatriate managers.

The purpose of the visit was described as part of a research project that aimed at understanding the operation of joint venture hotels. These employees were asked to respond to an anonymous questionnaire, which was originally written in English, but was translated into Chinese by a team of competent bilinguals. The questionnaire contained several sections which were concerned with different aspects of the operation of the hotels and information about the respondents and the hotels. The present is based on a set of items with regard to justice and job satisfaction. The items tapping these three justice constructs were taken from Moorman [1991], with modifications to render them more appropriate for a joint venture setting.

Performance-based distributive justice was measured by five items, and respondents were asked to indicate whether local employees were rewarded fairly. For items measuring procedural and interactional justice, the word "supervisor" was changed to "overseas manager." Procedural justice was tapped by seven items, and interactional justice by six items. In comparative distributive justice, following Rice et al. [1990], comparison with each referent group was measured by one item. A total of three items were developed, each targeting one of three referent groups, namely, overseas employees, local employees in other joint venture hotels, and local employees in state-owned hotels.

Finally, job satisfaction was measured by four items, which were taken from Cole [1979]. It should be noted that the fairness items asked subjects to make fairness judgments, whereas the satisfaction items are concerned with how satisfied the subjects were with their job in general. These two types of items are distinct from each other. All items were based on five-point Likert scales, with end-points labelled "strongly agree" and "strongly disagree." See Table 1 for the items used.

Reliability of Instruments

The reliability of the scales was assessed by Cronbach's alpha. Cronbach's alphas for performance-based distributive justice, procedural justice, inter-actional justice, and job satisfaction are .83, .67, .83, and .79, respectively. The alpha for procedural justice is marginal, but those for the other scales are satisfactory. For each scale, a composite score was formed by averaging its constituent items.

A series of regression analyses were used to test the hypotheses proposed. Missing values were handled with case-wise deletion in all analyses reported below. See Table 2 for the intercorrelations among the variables. First, to assess the impact of justice perception on satisfaction, performance-based distributive justice, procedural justice, and interactional justice were regressed on satisfaction. Results showed that only performance-based distributive and procedural justice showed a significant beta weight, and that the beta weight for interactional justice was not significant.

To test the effects of comparative distributive justice, a second set of regression analyses was conducted. In the first step, the three justice constructs were entered. In the second step, one of the three CDJ items was entered, and the crucial statistic was the change in the multiple R. If the change was significant, the CDJ item was able to add to the prediction of satisfaction over and above the effects of the three justice constructs. Consistent with Hypothesis, results showed that comparison with overseas employees was unable to explain additional variance. In contrast, comparison with local employees in other joint venture hotels or in state-owned hotels was able to explain a significant amount of additional variance.

Perceived Justice and Rank of Local Staff

A series of ANOVAs was used to test the effect of rank on perceived justice and job satisfaction. The respondents were divided into three groups based on their description of their rank: senior managers, middle managers and supervisors. Consistent with Hypothesis 2, the higher the rank, the less positive was perceived procedural justice, F(2, 128) = 5.97, p [less than] .05.

However, multiple range tests showed that the supervisors reported a significantly higher level of perceived procedural justice than the senior managers, and that the other group differences were not significant. With regard to interactional justice, the main effect of rank was also significant, F(2, 127) = 6.57, p [less than] .05. Multiple range tests showed that senior managers showed a significantly lower level of perceived interactional justice than middle managers and supervisors, which did not differ from each other significantly. Contrary to our expectation, rank did not show any effect upon performance-based distributive justice, $F(2, 128) = 2.26$, ns.

The effects of rank on each of the items in comparative distributive justice and satisfaction were also explored. No significant effects were found, except for the item concerning the comparison of one's salary with the salary of employees in state-owned enterprises. The means showed that middle managers showed a higher level of perceived justice than senior managers and supervisors. However, multiple range tests showed that no two groups were significantly different from each other.

Differences in Justice Perception and Satisfaction as A Function of Cultural Origin of Expatriate Managers. Participants were asked to indicate the cultural origin of the expatriate managers with whom they had the most contact. Three groups were formed based on the cultural origin of the overseas manager. The first group worked with overseas Chinese managers from Hong Kong, Taiwan and elsewhere. The second group worked with managers from North America and Europe.

The third group worked with Japanese managers. Results contradicted Hypothesis and showed that the group working with Western managers had higher means on several variables, although some of the differences were only marginally significant. Specifically, the two groups with Japanese and overseas Chinese managers showed a lower level of satisfaction than did the Western group. It is interesting to note that the three groups did not differ with regard to procedural and interactive justice.

However, the overseas Chinese and Japanese groups reported a lower level of performance-based and comparative distributive justice than did the Western group. That is, the overseas Chinese and Japanese groups perceived that they were rewarded less fairly in relation to their performance inputs and in comparison with overseas employees and local employees in other joint ventures hotels or in state-owned hotels.

These results suggest that differences in satisfaction as a function of the cultural origin of expatriate managers may be due to differences in perceived performance-based and comparative distributive justice. To test this notion, an analysis of covariance was conducted, with cultural origin of expatriate managers as the independent variable, satisfaction as the dependent variable, and performance-based distributive justice and the three CDJ items as covariates.

Consistent with Hypothesis the marginally significant difference in satisfaction across the three groups disappeared when the covariates were included $F(2, 116) = 1.48$, ns. This result supports the justice hypothesis and suggests that the difference in satisfaction across the three groups is likely to have been produced by differences in performance-based and comparative distributive justice. Once these differences were equated statistically, the difference in job satisfaction across the three groups disappeared.

Procedural justice and performance-based distributive justice were found to be predictive of job satisfaction. However, unlike American results, interactional justice was not. At this point, it is unclear why interactional justice was not related to job satisfaction in joint ventures in China. It is possible that because of the higher acceptance of hierarchy and authority figures in Chinese organizations, the level of interactional justice required by Chinese employees from their superiors may be lower.

This possibility obviously needs to be verified, but this finding makes it clear that justice theories, developed and confirmed in the U.S., should not be automatically assumed to be valid in different cultures.

As predicted, the comparison with expatriate staff did not account for additional variance in the prediction of job satisfaction. Clearly, local staff did not regard them as a meaningful referent group for social comparison in the perception of distributive justice. In contrast, the comparison with other local staff was able to add to the prediction of job satisfaction. This finding highlights the importance of social comparison in fairness judgments in joint ventures. The conceptualization of distributive justice, as a comparison between performance inputs and salaries, is too narrow in joint ventures and needs to be broadened to include social comparison processes.

Why is social comparison important in joint ventures? Several referent groups are clearly identifiable in joint ventures, namely, expatriate staff, local staff in joint ventures, and local staff in locally owned firms. It is possible that the salience of these groups accentuates the tendency to rely on social comparisons in making fairness judgments and in the formation of job attitudes. This line of reasoning deserves serious attention in future work.

As expected, senior managers showed the lowest level of perceived procedural and interaction justice. This pattern of results suggests that senior staff probably expected decisionmaking processes to be fairer, and interpersonal treatment received from expatriate staff more positive. The use of higher standards by this group probably has lowered their perception of these two justice constructs. Contrary to expectation, rank did not show any effect on performance-based distributive justice. This null finding probably reflects the fact that all levels of staff in these joint ventures are paid at a comparable level based upon their performance inputs.

Rank did not have any effect on two of the three comparative distributive justice items. It is interesting to note that the only significant effect involves the comparison with local employees in state-owned hotels. Middle managers reported the highest level of perceived justice, whereas senior managers and supervisors regarded their pay as less fair in comparison with local staff in other state-owned hotels. A plausible explanation for this unexpected finding is that senior managers and supervisors in joint ventures probably regarded their performance inputs as much higher than those of local staff in state-owned hotels. Thus, although they are usually paid at a higher level than staff in state-owned hotels, they probably think that they should be paid even higher.

The cultural match hypothesis is not supported by the results. Local employees who worked with overseas Chinese or Japanese staff were less satisfied than those who worked with Western managers. The similarity in cultural background between expatriate and local staff seems not to be a major factor in determining job satisfaction.

This pattern of results actually supports the justice hypothesis. In addition, the three groups also showed significant, or marginally significant, differences in perceived performance-based and comparative distributive justice. When group differences in performance-based and comparative distributive justice were controlled in an analysis of covariance, the group difference in job satisfaction disappeared. This result suggests that distributive justice was able to account for the group difference in job satisfaction. In short, fairness of pay seems to be a more important factor than cultural similarity in determining job satisfaction.

A number of practical conclusions can be drawn from the present results. Staff turnover has now become a serious problem in major cities in China. Sensenbrenner and Sensenbrenner [1994] reported that approximately 15% of employees changed jobs in Shanghai in 1992-1993. It is well known that job satisfaction is closely linked to turnover behavior. To reduce staff turnover, one effective way is to find ways to enhance the job satisfaction of local staff, and several approaches can be derived from the present findings.

First, pay is often emphasized in reducing staff turnover in joint ventures. The present findings corroborate this argument in that distributive justice shows a significant impact on job satisfaction. However, the results suggest that procedural justice is crucial as well. Management of joint ventures should try to establish decisionmaking processes that are consultative, open and responsive to feedback and suggestions.

Second, the present findings suggest that job satisfaction can be enhanced by carefully monitoring and influencing the social comparison processes that local staff may engage in. Expatriate managers must be updated about the salary levels of other joint ventures and state-owned enterprises in the same industry and their job requirements. Effort must be made to communicate to local staff, directly or indirectly, that their salary level is fair in relation to other joint ventures or state-owned enterprises. Failing to do so, local staff may be dissatisfied with their pay, regardless of their actual salary level, and quitting is likely to follow.

Third, the present findings suggest that senior local staff reported a lower level of perceived procedural and interactional justice. As explained before, compared to low-level staff, this group may expect fairer decision making processes and better interpersonal treatment from expatriate managers. Effort must be made to involve this group in decisionmaking processes, recognize their inputs, and treat them with dignity and respect.

Fourth, a number of authors have written on the problems created by cultural differences between expatriate and local staff. These concerns are real and must be tackled in order to build a culturally diverse team that is effective and cohesive. However, because cultural differences between local and expatriate staff are salient in a cross-cultural situation, it is easy to attribute difficulties encountered in a joint venture to cultural differences without a thorough analysis of the non-cultural causes of the difficulties.

The present results argue for a simultaneous consideration of both cultural and non-cultural issues when managerial problems are encountered in a joint venture. In fact, the present results suggest that for job satisfaction of Chinese employees, the cultural origin of the expatriate manager did not matter. Rather, a lower level of perceived performance-based and comparative distributive justice seems to be the cause of the lower satisfaction of Chinese staff who worked with overseas Chinese and Japanese managers. This finding highlights the possibility that cultural issues sometimes may not be a major cause of some difficulties encountered in joint ventures in China.

It is well known that job satisfaction is multifaceted. General job satisfaction was measured in the present study, and in future work, a more refined measure of job satisfaction could be used to examine how different facets of job satisfaction are related to different types of justice. Another area that is worth probing is the provocative argument that job satisfaction of Chinese employees has little to do with the cultural origin of their expatriate managers.

It is possible that in addition to justice issues, the three expatriate groups also differ in their managerial styles, which may affect the job attitudes of the local employees. Another possibility is that local staff may have different expectations regarding the behaviors and managerial styles of these three groups of expatriate managers. These expectations may also affect their job attitudes. Both possibilities should be explored in future research.

The Hospitality of Hotel Security

Owners and general managers of lodging facilities, regardless of the property size, have a responsibility to ensure that guests are provided with safe and secure accommodations. No less important is the protection of the employees at each site, as well as the security of their personal property and, of course, the company's assets. An annual review of security exposures provides a fresh look at potential problems and the procedures that may need to be implemented for effective protection. Proper evaluation requires information from many sources.

One resource is the police. Law enforcement agencies help businesses improve their protection by providing them with information concerning the number and types of crimes that occur in the area around the property and on the premises. They may even volunteer to inspect the hotel and provide recommendations for improvement.

Additional information about local crime conditions can be obtained from the newspaper and by meeting with the operators of other neighborhood businesses. Employees of the hotel who live in the area can provide further insights. A review of high-security protection at nearby properties, or the absence thereof, can indicate which defensive measures are considered appropriate for the location.

To determine on-site problems, the security manager has to examine the incident reports. It also helps to question employees, such as the front desk clerks, who have close contact with the guests and who would receive complaints. Incident reports and information tactfully gathered from guests provide a basis for evaluating procedures and implementing action.

A minisurvey of the property is the next step toward determining if a complete physical survey would be warranted. The security professional conducting the survey should begin with the street access to the property. Guests require a clear, well-defined, and well-illuminated route from the street to the hotel's guest entrance doors. All exterior lights should be checked on a daily basis for full illumination. Inoperative fixtures should be changed immediately upon discovery.

Heavy foliage reduces adequate exterior illumination in many instances and, therefore, should be trimmed. Perimeter barriers, such as fencing, need to be intact, and the ground needs to be firm and not eroded to prevent unauthorized ingress or the exodus of personal property or hotel assets, such as money or materials, that can be passed under the fence. During the late evening and early morning hours, securing remote driveway and pedestrian entrances is essential. Clear instructions about the nearest open entrance should be posted.

Foot patrols should check all exit doors. Those doors that should be secured in accordance with hotel instructions must be locked and have a panic bar on the inside for easy egress in an emergency. Entrances to employee work areas should have identifying signs prohibiting unauthorized entry. Directional signs to the elevators and exits should be highly visible. Access to the guest residence area of the hotel through the garage entrance should be controlled to deter trespassers.

Many hotels today still use metal or mechanical keys. These keys are more vulnerable to a breach in security, such as a loss or theft, than electronic keying systems, because electronic systems can be canceled or changed with a touch of a keyboard. Whatever the hotel's key arrangement, certain basic security measures are essential for safety.

When presenting any kind of key to a guest, the clerk should not announce the room number because it may be overheard by others nearby. Instead, he or she should use envelopes for the keys and point to the room number placed on the envelope for the guest to read.

Hotels are starting to convert from placing room numbers on keys to coded numbers and letters. The actual room number is put on the key envelope or, in some cases, on the guest's copy of the registration receipt. Should the key be lost or misplaced, it can only be identified by the key custodian or the front desk. Under no circumstances should guest room numbers be given out. Telephone calls can be connected to the room without divulging the location, and individuals can be directed to a house phone through which the operator or front desk will contact a guest for a visitor.

Guest room key accountability is not easy but can be made less difficult if the hotel engineer, the housekeeper, and the front desk manager work as a team and follow set procedures. The front desk manager should keep an inventory of the number of room keys maintained at the front desk. When the established supply for a room is almost depleted, the engineer should change the door lock, retrieve the remaining room keys, and provide a set number of keys for the new lock. Additional duplicate keys should not be made in lieu of changing the lock.

When checking out at the front desk, guests should be asked for their room key. If they are returning to their room, they should be instructed to leave the key on the dresser. Guests, in a hurry to leave the hotel with all their belongings, will consider returning the key a low priority and will probably take it home and throw it away. When it is time to clean the room; the key should be picked up by the maid and put into a locked key box affixed to the cleaning cart for security. The housekeeping supervisor should collect all keys from key boxes by 1:00 p.m. and return them promptly to the front desk.

This gives the desk clerks time to restore the keys in their slots before the afternoon rush of new guests. With the three departments cooperating, loss of keys can be reduced and security for guests increased. If department managers secure their keys in a locked hotel cabinet at the end of their shift, the chance of loss is minimized, and asset security is maintained.

A key custody log should be implemented. Usually the manager on duty or a designated person will have access to the secured keys in an emergency, and keys in use will be logged out.

Safe deposit boxes must be available when requested by guests; a hotel attendant should ensure that the boxes are otherwise properly stored and locked in a vault. Having only one guest key to access each safe deposit box, coupled with the guest's written agreement to bear the cost of removing the safe deposit lock if the key is lost, should be considered. The master or guard safe deposit key should be secured by the designated custodian, with monitored controlled access.

Guests should not have access into the cashier's area at any time. The entrances from the public area into the administration offices should be monitored during normal business hours by a receptionist. If this is not feasible, the access door should be equipped with a programmable combination lock, and the combination should be given to employees on a need-to-know basis.

Where possible, cashiers should have individual banks and retain their access key, with a duplicate held in the controller's safe. Unscheduled bank audits should be carried out by the controller with one witness. Each cashier should close out in privacy in the office at the end of his or her shift. Cashiers, with their bank, should be escorted by security from their station at the front desk to the office counting area. When each cashier's closeout is complete, the drop into the drop safe should be witnessed and certified in the deposit drop log. Dual access to the drop deposit with two keys or a combination and key is recommended.

When the hotel's daily deposit is being prepared, it is best done in a locked, private area with no visitors. The completed deposit should be stored in a locked safe, not a locked desk drawer, until an armored car service or management representative is ready to take it to the bank. When a representative is handling the bank deposit, routes and hours should be varied and a second person should accompany the representative making the deposit. Nothing identifying them with the hotel should be used.

Some hotels have a magnetic locking bar or electric strike latch installed on the main entrance door from the vestibule to the lobby during late evening and early morning hours. This allows egress but secures the doors from ingress. This should be supplemented with a two-way voice communication system between the vestibule and the front desk, accompanied by a buzzer visitors can use to summon the clerk when no one is at the front desk. If the potential guest in the vestibule cannot be seen from the front desk, CCTV is necessary. The door lock should be controlled by a switch at the front desk.

People tend to deviate from their normal protective guidelines when at a hotel. To remind guests to be aware of security measures, many hotels place a tastefully worded notice in each guest room in a highly visible location, such as on the bed, dresser, desk, or door. Some recommendations to consider include the following:

- Park your car in a well-lighted, visible area of the parking lot or garage.
- Do not leave any valuables in the car in a visible location.
- When checking in or departing, keep luggage in your personal possession or with the bellhop.
- Keep room keys in your possession at all times. If the key is lost, notify security and the front desk so that the lock can be changed promptly.
- Be wary of friendly strangers, especially those who display great interest in the room number.
- Engage the dead bolt and chain latch or bar provided on the entrance door when in the room. Do not leave the door ajar when leaving the room for ice, visiting a nearby room, or expecting a visitor.
- Before opening the door, use the peephole to identify the caller.
- Do not leave handbags, coats, or personal belongings unattended.
- When leaving the hotel on foot, ask a hotel employee about the safety of the area and whether it would be preferable to take public transportation. If in doubt, do not walk. Take a cab.

A security officer should have successfully completed all training courses required by the state and local authorities and should be capable of performing all hotel security functions. Proof of past security experience is recommended, and appropriate background checks should be completed prior to hiring. Although a security officer's basic knowledge may have been well established, to work effectively in a hotel requires additional training. Because of the presence of a high volume of people in a hotel, additional security responsibilities require tact and diplomacy.

Security officers must be alert to assist lost guests, those who display large sums of money in public, or those who attract attention to themselves in some other manner that could cause them to be victimized. Courteous and helpful guidance given to guests for their protection can resolve a problem before it materializes and ensure a continued pleasant stay in the hotel.

It is the duty of security officers at times to question persons in the hotel and on surrounding grounds. Officers must be tactful to obtain the desired information without offending the guest. Security patrols of the hotel property should include all interior and exterior areas, not just the buildings, parking areas, storage, receiving, and trash disposal locations. Every guest room door should be passed to verify that the doors are closed and no key is left in the lock or dropped on the floor. Listening for sounds of room smoke alarms is also essential.

Key security points throughout the facility should be identified, and checkpoints should be installed at every point to document the security officer's presence at hourly intervals. The route should be prepared to allow deviation from the path without missing any of the checkpoints. Variation of the routes as well as the hour patrolled is critical to avoid any pre-determined pattern.

Security reports and patrol logs should be reviewed daily by the general manager or the director of security. Hotel management staff and security staff should discuss policy and procedures at periodic meetings. While lodging security professionals must always be alert to new technology that allows them to better fulfill their mission, it is also vital that they constantly evaluate the basic protective measures. These measures can be even more effective when all employees at the hotel have been trained and encouraged to practice security and safety awareness for the protection of the guests and themselves.

The Current Scenario

The Indian economic bubble has managed to achieve a commendable feat of growing bigger and bigger without bursting. The consequences are there for all to see. The Bull Run in the Indian stock markets has been unstoppable and the much ridiculed spending power of the average Indian has touched new highs. Above all, the Indian economy is showing no signs of slowing down, and promises to grow at an incredible rate. This scenario has been particularly favourable for the hotel and hospitality industry.

The Incredible India! Campaign, cheaper airfares, and eased security concerns because of improved relations with Pakistan, have together added more fuel to the already booming tourism industry. Lack of hotels in India But unfortunately, the hotel and hospitality industry here has yet to catch up with this growth. The introduction of the bed and breakfast scheme - which offers tourist accommodation at houses that have rooms to spare - is ample proof of the scarcity of hotel rooms in India.

The demand for rooms is pitched at 90,000 rooms, which can hardly be met by the supply of 61,000 rooms. To add to this, the demand-supply difference is expected to rise, taking into account the growth in the tourism industry. Today, the tourism industry is in the want of 2,00,000 more rooms.

The requirement of hotels We are in the process of unveiling the power of India to the world. Be it in culture tourism, business tourism, or medical tourism, India has already gained place on the world map. And we definitely do not afford to lose our position because of the lack of availability of hotels for tourists to stay in.

Though the current growth rate of the hotel industry on the whole is a stupendous 40 per cent per annum - with Bangalore experiencing the highest rate of growth - we are in dire need of hotels in various categories, including luxury five star hotels, business class hotels, and reasonable accommodation catering to the domestic traffic.

The causes for increased demand The rise in the disposable incomes of the increasingly affluent middle class of India has been one of the causes of the increased demand for hotel accommodation, apart from the easy visa rules, public freedom, and copious low fare airlines on the platter. The new corporate culture with travel incentives and the mushrooming of blue chip companies in India have all contributed their own bit in the increased demand for hotel accommodation in the country. Government measures to meet the demand The government has increased the foreign direct investment (FDI) in the industry to 100 per cent, in May 2001.

Considering the numerous opportunities for hotel owners here, the sector is seen at the top slot among sectors vying for FDI. Though this has surely paved the way for foreign hotel giants to set shop in India, the lack of infrastructural facilities, red-tapism and anarchic land laws are a deterrent to many. The government, while focusing on reviving tourism, must also take care to provide the necessary groundwork that is required for the gestation of new hotels.

The hotel taxes in India are more than in most of the other Asian countries. This needs to be addressed urgently. The domestic tourism What can be better news than the hotel industry stalwarts from the world over waiting to set shop in India to experience a piece of action of its booming economy, and in turn fulfilling the demand of accommodation for tourists? Consider this - The Indian domestic market is one third of the total international arrivals at all the global markets taken together.

Religious tourism and the destination campaign of the Incredible India initiative also account for the growing domestic tourism industry. The International tourism market in India The number of international visitors in India has been steadily increasing over the last decade due to a number of reasons. With multinationals converging upon India to set up business operations, there has been an upsurge in the business travelers from diverse parts of the globe.

The Indian culture has played an important role in attracting leisure tourists to the holy land, while the splendid beauty of our virgin countryside and the unparalleled monuments make for an interesting trip. Religious tourism too is catching up, with induced circuits in Buddhist travel attracting Japanese tourists in hordes. The fillip that medical tourism has seen in recent years can be attributed to the low cost medical treatments at the hands of some of the most intelligent brains of the world.

The challenges ahead of us Experts are not completely wrong in painting a rosy picture of our hotel industry in the years to come. But they are not completely right either. We can assist brands in setting up hotels here only when we improve upon some of our drawbacks. Our deteriorating infrastructure needs to be fixed up before we expect the trickle of foreign visitors to turn into a deluge.

The dilapidated roads, never-on-time railways, and not-getting-any-younger airports are some of the first hurdles in receiving international traffic. The esoteric business practices and the corruption, too might shoo away foreign investors. Bottomline The fact that there is a huge demand for hotels in India being true, we are at a junction where leaping ahead is a matter of coping up with the challenges associated. If we can do that successfully, we will reap its benefits; if not, we are losing on one of the biggest opportunities facing us.

A Christian Perspective

When I was assigned the topic of love and sex (and I decided to add lust/desire as the link between the two), I immediately consulted with a number of my colleagues at the Boston University School of Theology. The response of my colleagues was uniform. Representing different theological disciplines and denominational backgrounds, they noted that the answer as to the Christian perspective on sex was simple: don't; but if you do, be sure not to enjoy it.

If this seems a vast and hasty overgeneralization, please consult Mark Jordan's new book (2002) on Christian sexual ethics to see that this confident and consistent rejection of sex and pleasure has been the dominant and main position for the entire history of the cumulative Christian tradition. As Clifford Bishop has noted, the West has held "a wounded body" in ambiguous embrace as chronicled by the history of its written discourse and artistic representation of sex.

Once my colleagues had delivered this ironic teaching, they did go on to give me good advice as to how to grapple with the topic, as well as to wish me well in the attempt.

I then decided to take solace in Daoism, often a good idea for a despondent Christian with strong Confucian tendencies, but came across this quote from Livia Kohn's new study of the tradition: "Anyone who commits debauchery and indulges in sex will suffer from insanity. Having passed through this, he will be born among the sows and boars." So much for differences between Daoism and Christianity – though I should point out that Kohn blames Buddhist influence for such a retrograde teaching. One wonders what will happen to women who act in a similar fashion.

However, I was cheered in my search when I read the great Tiantai master Zhiyi's account of the matter: "It is like fighting bandits. Bandits are the root of glory; it is because a general is able to destroy bandits that he attains fame and reward. Infinite lust is a seed of the Tathagata in just the same way. It makes the bodhisattvas come up with an infinite number of Dharma-ages in response."

According to Mark Heim, Dante had a slightly more charitable view: "Lust is a type of shared sin; at its best, and so long as it remains a sin of incontinence only, there is mutuality in it and exchange." At least Dante thought we were in it together. Moving on to a history of early modern Christian views of sex, which makes sense because this is probably the set of views that informs the modern period as well, I discovered why mainstream Christians were so concerned about the proper teaching of sexual ethics when I read the following: "... as the Ranters in seventeenth-century England proclaim, 'What act soever is done by thee in light and love, is light and lovely, thought it be called adultery.... No matter what Scripture, saints, or churches say, if that within thee do not condemn thee, thou shalt not be condemned.'"

If Daoists, Buddhists, and early modern Christians all agree and then disagree, then this is serious business indeed. Then I started to read about the contemporary history of sex, which I discovered was born, with a vengeance, about the same time as the new theology of dialogue, circa 1970. Even the scholarly, and hence most serious in tone, literature on sex is vast. I commend it to anyone who is not convinced that we have lived through and probably are still experiencing a new paradigm shift in the Christian worldview. My thesis is that the worldview transformation is the imaginative articulation of the shifting social grounds that have cried out for a new ethics of sex.

But perhaps things are not so simple. Does the sexual revolution of the 1960s and 1970s demand a new worldview or did a new worldview allow for the radical new adventures in sex? Both, probably. Worldviews arise out of changed social conditions, and new social conditions allow for the articulation of imaginative descriptions as philosophic and theological worldviews. If the historians of sex are to be believed, human beings have always been fascinated by sex, even if the definitions of sex, much less gender, have been highly contested. What adult over the age of forty would not suspect as much?

How do worldviews change? They change when the lifeworlds of women and men change such that the theologies and philosophies that serve to articulate the hopes and dreams of a people no longer work; the result is cognitive dissonance. Of course, people cheerfully live with cognitive dissonance all the time, but when a disconnect between how the world is believed to be and how it is described in second-order cognitive disciplines such as philosophy and theology opens up to dramatic proportions, public intellectuals play the role of prophets of new days. I do not want to be misunderstood.

People do not read Part I of Process and Reality, for instance, and then decide to act differently. Rather, people realize that their inherited philosophies and theologies need to be brought into line with contemporary worldviews and set about to create new visions of new worldviews.

This account of why people change worldviews is actually neutral as to why the perceptions between reality and worldviews change. On the one hand, changing worldviews can be given a purely naturalist interpretation. A Marxist affirms that philosophy and theology are only epicycles of the material basis of civilizations. A follower of Durkheim argues that religion is simply a projection of a social reality into an image of the divine. But on the other hand, pious Christians and Muslims can read the hand or word of God at work in the changing visions of the people. A savior can be born that demands a new vision of earth, heaven, and hell; a final prophet finally helps people understand how the world was created and to what end they must strive for in this veil of tears. However, both secular intellectuals and theologians have explanations of why new theologies arise and why worldviews are transformed.

Feminist scholars argue that human beings will have to change their worldviews once the voices of women re incorporated into self-conscious philosophic and theological discourse. (10) Nowhere is this more evident than in the discussion of sexual ethics. Women point out that they are sexual beings and not just passive objects of male desire. Women have become sexual agents and demand that any new sexual ethics include their insights into what conduces toward human flourishing; and in this case, not just the pleasure of the male half of the human race.

Along with questions of changing worldviews, I also need to address the demographic question of audience. The Christian movement in North America, at least among Protestants, has become more and more divided these days between its liberal, moderate, and conservative wings. Therefore, I have decided to be honest, as my colleagues in social critical studies would say, about my social location. I am a liberal Christian.

This means, if scholars such as Roof and Wurthnow are correct in their studies of religious demography, that I am speaking for and about approximately 20 percent of the Christians in North America. I have come to the conclusion that it no longer makes any sense for me to try to write for all North American Christians because they simply belong to very different religions even though they call themselves Christian. In terms of David Tracy's tripartite division of the theological discourse, I am writing foundational and perhaps even systematic theology for liberal modern and postmodern Christians.

When I address other Christians I need to write in an apologetic mode, if I choose to address them at all. In terms of affinity of worldviews, I will have more in common with modern and postmodern Buddhists and Confucians than with fundamentalist Christians.

Beyond the label "Christian" there is not much that connects (all right, the Bible is still the main text for all Christians, as well as a shared history or tradition to a more limited extent) the leadership of the Southern Baptist Convention and Christian Unitarian Universalists or the liberals within the United Church of Canada or the United Church of Christ. Trying to write something that represents the thought of all Christians in North America would be to write something so banal as to be completely uninteresting. Moreover, I think that it is time that the different wings of the Christian movement in North America begin to define their own yanas in terms of what they really believe rather than what they think will simply serve not to offend anyone else.

The news bulletin that we are living in a time of redefinition for many aspects of human culture is not new. However, I think that such a shift in fundamental perceptions of God-world relations lies at the foundation of the raging debates over sexual congress and sexual ethics in the modern world—and for many other battles of the "culture wars" that so threaten to engulf not only the church but also the academy. As the historians of sex now narrate, human beings have engaged, worried about, and enjoyed various forms of sexual activity as long as we have been human.

And if the primatologists are to be believed, the line of descent that gave rise (only a slight pun intended) to humans, chimps, and bonobos share diverse erotic activities and imaginations. There is nothing new about sex per se—though it is fascinating to see modern historians of sex chronicle how human beings have thought ever so different things about sex and gender even within the cultural sphere of the North Atlantic world.

My concern is perhaps even more foundational: the shift in God-world relations that characterizes the rise of the late modern world. Such a shift, I will argue, goes on unabated in late modernity and into postmodernism regardless of whether we assume that there is something in postmodernism that merits its separation from late modern sensibilities. My colleague Robert Neville has ironically called this "paleo-Galactic," because who wants to be at the end of anything when it is much more enjoyable to be at the beginning of something new?

That public intellectuals are busy writing and publicizing shifts in worldview analysis and are eagerly engaged in formulating new philosophies and theologies should also come as no surprise. In fact, such searches for new philosophic theologies should alert us to the fact that the world has changed for many people. As I noted above, the shift has been most dramatic for young women in the North Atlantic world. Such changes in lifeworlds demand new forms of ethical engagement. Sex is merely one area of human life that cries out for better understanding and the articulation of sound ethical theories. The praxis of the liberation of women is creating, again to follow Tracy's division of the theological sciences, new systematic and foundational theology. Lifeworlds change and theologians scramble to keep up; if theologians do not keep up they are simply ignored. For instance, the hierarchy of the Roman Catholic Church endlessly complains that the faithful are no longer following the teachings of the church about items such as birth control.

In order to summarize this particular philosophic and religious paradigm shift, I will recall a famous article by Robert Bellah reprinted in Beyond Belief on global religious evolution. Bellah is asking us to look not at changes in specific doctrines or teachings from various religions—in his case most specifically from early modern and modern East Asia and Europe—but rather at the profound transformation of religious sensibility per se. If you would like an even more evocative example, call to mind David Lodge's fantastical description of the loss of hell for a group of English Roman Catholic graduates students in The British Museum Is Falling Down. The characters in Lodge's novel wake up one morning to find that they have lost hell, literally. The very idea of such a place as hell, which the students recognize as part of the religious life view of their parents and grandparents, has simply become so alien that they cannot imagine that they have lost hell because hell no longer makes sense to them.

Bellah's point is less literary but as telling. In short, Bellah argues that one of the chief characteristics of global religion, at least since the Axial Age, has been the pervasive sense that God or the religious ultimate is or becomes ever more distant from the world of human beings, leading to doctrines of God as the wholly other. A doctrinal version of this sensibility is the notion of strict transcendence as it has been defined in early modern Christian theology by both Protestants and Catholics (though this pertains to Catholics less so at least in terms of formal academic theology).

Strict transcendence means that God is God and does not depend on the world for anything at all, though the world is believed to depend perfectly for its very existence on the gracious creation and support of God. Joseph Bracken, in a discussion of Thomas Aquinas's unwillingness to apply Trinitarian theology to God-world relations, writes "Rather, in line with the philosophy of antiquity as carried forward by Origen and Augustine, he conceived God as the transcendent Creator of the world to be utterly simple and thus lacking in any intrinsic relationship to creation."

There are all kinds of philosophic problems, no doubt, with such a monodirectional view of God-world relations, but these will not detain us here. The real problem is that, along with the ontocosmology of such a strict view of transcendence, all kinds of other visions of reality (and sexuality) trail along in its wake. If God is spirit, for instance, and the world material, and if God is good and the world at best highly suspect, things of material nature are ethically problematical.

The rest of the list of problems with the logocentric philosophies and theologies of the West is well known; feminist theologians have been in the forefront in showing how this radical separation of God and the World has induced a denigration of women in general and sexuality in particular. There is a world of pure ideas, the world of men, and then there is the world of women, of matter, of dirt, of impurity, and so it goes. One after another historical study has attempted to demonstrate how a set of views of God-world relations has implacable implications for real women because women are depicted as more earthly (and therefore, ungodly) in their essential beings. It clearly has implications for the sexual relations of human beings as well.

Bellah then goes to note that something is happening to perceptions of God-world relations in late modernity. Unlike our Tokugawa Neo-Confucian scholars and Puritan New England divines, late modern or postmodern people conceive of God-world relations on a dramatically different model. It is as if, Bellah writes, strict transcendence collapsed sometime after the Enlightenment. Somehow it does not make sense in the twenty-first century that God is absent from the world as would be the logic of a radical doctrine of divine transcendence.

There are flurries of theories that try to explain what has happened. Bellah, for instance, notes that the late modern view of God-world relations now resembles the early religious sensibilities of human beings when the God/s and the world were co-implicated in one organic connection. Early modern Western missionaries called this primitive thought, but their great-great-great grandchildren embrace such a view of God-world relations as New Age spirituality. As above, so below, and the two are now intimately interconnected once again.

Nonetheless, I need to stress an important caveat here about the trait of transcendence. Whitehead once wisely wrote that an adequate philosophy was one that explained objects and events and did not seek to explain away things that were not initially convivial to the contour of its own categorial system. Just because modernist and postmodernist theologies reject one notion of transcendence does not mean that such new imaginative reconstructions of tradition theology do not need to be able to explain what transcendence meant for Augustine, Aquinas, Duns Scotus, and Calvin—much less Barth and Tillich, Huston Smith passionately declaims, if a modernist sensibility rips the twin pillars of classical Western theistic theology, transcendence and revelation, from the bleeding body of traditional spiritual lore, we are left not with a living religion, but only with a mangled relic of a past form of spiritual life. However, even in respecting the theological sedimentations of the revered past, we must boldly explore the alternative logics that lead inevitably to a different bricolage of spiritual discernment into the present state of our embodied religious consciousness. Description and articulation of present religious experience is just as foundational as historical hindsight into the various trajectories of theological ethics.

It is especially important when modern sensibilities appear to be dramatically divergent from the second-order normative prescriptions of classical systematic theology and the ethical injunctions that flow from those classical teachings. Why stress the notion of a paradigm shift in thinking about

God-world relations when we are thinking about sex, love, and lechery? First, such philosophical and cultural reflection saves us from the tyranny of the present moment.

For instance, many people (at least in North America) assume that the sexual revolution of the 1960s and 1970s was an unprecedented upheaval in terms of human sexuality. Any reading of the literature on the history of sex should disabuse the thoughtful reader that this indeed was the case. There have been sexual revolutions before; a perfect example would be the late Ming period in China for instance. People have been experimenting with gender roles and the pleasures of sex for a long, long time. Sexual revolutions are simply part of a larger cultural history, though they have often been ignored or censored for all kinds of reasons. Nonetheless, cultural revolutions often indicate changes in worldviews in any society and I think that this is what has happened in the modern West.

Let us consider another example about paradigmatic worldview shifts. I have found that many of my theological students now deeply appreciate the various teachings of Native American elders or other representatives of the primal religious traditions of the world. There are obviously a number of reasons why this is the case, but I believe that worldview transformation is very much part of the picture. The reason for this is that many Native America elders enunciate, in highly diverse forms, a worldview wherein the divine reality and the mundane world are part of a continuum of interaction and intersubjective self-formation that fuses the immanent and transcendent inextricably.

This sense of the absolute connection of the divine and quotidian is immensely appealing to my students because, without putting too fine a point on it, it is the way they now see the world. A completely transcendent deity simply no longer makes no sense to them. When they read Calvin or Barth, the early and late modern Christian acceptance and worship of a totally transcendent deity no longer seems to fit their sense of God-world relations. The Native American elder better expresses their understanding of God-world relations than many Christian theological giants. In short, my students have a felt need to readjust their notions of what constitutes transcendence in a fashion that appreciates rather than disregards the spiritual teachings of the primal religions of North America (and other parts of the world as well).

This kind of interfaith encounter, of course, is problematic for the more conservative and orthodox Christian students when they realize that they actually rather appreciate what the native traditions have to teach on some topics, especially in ecological theology and ethics. They express a sense of considerable cognitive dissonance when they realize that the elder makes more sense than Christian theologians when the conversation moves to respect for the natural world. One of the components of being bathed in the acids of modernity is to encounter alternative worldviews; but more than mere encounter, there is a willingness to take the worldview of the radical "other" seriously.

What is going on here? I explain that this probably has something to do with the relationship of their worldview and what they believe the Christian churches have always and everywhere taught. The easiest way out of the predicament for my perplexed students comes when I try to show that their relationship to a religion and to a specific worldview is not always the same thing; I explain that worldviews qua philosophic doctrines come and go whereas the great Axial Age religions have demonstrated a tremendous staying power. Christians, for instance, have made use of Stoic, Neo-Platonic, and Aristotelian and various early modern philosophies, and can certainly make effective use of different or new philosophic traditions when the need arises.

The trick is to make use of a worldview or philosophy for the specific needs of a cumulative religious tradition. I go on to state that African-, Native American-, Buddhist-, Daoist-, and Confucian-derived worldviews do and will sustain the articulation of the Christian gospel in the twenty-first century. My Korean students and I enjoy, for instance, creating

Christian systematic theology based on the daoxue of Zhu Xi, T'oegye, and Yulgok. My internal Christian apologetic argument is that evangelism is not revivalism; when a worldview is dead, there is little purpose in continuing to use a theology yoked to the corpse of a previous living faith. Real evangelism is the confrontation of the living Christian gospel with new historical and cultural circumstances, and shifts in deployment of global philosophic resources is to be not only expected but also applauded.

Without such transformation no religion ever crosses over into a new or different cultural scene. One question almost immediately follows from such explanations of how we go about foundational theology in a pluralistic age: What makes this new amalgam Christian in anything resembling a commonsensical understanding of a cumulative faith tradition? A hasty sketch of such a warrant for the use of Christian for a new theology is this. The version of the worldview that I am describing can affirm three traits that link it to the history of the Christian cumulative tradition.

First, there is a profound sense of the divine eros for the world and the creatures of the world in the new worldview. This is something that eludes precise theological definition in dogmatic rubrics that is not just assertive, but also exhibitive and even active, a combination of all three modes of human query and imaginative reconstruction. It is that sense of the "More" that James wrote about qua the peripheral awareness many people have of the divine eros that lurks on the edge of their focal awareness. The divine eros surrounds us though we are unable to give a precise assertive or perfected prepositional account of what this means; or, as Calvin taught, the finite cannot encompass the infinite. This is why so many theologians embrace negative as well as positive theological discourses. Second, this new worldview embodies a truly radical sense notion of incarnation.

The story of the Word becoming flesh is no longer the story alone told about Jesus of Nazareth but about the universal action of the divine reality for the whole created order. Third, the interaction of the finite creatures and the divine reality makes all things new (this new worldview even has a place for the Book of Revelation). An added benefit of this new interpretation of the divine eros, the doctrine of incarnation, and the radical reformation of the cosmos is that it allows Christians to enter into a fruitful dialogue with such diverse fellow pilgrims as Native American elders, Confucians, and Daoists—just to mention a few of the possible extensions of such a philosophic theology that takes the religious, artistic, scientific, and technological sensibilities of the modernity and postmodernity into account.

Another caveat. I have provided this list of three theological rubrics that show the connection of my imaginative reconstruction of modern spiritual sensibilities in terms of three traditional Christian motifs. However, I must be cautious. Comparative theology—and this includes comparisons between and among different worldviews within one overarching religious tradition called Christianity—is prone to the charge of seeing similarities via the conceptual magic of comparison. As all the authors, beginning with Jonathan Z. Smith, note in A Magic Still Dwells, it is dangerous to assert prematurely where the lines of connection can be divined between different religious traditions. For historians of religion, philosophers, and theologians, the need to pay careful attention to difference is as important as the recognition of similarities.

If there is actually a real paradigm shift in religious sensibility going on in the twenty-first century within the Christian movement, I would expect that any new articulation of the doctrines of God as the divine eros, the incarnation, and the trait of semper transformata will be. different from previous Christian narratives. Whether these new articulations of spiritual insight even remain within the Christian historical movement is something that only future generations will judge. Some wonderful new ideas have become the cherished dogmas of various Christian churches, whereas others, such as the radical Gnostic separation of spirit and flesh, have been roundly condemned as not being worthy of reception by the Christian faithful.

What would be a possible way forward in framing an equally inclusive modern Christian rubric for sexual ethics? What aspect of the tradition can be imaginatively revived and revised to propel forward Christian thinking about sex? Thomas Ogletree said that there is indeed a dominating root metaphor for Christian thinking about ethics. This is the imperative to show hospitality to the stranger. We are all strangers to our lovers, and even to our own sexual desire, fantasies, and actions. Strangers arrive within our purview and we must find a way, so Ogletree argues, to show them hospitality. "Strangers need shelter and sustenance in their travels, especially when they are moving through hostile environment. On the other hand hospitality designates occasions of potential discovery which can open up our narrow provincial worlds. Strangers have stories to tell which we have never heard before, stories which can redirect our seeing and stimulate our imaginations."

Moreover, strangers can stimulate more than our imaginations and become our friends, lovers, and partners for life. We enter a novel ethical/sexual world through hospitality. Traditional Christian motifs and root metaphors can become alive again in a transformed world of new relations between and among men and women and all the other various combinations of human sexual imagination.

Debates about sexuality, therefore, become a corollary of a massive paradigm shift that becomes articulated in a variety of new worldviews, which in turn become embodied in new systematic philosophic and theological reflections. The case of fleshly pleasure, surely a key concept for the analysis of sexuality, bears contemplation. If God creates the world, and if God is immanent in the world in a major way, and if the world is one wherein pleasure is found in sex, then God created pleasure as part of various sexual acts.

The quotidian becomes the locus of the divine, or as Herbert Fingarette so aptly titled his study of Master Kong, the secular is the sacred. And if the secular is sexual pleasure, then we need a doctrine of sexual pleasure as something positive. Here again my students, driven by the logic of new worldviews, refuse to think any longer that pleasure is evil. Along with the collapse of hell and the Totally Transcendent God, there has been an inversion of traditional views of pleasure. The modern world is much more openly hedonistic than ascetic. Moreover, there is now a reasoned defense of pleasure as part of the created order. We need redemption of pleasure, according to many of my students.

Christian theology, therefore, has a massive job of reconstruction on its hands. First, much of its inherited worldview analysis (read: both ontology and cosmology) no longer makes sense to the educated public in North America. Second, the various specific ethical teachings about sex that were predicated on the older worldviews likewise no longer make much sense to the same public. For instance, if sex is purely for reproduction, somehow the vast majorities of women in North America (and Europe as well) have not gotten the message or have simply chosen to ignore or reject this basic teaching. Women have long endured such lessons but are now able to pick and choose what they will and will not accept from a predominantly male clergy.

Any new theological ethics of sex must, therefore, be honest about what people believe. To formally teach one thing and then more privately explain away those teachings strikes my students as a form of hypocrisy. I try to explain to my students that hypocrisy is not always a bad thing, but they contend that it could never be the formal basis for their practice of ministry. I agree. Furthermore, any new theology of sexual ethics must be empirically sound. What I mean here is that theologians must take modern science and technology into account when they frame their new worldviews.

This means, for instance, that evolutionary theory in science and critical historical awareness in the humanities must be acknowledged—acknowledged such that theologians can no longer write as if modern science has never emerged after the seventeenth century, the Enlightenment, and industrial and technological revolutions of the nineteenth century. Theologians as diverse as Tracy, Kaufman, Jordan, Fortune, and Neville all agree on the need for honestly conjoined empir soundness; piety must be extended to the new story of the hidden heart of the cosmos, to borrow the evocative book title by Brian Swimme.

Actually, the call for empirical soundness is part and parcel of the paradigm shift qua worldview transformation that demands a radical re-analysis of the God-world relationship for Christians. If God is dramatically immanent in the mundane world, then God is part of the empirical nature of the world. It is not without reason that the American pragmatic and naturalist traditions and process thought have become favorite philosophic resources for reforming Christian theologians in North America. (23) Pragmatism, naturalism, and process thought have the benefit of being indigenous to North America and dedicated to being empirically sound philosophies.

What forms of classical Christian sexual ethics merit restoration or retrieval for a modern Christian who has been captured or persuaded by the new sense of inextricable immanence of contemporary God-world relations? My very blunt answer in regard to most formal teachings about sex is: almost nothing. This harsh judgment begs for immediate interpretation. Religions live by their traditions, and if the whole tradition is jettisoned, then what is left? A radical proponent of reform might retort that nothing need be retained save the most fundamental commitment to being a member of that particular community of faith.

Though I admit my memory may be faulty, I remember that Wilfred Cantwell Smith, at a conference in Toronto in the early 1980s, basically said, in response to a similar question about the necessity for tradition in religion, that a Christian was someone who said she or he was a Christian, period. Nonetheless, Smith was a champion, among other things, of a complex definition of human religious history that included, again among other items, the faith of the person and the cumulative tradition into which the person was born or which that person adopted. Raimon Panikkar, in an essay soon to be published on the question of Christian identity in a pluralistic age, has proposed a parallel thesis about Christian identity that I think Smith would have approved of.

In the first instance, Panikkar agrees with Smith that whether or not a person is a Christian is defined by the self-conscious confession of the person to be a Christian and that this confession of faith be "validated" by the recognition of the same community that this person is a Christian. This would satisfy both the sense of existential commitment that Smith deems makes for religious faith as well as a role of the community of like-minded members of the cumulative tradition.

Mou Zongsan (1909-1995), the subtlest philosopher among the last generation of New Confucians, argued that any religious Way—and he included Confucianism among the religions of the world—was structured around vertical and horizontal dimensions. The vertical dimension constitutes the human encounter with the divine reality, which Mou recognized as "God" in Western religions and terms such as "Dao" or the "Supreme Ultimate" in Confucianism. According to Mou, it is this engagement with the divine reality that makes a tradition religious as opposed to merely philosophic in the sense of technical reason. Mou wanted to include reflections on the vertical dimension of human experience because he defended the notion that there was a profound religious dimension to be found in the Confucian Way. Mou believed that you could not fully understand Confucianism without recourse to an analysis of its vertical dimension.

Mou also posited a horizontal dimension to the great world religions. Religions not only foster an encounter with divine reality but also have devised various complicated systems of ethical and social norms that guide the lives of their members.

Each tradition, therefore, gives ethical advice to its members based on its understanding of the interplay of the vertical and horizontal dimensions of human life. Mou himself would often philosophically define the vertical dimension of Confucian religiousness as the embodiment of creativity itself. The horizontal realm Mou concurrently defined as the ceaseless deepening of human intersubjectivity such that concern for self and others was embodied in various codes of human ethical conduct.

In traditional terms, this was the way Mou would link ren, or humaneness, as the highest virtue with li, or ritual, as the expression in human life of the embodiment of humaneness as the expression of deepened intersubjectivity as creativity itself. I go on at length about Mou because I think that he illustrates cogently, albeit from the Confucian viewpoint, the reason why no religion can jettison ethical reflection and remain a living religion in anything like the sense of achievement of the great traditions of the Axial Age.

Actually, Mou would expand his claim to hold that no religion can abandon comprehensive reflection on human flourishing in all its dimensions, the ethical being a crucial but not the only proper form of horizontal human activity, but this would take us too far astray into the study of New Confucian social theory. I also want to make another point by including Mou in this conversation, namely that he has already become a resource for the renewal of Christian theology. Mou informs the thought of more and more younger Chinese and Korean theologians, and hence has become part of Christian history.

This is probably not well known because most North Atlantic theologians have no clue as to who this Chinese Confucian scholar is, or why they should be interested in him. My hypothesis is that Mou will become part of the Christian lineage as surely as Plato, Aristotle, Augustine, Thomas, Cusa, Luther, Calvin, Kant, Hegel, Barth, Whitehead, and Tillich. As more and more young East Asians no longer must submit to a deracinated version of global history, important East Asian intellectual resources will join the narrative of the Christian gospel—and will enrich and transform the gospel in the process.

So what ethical aspects or traditions are worth trying to retrieve? I will suggest one candidate, namely the classic tradition known as casuistry. Most modern, and especially Protestant, theologians probably consider casuistry a dead tradition; moreover it is a tradition that owes its demise to humor and not the to the fires of the heretical stake nor the dialectical refutation of sound theological discourse. Pascal, rather like Cervantes for the adventures of knights, is assumed to have ridiculed the art of casuistry to such an extent that it never recovered from his criticism. To a large extent, this proved to be historically accurate, though casuistry survived in both Roman Catholic and Anglican versions into the early twentieth century.

Moreover, there has been something of a revival of interest in casuistry in more recent periods. At least one reason for such a renewed concern is that casuistry appears to be a form of ethical reasoning suitable for a pluralistic age. Much of the recent interest in casuistry derives from the 1988 work of Albert Jonsen and Stephen Toulmin, The Abuse of Casuistry: A History of Moral Reasoning. Stimulated by Jonsen and Toulmin, many other ethicists have looked again at a tradition long assumed dead. For the purposes of pondering a prolegomenon to any future Christian ethics of sex, I will follow Jonsen and Toulmin's definition of casuistry. They write that casuistry is "the analysis of moral issues, using procedures of reasoning based on paradigms and analogies, leading to the formulation of expert opinions about the existence and stringency of particular moral obligations, framed in terms of rules or maxims that are general but not universal or invariable, since they hold good with certainty only in the typical conditions of the agent and circumstances of action."

Here we can see, for instance, a structural affinity between the modern ethics of casuistry and North American process, naturalist, pragmatic, and metaphoric philosophies in terms of the fallibilist sensibility. This is also one of the things that most annoyed Pascal as a Jansenist theologian about the casuist tradition: it refused to provide a perfect dictionary of ethical norms for moral decision making. Pascal wanted something better than "more or less," but this probabilism may indeed be the case for modern moral philosophizing in a pluralist age. As I have argued elsewhere, a great deal of Song daoxue moral theory can be read as a Confucian version of casuistry.

The great Song Confucian masters such as Zhu Xi (1130-1200) recognized that the moral maxims of classical Confucian thought needed to be balanced by quan, or learning, to balance the Way in difficult cases, often translated into English as the expedient. I would further argue, but not here, that casuistry as a moral tradition is compatible with the North American philosophic traditions of pragmatism, naturalism, process philosophy, and modern metaphoric body philosophy. At its best, casuistry is dedicated to respecting history and the recognition of novel or difficult ethical situations.

It can be traditional and empirical at the same time, and in fact demands that any sophisticated moral advice had probably better keep an eye on tradition and innovation if it is going to make any sense whatsoever. As I reviewed the liberal Christian literature, I discovered than many pastoral counseling manuals could, without stretching the definition too much, be considered modern casuistry. As Jonsen and Toulmin likewise noted, there is the suspicion that any sensitive moral guide will often resort to something like classical or contemporary casuistry when the normal rules do not apply. Such talent for giving sound moral advice that goes beyond the mechanical application of rules has been a part of Christian (and Confucian) lore for a long, long time. Given the complexities of human sexuality, I believe that some form of casuistry will remain part of the practical moral practice of Christian ethicists and counselors for an equally long, long time.

For most of this paper I have stressed questions of cosmological paradigm shifts and second-order methodological ethical considerations. I will now reverse directions and discuss a concrete set of guidelines for consensual sex among adults provided by Marie Fortune. (27) Fortune, who is well known for her work on the issues of clergy sexual abuse, wrote a small book in which she tried to summarize what she takes to be sensible advice about consensual adult sexual acts.

As an aside, and with approval as a Confucian-Christian, I found it fascinating that she framed her discourse in terms of "love does no harm"—Fortune's version of the Confucian negative version of the golden rule. Do not do unto others what you would not have them do to you. Tu Weiming has argued that while this is formulated as a negative rule, it is a good formal rule for a pluralistic social setting when we do not want people imposing even their most cherished "good" behaviors and rules precisely because they are not necessarily good rules nor virtues for everyone. For instance, though I am convinced that vegetarians have a strong theoretical point to make, I would not like to be forced to become a vegan against my will.

Even before Fortune outlines her five recommendations for consensual sex, she makes it clear that she is talking only about sexual acts between consenting adults. She wants to build a fence, a hedge as it were, around any kind of abusive sexuality that takes advantage of other people. She is concerned that in a complex society with strong differentiated social roles that parcel out power and prestige hierarchically, there is always the temptation to abuse social power and capital for sexual favors. Abuse of parishioners by clergy and of patients by counselors are perfect examples of the kind of social situations that Fortune believes cannot be classified as consensual sex. Here again a Confucian-Christian recognizes a version of the doctrine of the rectification of names. When a person takes on the role of clergy, for instance, that person abjures any possible sexual relations with a member of her or his parish; the same advice holds for a teacher with her or his students.

Another important part of Fortune's program is the fact that she is writing from within a Christian theological framework. For instance, Fortune reads the Song of Songs as an erotic love poem. Moreover, she also notes that it does not preclude a homosexual as well as a heterosexual reading. Fortune is one of a growing list of Christian theologians who are willing to defend homosexuality as within the purview of God's love. While it might not be the same framework of Billy Graham, or the leadership of the Roman Catholic Church, or the Southern Baptist Convention, or Jerry Falwell, Fortune does defend her ethical system in terms of its conformity with a liberal reading of Christian texts.

Fortune develops five rubrics for guiding decisions about sexual acts and relations. I make this distinction because it is part of Fortune's argument; although with the caveat that Fortune herself recommends (as actually does almost everyone else I have read) that sex and relationships appear to be part of primate behavior. Rubric I is that in seeking sex, we should choose peer relationships. She argues that in seeking a peer for sex we avoid the problem of abuse of person and power that is so rampant in our society. Rubric II is that we must seek authentic consent. Once we have found a peer partner, we need to make sure that she or he is genuinely interested in having some kind of sex without moral qualms. Or as Fortune says, "authentic success should not be confused with submission, the absence of non-consent, or acquiescence." The first two rubrics generally deal with the honest and ethical choice of a sexual partner.

Rubric III deals with what Fortune, again using Christian symbolism, calls the stewardship of sexuality. One concrete part of this rubric demands that we care about the health and well-being of our sexual partners; this includes concern for protecting others and ourselves against sexually transmitted diseases and also thinking carefully about the reproductive potential of heterosexual sexual acts. It also demands that we develop ways to talk to our partners about our needs and wants before, during, and after sex. Rubric IV follows from the third. "Am I committed to sharing sexual pleasure and intimacy in my relationship? My concern should be both for my own needs and those of my partner." I will return to rubric 1V later in the essay because it illustrates perfectly one major aspect of the how paradigm shifts in cosmology and the conceptualization of God-world relations have a direct impact on sexual ethics.

Without putting too fine a point on it, notice how pleasure moves from being part of the problem to becoming something to be honored and appreciated as a cosmological good. I suggest that rubrics III and IV discuss the "how" of sexual activity, namely care for health and then the pleasure of the act itself. Rubric V is about the need for faithfulness in sexual encounters. "Am I faithful to my promises and commitments? Whatever the nature of a commitment to one's partner and whatever the duration of that commitment, fidelity requires honesty and the keeping of promises. Change in an individual may require a change in the commitment which hopefully can be achieved through open and honest communication."

Whitehead once wrote that there is the need for a hope of rationalism within any philosophic system. Such a hope is not open to dialectic formulation, but it is there at the fundament of any search for meaning. This is what Fortune means with her fifth rubric. Here again we see the theological hardware and deep operating systems of Fortune's attempt to provide guidelines of adult consensual sex. Some modern philosophers would argue that if we can really communicate, then we would be able to be faithful. In practice this seems to be a hope rather than a possibility.

When you focus on Fortune's five rubrics, it is clear that adoption of these five guidelines would demand some radical changes in how Christians have viewed the world and how sexuality is part of that world. For instance, rubric III (stewardship) asks us to consider that sexual partners should understand and take precautions against sexually transmitted diseases and be aware of questions of reproductive choice. As Rita Gross has so often reminded us, dialogue between and among Christians and Buddhists raises the question of pronatal sensibilities among the Christians present. The point that Gross has been making can be interpreted on two levels.

The first has to do with the quality of particular human relationships. Does every human sexual act need to be reproductive in outcome? Clearly Gross believes, along with Fortune, that this is not the case. The second consideration has to do with our growing awareness that the pronatal policies of many of the great Eurasian Axial Age religions now have dangerous implications for the viability of the human species. Based on a rethinking of the notion of stewardship, is it time to rethink our ecological connection to the world as it relates to pronatal teachings? Therefore, does it make any sense to continue to think that human beings really do need, in all cases, to multiply without number and then dominate the created order? My answer to this rhetorical question is, no, we as a species need to rethink our stewardship of the created order and one of the most germane domains of such a rethinking would be in the arena of sexuality as it relates to reproduction.

The reflections listed above indicate how a change in thinking about something as intimate and personal as sexual acts can be transformed into broader community reflections on the very nature of human flourishing at a cosmological level. It is truly a case of the personal and the political as feminists have been alerting us to for a long time now. Also authors such as Fortune and Jordan, as homosexuals, draw our attention to the fact that the very nature of homosexual acts is not pronatalist—at least before the arrival of postmodern medical science.

Along with dialogue between and among religions, there is a concomitant need for dialogue between and among persons with different sexual orientations. The problems of framing a believable liberal Christian sexual ethics are complicated enough that Christians need all kinds of insights and to be as inclusive as possible in the dialogue. And nowhere is this more urgent than when we begin to try to find religious and ethical answers posed by the questions raised by the ecological crisis.

Where does all of this leave contemporary Christian ethics? Most specifically, where does it leave liberal Christian intellectuals as they attempt to revivify the cumulative tradition? If my analysis is correct, then it leaves Christian ethicists with a major problem. If they are honest, then most of the tradition is of little use. Some specific methodologies, such as a reformed casuistry, can be brought back into play. But even the deployment of casuistry is ironic because it again becomes a viable option for methodological reasons; content to be applied via the method is another question entirely.

Casuistry is viable precisely because Christians in North America no longer live in a "Christian" country. Although it is still true that Christians are the majority religion of North America, other groups, such as Jews, Muslims, Hindus, Sikhs, Jains, Buddhists, Daoists, Native American traditionalists, and even some Confucians, are growing in numbers.

But what is even more important than demography—and I do not want to discount demographic issues for a moment—is the growing voice of all the traditions in North America. Hegel once said that if you tell people they are free, they will begin to believe it and act as if they are free. If you tell people that one of the glories of North American societies is their religious freedom, which includes the right to speak out in public about matters that affect their communities of faith, then more and more different religious people will speak openly about their concerns. I am struck by how Muslims, after the tragedy of 9/11, are attempting to defend their religion against malicious attacks inferring theirs as a religion of war and terror as opposed to one of peace and justice. North American Muslims are just as appalled by 9/11 as any other North Americans, but they are unwilling to allow the actions of a few criminal terrorists to hijack the good name of Islam.

As Jonsen and Toulmin have argued, casuistry is a tradition capable of thriving in a pluralist environment. Casuistry, just like other forms of early modern Christian discourse, was not originally designed for this task, but it did have the feature of the recognition of a diversity of possible choices, and can be expanded to include a recognition of possible ethical choices informed by the consideration of a wider range of religious options. For instance, the ecological insights of many Native American traditions can now become the common discourse of all North Americans.

However, this still leaves us (the Christians) with the problem of some kind of starting place. Actually, we probably have the same starting place that every ethicist dealing with sexuality has: we have what we think are the main ethical rubrics, metaphors, and insights of our tradition and the human desire for sex. We will defer a discussion of the desire for sex for a moment, and ask, what is the root metaphor for Christian ethics? I will simply select a specified version of "love," though I confess I do so with some hesitation.

Nonetheless, if you have to rummage around for a key insight or metaphor within the vast majority of Christian traditions, some comment about love as a theological doctrine appears over and over again. Of course, just how Christian theological love and love as sexual desire are connected is another matter entirely. My specification of the doctrine of love is qualified by the reflections of Marie Fortune and Robert Neville. Both have written books that talk about how to practice the hermeneutics of restoration, to borrow a phrase from Ricouer. Fortune wants to retrieve something useful for a contemporary and responsible liberal Christian sexual ethics; Neville more broadly wants to restore the symbol of Jesus in all its riches for contemporary Christian theological reflection.

In both cases they specify "love" as a form of care, and in this focus on care as concern for the others they both repay major debts to feminist theoreticians of the ethics of care. I personally approve of this move, made on inter-Christian grounds by both Fortune and Neville, because it dovetails neatly with the Confucian insistence that care and concern for self and others resides at the center of human ethical reflection. As the Neo-Confucians taught, one must obtain the Dao for oneself in service to others. One, as the Quakers teach, has a concern for self and others. Mou Zongsan goes so far as to say that the chief Confucian sensibility is concern-consciousness, a way of looking at the world based on a profound intersubjectivity between the emerging self, other human beings, and finally the whole cosmos.

So I agree with Fortune that we can, at a minimum, not harm others in sexual acts. But according to Fortune and Neville we ought to do more: we should have a positive regard for others. We should love others because God first loved us. This is my root metaphor and becomes the rubric for one side of the task of ethical counseling.

The other side, as I mentioned just above, is sexual desire. Now, as I interpret it, sexual pleasure is a particularly intense subset of the larger range of pleasures of which a human being is capable. Of course, this would have been obvious to Christian ethicists from the very beginning of the Christian movement. However—and here is where it is important to reflect on paradigm shifts in cosmology—pleasure has shifted from negative to positive in liberal Christian worldviews. Liberal Christians accept that God created the world and saw that it was good. One vital aspect of this creation is pleasure, and sexual activity is surely an important pleasure for most human beings. Moreover, the liberal modern cosmology affirms that pleasure is good per se. There is nothing intrinsically wrong with the pursuit of pleasure so long as it is governed by the rubric of concern or care.

The cosmological paradigm shift or change in the liberal Christian perspective on God-world relations has transformed the equation of love/concern/care/pleasure from a dipolar relation of something good (love) and something bad (pleasure) into an equation of two goods. Of course, for the practical ethicist the problem still remains that sometimes two goods can conflict.

Moreover, Leibniz teaches us that we actually have a more difficult problem now with our two goods than we had with one good and one evil. Leibniz taught that it is easy to understand that we need to resist evil and embrace the good. Real problems arise when we have two competing goods, and this is precisely the new cosmological problem for contemporary liberal Christian ethicists. Love as cosmic concern-consciousness is good and sex per se is also good—

more or less. Confucian-Christians would have no trouble (something of a rhetorical flourish) with such a reformed understanding because the Confucian tradition has always had a much higher view of sex than has the Christian tradition. Although Confucians were hardly sexual swingers, they did recognize that sex was important to human beings and was something to be enjoyed within proper bounds. Rather like Christians, these proper bounds were defined in terms of heterosexual marriage. Some Confucians, at least from the Ming dynasty on, even defended the idea of a companionate marriage with sex being one important part of the equation.

Modern liberal Christian sexual ethics must now do much the same thing. Nor should this really be much of an intellectual scandal. It is clear that Christian theology has accommodated itself successfully to many different paradigm shifts. These cosmological shifts of philosophic opinion have also engendered major transformations of ethical teachings as well. For instance, Christians no longer accept slavery.

Modern liberal Christians will no longer define sexuality per se as evil and something to be eliminated, sublimated, or controlled as a negative fact of this all-too-human life. Rather, they will need to creatively devise a new set of ethical teachings that will make use of the theological rubrics of the tradition along with the new cosmological sensibility about pleasure. If Christians do not do so, more and more people will simply ignore the teachings of the Christian movement and find their ethical teachings somewhere else.

If Mou Zongsan is correct again, this would be a disaster for the Christian movement. And if Leibniz is right about the difficulty of balancing sometimes incommensurable goods—love/concern/care against sexual pleasure as positive elements of human existence—then we are in for some truly fascinating theological reconstructions. However, if we are honest about how cosmologies and religious metaphors and rubrics interact in the formulating of sexual ethics, we can do no other (with thanks to Luther for the end, as it were).

Chapter 4

Hotel Way of Life

URBAN SETTLEMENT

In conducting our historical review of the urban settlements for the single poor in Chicago and cities elsewhere, we emphasized three themes. First, that the residents of the Main Stem and Skid Row pursued independence with determination and vigor, an independence facilitated by the design and provision of SRO hotels. Second, that the pursuit of individual autonomy among those single men at the bottom of the urban labor market was made possible by their use of networks of community social ties binding the dependent and independent members of Skid Row together.

Third, that these residential communities declined precipitously in the 1960s, not only because the prosperity of the 1950s and 1960s reduced the number of the single working poor who would live there, but also because urban renewal programs leveled most of the SRO hotels. The residents contributed relatively little to the demise of Skid Row. Using these themes to revise the story of the rise of the Main Stem and the fall of Skid Row provides an important correction to the misleading accounts of Skid Row that gained popularity in the 1950s and 1960s. The accounts, which stressed personal failure, continue to shape public perceptions of the urban homeless today.

We realized, however, that historical revision alone might not prove persuasive to skeptics, who might accuse us of romanticizing the Skid Row community, or argue that although our account may have been true for SRO hotels in the past, the remaining hotels no longer offer the useful physical and social resources they once did. In order to test our beliefs, therefore, we devised a survey that would have the same scope of Bogue's earlier study but would include a sample of residents from all the SRO hotels in the city of Chicago rather than just the few hotels remaining in the original Skid Row area.

Our research is not without important precedents. As we mentioned in chapter 6, social order analysts classified SRO hotel residents using concepts of social community rather than social disaffiliation. Initially, the social order analysts avoided the political implications of their research, but the enormous social costs urban renewal imposed on residents of workingclass neighborhoods eventually inspired other research analysts, schooled in the same tradition, to put the community interpretation to political use.

For instance, studies by Marc Fried, Chester Hartman, Jim Ward, and others exposed the way labeling the residents of inner-city neighborhoods as "Skid Row bums" served the political purposes of local developers and officials looking for reasons to displace the low-income residents quickly and cheaply. Forcibly removing working-class citizens from the local community to which they belong, they argued, was a terribly destructive action requiring a great deal more compensation, care, and respect than redevelopment authorities had provided. Documenting the social costs of community destruction and the unfair burdens of forced relocation, these critics helped liberal lobbyists convince legislators to shift the focus of urban renewal from slum clearance to rehabilitation, and to increase relocation benefits to those people and businesses evicted as a direct result of federally funded development projects.

It is in the context of this research that individual SRO hotels became the object of studies conducted by social analysts critical of both the Skid Row stereotype and large-scale redevelopment clearance schemes. For instance, in 1975 analysts at the Western Behavioral Sciences Institute studied a sample of residents from twelve hotels in downtown San Diego, California.

Their purpose was to explore whether the nonwelfare poor living in hotels managed to avoid dependency. They found little in the way of social pathology and a great deal of social support among elderly residents. Other studies of SRO hotels came to similar conclusions about the usefulness and value of the SRO hotels as inexpensive living environments contributing to the autonomy of residents. New evidence on the social usefulness of hotels, however, did not inspire widespread revisions of the stereotype developed from the earlier Skid Row studies. Other than the San Diego case, most studies of SRO hotels used ethnographic in-depth analysis of individual hotels, which provided convincing detail about a single hotel but prevented the construction of unbiased inferences to all the hotels in a particular city. Hence, proponents of the Skid Row stereotype could dismiss the findings as valid, but exceptional. Furthermore, some in-depth studies of SRO hotels did not find benign systems of social supports, but instead found environments characterized by social isolation.

We designed our research study in order to test whether the sorts of social communities analysts found for individual hotels would exist for a sample of residents representing all the SRO hotel residents in a single city, Chicago. We first conducted a census of all the SRO hotels in the city and then randomly selected both hotels and rooms to ensure an unbiased as well as representative sample of residents whom we intended to interview. We stratified the sample by three geographic areas: North Side, Central (Skid Row and peripheral areas), and South Side. In all, we managed to collect 185 interviews with residents from eighteen hotels during the late spring and summer of 1985. Since we under sampled from the North Side and over sampled from the South Side hotels, we weighted the sample to correct for this bias.

The analysis of our survey findings provides a systematic assessment of the empirical foundations for the popular Skid Row stereotype. Our findings contradict the five most common generalizations about "Skid Row bums": that they are deviant, transient, lazy, dependent, and isolated. For example, we found that although the demographic characteristics of SRO residents do differ from the general population, these differences do not make them deviants. The frequent moves of SRO residents can also more accurately be ascribed to displacement than transience.

SRO residents are mostly poor, not because they avoid work, but because they earn low wages, cannot find work, or receive inadequate retirement or disability benefits. The social vulnerabilities of SRO residents do not predict their dependence. Despite considerable economic hardship and personal illness among the SRO population as a whole, these difficulties do not accumulate among such vulnerable social groups as blacks, women, and the elderly. Finally, the SRO residents maintain their autonomy not by isolating themselves, but by contributing responsibly to the well-being of others through ongoing reciprocal relationships. We conclude that the stereotype falsely attributes socially deviant or otherwise pathological meanings to the social characteristics and relationships of SRO hotel residents, and thereby hides the distinctive and valuable social benefits of the SRO way of life.

Different but Not Deviant

The SRO residents differ significantly from the general city population in age, sex, race, and other demographic characteristics. However, these differences are much smaller than those that marked the social distance between the Skid Row residents and other city residents in the 1950s. The residents of SRO hotels come mainly from the ranks of the working poor and so reflect the social characteristics of this population. Hence, comparisons with the general population offer exaggerated estimates of the size of these differences.

The SRO residents who perhaps come closest to maintaining the way of life associated with the real Skid Row (not the stereotype) are the SRO veterans. These were SRO residents who reported living in another SRO hotel before moving to their present address, hence the title of "veterans." SRO veterans were older and more likely to be white and to have never married than the first-timers. In these respects they more closely resemble the Skid Row population studied by Bogue. The SRO veterans lived mainly in the hotels near downtown (41 percent) and the North Side (56 percent). Barely 3 percent of the black South Side residents had a history of living in SROs.

The SRO hotel population remains overwhelmingly male, and because the residents rent single rooms, the majority live alone. The most surprising finding was that almost one in five shares his tiny living quarters with someone else. The above characteristics more than any others separate this population from the general city population. Alcoholism, the problem that figured so prominently in the Skid Row study by Bogue, appears to be much less pervasive among the SRO residents of the 1980s. Only 14 percent of the SRO residents drank alcohol as frequently as once a day or more, and 37 percent did not drink at all.

Almost 15 percent of the residents suffered from such life-threatening conditions as heart disease, emphysema, cirrhosis of the liver, tuberculosis, cancer, and paralysis due to a stroke. Another 22 percent lived with less serious but still chronically disruptive illnesses like diabetes, high blood pressure, cataracts, arthritis, asthma, or muscular dystrophy. Fewer than 5 percent of the SRO residents reported suffering from mental illness. Overall, 38 percent of the SRO residents endured some form of serious illness at the time of our interview. An additional 3 percent reported chronic minor ailments. The SRO residents reported twice the proportion of serious illness as the adult population nationwide.

The differences between SRO residents and Chicago residents in terms of race, marital status, schooling, and age are much smaller than they were thirty years ago. In part the change reflects the fact that the first-timers in the SRO closely resemble the typical single poor adults of all Chicago while the overall socioeconomic characteristics of the city's residents have fallen in comparison with those of the people in the surrounding suburbs. The SRO residents' choice of a single room accommodation necessarily places them in a distinct category of single-person households, a category that ironically is becoming increasingly popular among young single professionals pursuing the advantages of urban living by renting small studio apartments near downtown. In certain neighborhoods the influx of professionals has been so great as to pit the SRO residents against the wealthier newcomers in a bidding competition for scarce residential space, including the SRO hotels. The wealthier bidders always win. The SRO residents end up being displaced.

Transiency Reconsidered

We found that, contrary to the stereotype of rootless wanderers or transient alcoholics, about one-half of the SRO residents had lived in their present unit for two years or more, and 29 percent had lived there four years or more. The burden of moving, however, was not evenly distributed. Sixty-five percent of the women had lived in their current residence than two years, compared with only 44 percent of the men. Comparing the young with the overall population, we found that 80 percent of the residents below thirty-five years of age had lived in their current unit less than two years, but that only 48 percent of all residents had changed residences that recently.

SRO residents do tend to move more frequently than the general population. For instance, among all U.S. households, only 35 percent of the homeowners and 60 percent of the renters move every five years, as compared with 75 percent of all SRO residents. However, when compared with other unrelated individuals in midwestern metropolitan areas, the SRO residents do not differ much in their transience. Overall, 29 percent of unrelated individuals had moved between March 1982 and March 1983 (34.5 percent of those below the poverty line), whereas 37.8 percent of the SRO residents had moved during the year preceding the interview (summer 1984 to summer 1985). A greater proportion of the SRO residents than unrelated individuals in the Midwest move, but this difference reflects the peculiar pressures of hotel life as much as it does the characteristics of the tenants. SRO residents face far greater displacement pressures than do those individuals renting apartments or houses. When we analyzed each respondent's housing history, we discovered that moving depended less on initiative and desire than on pressures of physical, social, and economic circumstance.

When we asked respondents why they left their prior residence, 80 percent referred to conditions that pushed them out of their homes. One in five (23 percent) were evicted mainly because of closure or conversion of the building. In one instance, a man was forced out because "they condemned the building and turned off the heat." About one in three (31 percent) left for reasons of social pressure, usually either to avoid the dangers of ongoing social disputes with household members, local gangs, or landlords, or to accommodate changes in household organization. For instance, one respondent left her residence because her husband died, and an elderly black man complained that he moved because the bigoted landlord would not allow black people to visit.

Overcrowding, divorce, and other social pressures were also mentioned frequently, as in the case of the twenty-nine-year-old black man who moved out because "my sister's new apartment lease only allowed a certain amount of people to live there," or of the man on leave from work who told us that, after separating from his wife, "I wasn't getting an income and I couldn't afford the rent." An elderly black woman complained that she was forced to move away from her daughter because, as she put it, "My daughter was on AFDC and I was on General Assistance, and the Public Aid office told me I had to move because too much money was coming into one place."

Problems with the physical conditions of the prior residence or the pressures of decreasing income and increasing rent together accounted for only about 20 percent of the reasons respondents offered for moving. Rising rent was the most frequently mentioned economic pressure, followed closely by job loss. Environmental complaints included lack of repairs, the presence of vermin, and noise. One woman summed up her reasons for moving: "the management didn't service the building — no cleaning, spraying, painting or repairs were done."

Only one in five of the reasons respondents gave to explain their most recent move reflected a desire to change residence or express a preference. Those few who left without external pressure did so to pursue more advantageous employment (5.7 percent) or to obtain greater autonomy by living on their own (11.6 percent). Comments such as "I just need a place of my own" were frequently made. Although we interpreted these as voluntary choices, the desire for privacy was usually expressed by someone who felt confined living in a household with others. Someone seeking privacy and autonomy is obviously leaving a dwelling where these conditions are lacking and so is responding to the social pressures of shared living arrangements. The remaining 9 percent simply replied that they had left from another city to come to Chicago without specifying what attracted them.

When we call someone a "transient" we usually mean a person whose frequent moves reflect a chosen life-style of constant migration. These residents do not choose to move but move because they are forced to do so. In other words, SRO residents in Chicago face powerful displacement pressures at a level far greater than does the general population, so their frequent moves should not be mistaken for transience.

At the time of our census in 1984, SRO hotels provided about 11,800 units of affordable housing. We knew the spaces were small, but we also measured other characteristics of the room to assess the quality of the space. We utilized a measure of overall room quality with a high score of 11 and a low score of 0. Each room received 3 points for a bath, 2 points for a closet, and I point each for the following: sink, heater, window, stove, phone, and television set. We discovered that the hotel rooms with the lowest scores clustered in two cubicle hotels. Rooms in these hotels had an average score of 0. 85, whereas the private rooms in the other SRO hotels averaged 9.60. The cubicle hotels in our sample accounted for only 5 percent of the units and 3 percent of the hotels in the city. In contrast, cubicle hotels accounted for almost 85 percent of the 11,943 hotel units and 32 percent of the hotels on Skid Row in 1958.

Most SRO residents actively choose their housing, selecting an SRO not simply as a haven of last resort, but as an urban home. The socially and economically diverse clientele of SROs report a correspondingly complex assortment of reasons to explain why they chose their present residence. We had expected to find that most tenants would, like the cubicle tenants, claim low rent as the primary reason they chose an SRO residence.

Though a plurality did offer economic reasons for their choice (39 percent), only about half of these reported low rents (23 percent). Most of these were the tenants in cubicle hotels. Typical of the reasons offered by these residents was the explanation offered by one elderly man who declared, "I can't afford to pay a lot of rent or utility bills." Interestingly, a few of the more prosperous and discriminating residents (4 percent) contend that their present SRO provided better quality shelter than competing hotels; for example, one man stated, "This is better than other hotels. It's cleaner, kept up better, and quieter."

A substantial portion referred to social relationships as the primary reason for choosing their present living arrangements in an SRO. Some wanted to live near friends (7.6 percent) or relatives (4.2 percent), as in the case of a son who moved to his present address because, as he put it, "My father lives across the street and it's convenient to cross and take care of him." Many based their choice on the referral of a trusted friend (11. 6 percent). A few mentioned that they had rented in the SRO before or knew the owner (6.9 percent).

The most unexpected finding popped up in the "Other" category. Slightly more than 15 percent chose their hotel accommodation because of its convenient location. Convenience meant various things to people. For instance, one woman specified: "It has a convenient location because church is close by and anything you would need for living you can find in this area."

Another woman defined convenient as "being close to where I work and close to good transportation." Access to employment and services (especially good public transportation) at affordable prices makes SRO living an attractive residential option for low-income renters. This was akin to the situation at the turn of the century when most SRO hotels were built to accommodate low-income workers and transients. Although the present residents are not hoboes, tramps, or bums of years gone by, they nevertheless rely on the accessibility of the hotels to city services and activities just as their predecessors did.

Others admitted that, despite searching, they chose their present SRO hotel because it was the only one with vacancies at the time. One woman lamented, "I had gone to five different places and they were all filled and this was the first one which had a room, so I took it." Fewer than 8 percent gave no reason for their choice.

Finally, only about 4 percent found their present accommodation by referral from a social service agency. At the present time the use of SRO hotels in Chicago as residential placements for social service institutions is not as widespread as in the past or in other cities. This contrasts with common practice in New York or Los Angeles, where SRO hotels are routinely used to house welfare recipients through use of rent vouchers. The hotels included in our sample got their residents from the rental market, not the state.

Poor but Not Lazy

According to the Skid Row stereotype, SRO hotel residents will likely prefer irregular or even criminal employment to a steady job. They will act like bums, seeking free handouts and welfare in order to escape the burdens of work. But do SRO residents actually exhibit an aversion to work and a desire to live off the system? Our evidence disputes this image. The interviews made it clear that residents not only acknowledge the value of work but that economic necessity provides a powerful incentive for them to stay in the labor market as long as possible.

The SRO inhabitants work or pursue work if they can. At the time of our interviews 42 percent had permanent jobs, 23 percent were searching for work, and only 35 percent remained outside the labor market. Furthermore, among those who were neither employed nor searching for work, 24 percent claimed retirement, 55.5 percent permanent disability, and 9.5 percent other conditions as reasons why they did not seek work. Only 11 percent received public aid payments. That leaves a small fraction of people who might fit the stereotype of the shiftless bum, though even in this category most cases could not be described as "shiftless." This group included two single women with children not on aid, a housewife, a student, and a part-time day laborer. Only one person claimed that he wanted to work but just was not able to find it and had given up.

The key to independence and autonomy is a secure source of income. The SRO residents who enjoyed full-time employment, as well as those who received Social Security, Supplemental Security Income (SSI) benefits, or pension funds, could rely on the predictability of their checks, even if the amounts were modest. Those who worked part time at low-wage jobs or were unemployed and on public aid faced a more precarious economic condition. These were the dependent poor, most of whom struggled to obtain access to employment and a few of whom sought a more dependable and substantial public source of aid (such as SSI) other than General Assistance (GA) grants.

About 60 percent of the SRO residents enjoy modest economic security that makes independent life in the SRO hotel a viable living arrangement. The remaining 40 percent, however, include those who must routinely face serious economic and hence shelter uncertainty. We calculated the predominant income source for each resident based on the proportion of income from each of three sources: earnings from wages, previous earnings (mainly disability, Social Security, or pension payments), and unearned aid (usually General Assistance). Wage income offered the most secure source of income and hence the greatest freedom from want, whereas reliance on unearned income left recipients at the mercy of their scrutinizing benefactors.

The residents who rely on earnings-related entitlement income such as Social Security tended to fall between the other two groups, although they were much closer to the aid recipients than to the wage earners. Three out of five SRO residents support themselves solely on earnings-related income. Almost one in four (24 percent) who are looking for work use General Assistance and food stamps to make ends meet while they search. Most of the remaining residents receive disability payments.

The occupational profile of the SRO residents reveals their roots in the working class. Only a tiny portion of the residents had worked as professionals or managers, compared with more than one in five of the city work force. The residents labored mainly in service occupations (52 percent) or as operatives (17 percent) and laborers (9 percent). This again squared with historical analysis, which indicated that most SRO tenants provided low-wage service labor to the city's office and commercial districts.

Low-status jobs usually meant low-paying and insecure jobs as well. Less than half of the SRO residents employed at the time of our interview received medical insurance coverage (42 percent), life insurance (36 percent), workers' compensation (50 percent), or unemployment benefits (51 percent) as part of their employment compensation. In addition, 50 percent worked on an hourly or daily wage rate, and 26 percent worked part time. Although the employed residents had on average held their present job for four and a half years, 43 percent had done so for only one year or less.

Part-time employees earned on the average about $634 per month, compared with $910 for all employed residents and $1,134 for full-time jobholders with benefits. In effect, full-time employees with benefits earned almost twice the monthly income of part-time employees without benefits. But only a tiny portion of the SRO residents enjoyed such jobs. The majority made just about enough to make ends meet, and a substantial minority (40 percent) earned less than the official poverty threshold.

The most substantial source of formal aid for SRO residents comes from the federal and state governments in the form of transfer payments. Thirtyfive percent were receiving public assistance from such programs as General Assistance (GA), Supplemental Security Income (SSI), food stamps, Medicaid, and Aid for Dependent Children (AFDC). These residents had managed to reach the safety net of the welfare state. However, their position was precarious, as most were receiving GA benefits that in 1987 provided a maximum of $154 per month. Overall, the 35 percent who got aid received only 17 percent of the total income received by all SRO residents. The relatively small amount of aid, given the high cost of living, made sustained provision of rental housing even in the SRO hotels extremely difficult.

Conditions of economic dependence are far more common among the homeless. A 1985 survey of street and shelter homeless in Chicago conducted by the National Opinion Research Center (NORC) found that 22 percent had received GA, 6 percent AFDC, 6 percent SSI, and 2 percent disability payments, or less than 36 percent overall after controlling for overlap. Although one in three was receiving aid, these recipients were still unable to secure rental shelter in the housing market. Furthermore, the NORC analysts compared actual use to eligibility for GA and AFDC and discovered that almost two out of three of the homeless who were eligible for GA benefits were not getting them._Not only are people on the streets and in shelters falling through the mesh in the public aid safety net for the poor, but even when they manage to grab hold, the benefits are still too little to cover the lowest market rent.

Vulnerable but Not Dependent

Instead of treating the vulnerabilities of SRO residents as direct and unmediated indicators of dependence, we analyzed the relationship between economic status and individual hardship. We expected the distribution of hardship to follow the contours of economic status. Thus, we first analyzed the incidence of economic hardship among SRO residents and then traced its distribution according to the social vulnerabilities associated with being a woman, black, or old. The burdens of different economic hardships among the SRO residents, we argue, do not pile up disproportionately upon the vulnerable, but upon those with the lowest income.

At the time of our interview almost one out of three residents (32 percent) carried a rent burden of greater than 50 percent; 15 percent had been displaced from their prior residence because of economic pressures sometime during the most recent six months, and almost one in ten (9.5 percent) had slept outside or in an emergency shelter at least once in the previous six months. The incidence of hunger was quite high among SRO residents. 'We asked residents whether there had been any time in the past six months when they had been unable to buy food for themselves; 31 percent answered yes. More than half (51 percent) of those dependent on unearned income from others had found themselves in such a plight.

To measure the cumulative economic hardship among the SRO residents, we assigned the presence of each economic hardship a value of 1, summing these to produce an economic hardship score for each resident. The maximum score was 3. The unfortunate resident who received this score had, during the six months preceding the interview, been displaced from his residence for economic reasons, been forced to sleep outside, and gone without food at least once. Furthermore, the same resident at the time of the interview was paying more than 50 percent of his income in rent.

Economic hardships were evenly distributed by race and age. However, women were more likely to suffer economic hardships than were men. In particular, women carried heavier rent burdens and were subjected to displacement for economic reasons twice as often. However, women endured these economic shelter-related hardships, not out of discrimination, but choice. Women were unwilling to rent poorer quality (and usually less expensive) rooms than were men with equivalent incomes. Furthermore, women residents were far more likely (57 percent) to be sharing their room with a spouse, friend, or close relation than were men (8 percent). An additional roommate translates into a higher rent. If one of the roommates makes little income, this means the higher rent will likely impose a greater rent burden on others in the household. Thus, women endured a greater share of the housing difficulties for economic reasons, not because they were women.

The distribution of economic hardship, predictably, was closely related to source of income. However, women, blacks, and the elderly – frequently discriminated against in the distribution of economic resources – did not endure significantly more economic hardship than did others who were younger, male, or white. Although their resources are meager and the presence of some hardship likely, most SRO residents do not suffer from the cumulative maldistribution of economic hardship because of their social vulnerabilities. The social diversity of the SRO environment helps vulnerable residents avoid the dependence that befalls those who must live in institutional settings that concentrate people with the same vulnerabilities (e.g., nursing homes or high-rise public housing projects).

Independence as a Way of Life

Perhaps the most serious misconception of the SRO residents places them among the ranks of the disaffiliated. Our research disclosed that most SRO residents possess a variety of social attachments to kin, friends, and neighborhood life. Though the existence of such attachments has been documented in studies like those of Bogue and Bahr, analysts have missed the significance of their own findings in their search for disaffiliation. We take a different tack, arguing that SRO residents belong to communities that not only nurture social identity but help them cope with economic hardship.

We asked residents in our survey to give the names of all the relatives and friends they felt closest to and to indicate which of these they had contacted at least once in the past year. The two lists, with few exceptions, were the same. Residents seldom mentioned close relatives or friends whom they had not contacted during the previous year. Almost as many respondents mentioned relatives (133) as did friends (127). Combined, the personal social networks included 666 close relationships distributed among 85 percent of the respondents.

Overall, the average number of ties with both relatives and friends was about four per resident. The size and composition of the social networks varied with the social characteristics of the residents. Women and blacks had much larger networks of close personal relationships (5.02 and 5.21, respectively) than did the elderly (3.58). Relatives predominated in the networks of women and blacks. Only 15 percent of the SRO residents reported having no close personal relationships.

Although the number of personal social relationships per SRO resident may seem small when compared with the social networks of middle-class households, the figure is close to the average number of social ties among working-class respondents also interviewed in a study of three Chicago residential neighborhoods in 1985. The fact that a variety of workingclass households had social networks only slightly larger than those among SRO residents suggests that the small network among SRO residents reflects their class position rather than some sort of disaffiliation.

Besides their personal networks, we also identified the less intimate social ties residents used with others in the SRO hotel and surrounding neighborhood. We constructed an SRO social network index to provide a composite summary of the number of social ties linking each resident to others inhabiting the SRO world. The classification scheme is outlined in appendix C and includes the description of each type of social tie.

About 84 percent of the residents had some SRO network ties. However, more than half of the 375 ties (57 percent) included ongoing contact with hotel staff. These staff ties predominate among those residents having no close personal network but some SRO relations. Eighty percent of the social contacts within these SRO networks were with SRO staff. Clearly, the hotels provided an important social milieu for the SRO residents who had few personal or no close ties. These residents come closest to fitting the social conceptions of the Skid Row isolate featured in earlier studies of Skid Row. However, we are much less willing to call them disaffiliated than were earlier researchers.

Although almost 15 percent of the SRO residents appear to be attached exclusively to the local social world of their SRO, possessing only a few local social ties does not mean they are isolated and dependent. Many have chosen to live alone and enjoy the autonomy and anonymity of hotel life. Compared with the hardships of illness and poverty, the lack of close social relationships may be a relatively minor problem. In some cases these close relations contribute to the economic and social marginality of SRO residents who use the hotel as a haven from troublesome and even dangerous relations with kin or gangs.

SRO residents proved to be resourceful and capable individuals despite their modest means and considerable hardship. We believe their autonomy was possible in large part because most possessed informal helping networks among relatives and friends, as well as knowledge of formal service providers. The close personal relationships residents enjoy with friends and relatives provide an important social resource. More than three out of four residents with close personal ties claimed that some sort of helping occurred among friends and relatives. On the average, three out of five personal relationships involved some sort of help during the past year.

Despite the frequency of such helping relationships, the SRO residents gave little indication that they were dependent partners. If SRO residents perceived themselves as passive victims or self-centered sociopaths, we expected them to report receiving help much more than they gave or shared it. However, such was not the case. They were primary recipients in only 24 percent of the relations, and major contributors in the remaining 16 percent. Respondents reported giving and getting help equally with other members of their network in 60 percent of the helping relationships. Their preference for reciprocity reflects not only a basic attachment to the cultural value of autonomy but more important, the protection and enhancement of this independence through the social bonds of mutual aid. The autonomy of SRO residents, like those in other social communities, rests on a foundation of security obtained through social interdependence, not social isolation."

The relationships between different helping interactions (e.g., reciprocity) and type of social tie (e.g., kin) among SRO residents resembled the patterns found among residents of diverse working-class households in Chicago. Interviewed at about the same time as part of a different study, these residents lived in apartments or single-family dwellings clustered in three ethnically distinct neighborhoods.

For instance, for both samples the proportion of helping network ties with kin was almost identical: 53 percent among SRO residents and 55 percent for neighborhood residents. The residents of SRO hotels possess helping relationships like those of respondents from other working-class households. The modest differences indicate the inaccuracy of pinning the label of disaffiliation on SRO residents. Furthermore, these helping networks reflect the presence of a social community whose members utilize complex moral judgments to justify each helping relationship.

Thus, when we asked residents with helping relationships why the particular form of helping interaction had turned out that way, we further discovered a complex set of moral bonds. Most SRO residents, it seems, did not follow a particular moral scheme, applying, for instance, the Golden Rule to all their relationships. Instead, residents based their moral assessments on the kind of relationship that tied them implicitly or explicitly to each person. The moral quality of the helping interaction depended on the type of social relation they shared with each member of their network.

The norms guiding the provision of informal help tended to reflect the social differences between kinship and friendship ties. Most ties with close kin involve duties based implicitly in the social requirements of the particular kinship bond (e.g., "She's my mother, that's why I give more to her") or based on additional considerations of relative strength (e.g., "My brother is older and looks out for me") and need (e.g., "My mother is blind, so I give more to her"). These can be distinguished from the voluntary obligations that characterize the reciprocity of friendships based either on comradeship (e.g., "We found something common. We're friends"), intimacy (e.g., "We love, care, respect, and appreciate each other"), or fair exchange (e.g., "We just take each other places if needed").

The relationship between helping interaction and type of moral reason, which sorts the reasons for each helping relationship into two groups: those based on voluntary obligation and those based on the stronger sense of duty. When residents get help from others, they mostly claim that others owe it to them not only out of a sense of prescribed duty (41 percent) but because of the altruistic strength (usually economic) of the giver (27 percent) as well.

Few residents contended that they got help because of their need (14 percent); slightly more residents (15 percent) admitted that they got more help in a relationship because the other valued them as a lover, intimate, or comrade. In contrast, residents reported that they gave help mostly because they felt obliged by the other's need (38 percent), their own relative strength (19 percent), or prescribed duty (31 percent) based on the bonds of kinship.

The pattern in these reports by respondents points (whether accurately or inaccurately, we do not know) to a strong desire for autonomy in the context of unbalanced helping relations. Residents who were recipients of help in a relationship claimed that the moral bonds of duty or the voluntary obligation of altruism on the part of prosperous and capable kin entitled them to aid. They seldom mentioned their own need and the dependency associated with it, even though low income and frequent hardship makes such reasons likely.

However, when the situation was reversed and residents acted as the primary giver, they claimed that they gave help mainly in response to need and out of their own relative strengths rather than in response to the duties of kinship or the bonds of comradeship. Residents perceive themselves as actors motivated to give out of a sense of responsibility and to receive out of a feeling of solidarity. Thus, the moral sensibilities residents reported dispute claims of disaffiliation, since these are clearly not the sentiments of sociopaths or anomic derelicts.

Reciprocity in helping was based mainly on the voluntary obligations of comradeship and intimacy (61 percent) or contract (6 percent). Clearly, the very meaning of reciprocity in our culture is so closely tied up with the practice of sharing that the connection fits our common sense. Less obvious are the reciprocal helping relationships based on involuntary duty (29 percent). Here, residents usually referred to the implicit expectation of mutual aid associated with kinship bonds. Thus, although reciprocal aid may not be based exclusively on voluntary obligations (and rarely on instrumental exchanges common among the helping networks of the middle class), it does not seem to be based on shared strengths or needs for SRO residents.

The distribution of different kinds of informal help within the personal networks of residents is complex, following paths organized by both the kind of social relationships and type of helping interaction. Thus the significance of the social tie and the nature of the helping interaction shape not only how informal help is delivered but what kinds are delivered. Unlike the formal care-giving system with its requirement that recipients be needy, with care organized in functionally discrete and coherent categories, informal care is relational and complex. SRO residents do not have to demonstrate their eligibility to friends and kin to deserve aid; they receive this entitlement (or at least claim they do) as part of the moral bonds that make up the various social relations they inherit, maintain, and create.

Within their personal social networks SRO tenants play active roles, usually sharing aid, seldom just getting it. Help is also defined on a complex situational basis rather than in limited, carefully defined categories. The residents justify and interpret their helping relationships in terms that display moral schemes sensitive to the needs of others, responsive to reciprocal exchanges based in mutual trust, and wary of the stigma and disgrace of dependency. Though their reasons for sharing help may differ from those of middle-class service providers, officials, bureaucrats, and the likes, SRO tenants offer reasons that justify a coherent and generous reciprocity that enables them to get and give help without sacrificing their often fragile independence.

Many SRO residents (about 15 percent) had no close personal relationships, and some of those who did got no help from either close friends or kin. Overall, 36 percent of the tenants had no personal helping network. Most of these residents, however, were neither isolated nor dependent. They received aid from others in the SRO hotel. About 70 percent of the SRO residents without personal helping relationships got help from others in the SRO hotel at least once during the year preceding the interview. Although they did not describe close and ongoing relationships with their helpers, the residents who relied on others in the SRO for aid got help mainly from friends and SRO staff, usually in the form of referrals to jobs, shelter, or medical care. (See appendix C for a detailed description of the kinds and amounts of help, controlling for the presence of close personal relationships.)

Putting these referrals to good use requires a minimum threshold of independence, so when residents lose their capacity to act autonomously, they no longer can take this information and put it to good use. They fall outside the boundaries of help within the SRO world. This seems to be happening to some of the poorest and most physically vulnerable SRO residents (about 11 percent of the SRO residents). Since they have no personal helping network, they have no alternative but to turn to the formal care-giving system for help.

Thus, when residents become too economically or physically dependent, the SRO social world cannot substitute for the close ties of family and friends or the resources of formal helping institutions. Instead, the SRO network provides an informal linkage between residents and the formal system of jobs and services. We explored therefore the extent to which residents rely on formal services. The most important question was whether those residents who lack any informal helping ties, either personal or SRO based, receive aid from the formal care-giving system.

We found that the most frequently used formal nonprofit services were local hospitals and clinics. Despite the lack of medical insurance, most residents with serious chronic illnesses (93 percent) had used nonprofit hospitals or clinics to obtain health care. About one in three had sought such aid using referrals from friends and relatives; the others relied on their own knowledge and experience in selecting where they went.

Residents were less successful at using the food distribution network that has expanded rapidly since 1982 with federal funding authorized by the Federal Emergency Management Act (FEMA), supplementing donations from churches and philanthropic foundations. Only 60 percent of the hungry SRO residents knew of a place they could go to obtain free groceries or a free meal. Another 15 percent reported that they got most of their clothes free from church and nonprofit charities in order to avoid the expense of purchasing their own.

Aid for those burdened with excessively high rents or recently displaced from their prior residence was virtually nil. However, two out of three of those who had been forced to sleep out sometime during the first six months of 1985 did receive aid, either sleeping in an emergency shelter or receiving an agency referral to the SRO hotel where they resided at the time of the interview.

We prepared a composite measure of residents' use of formal care, mainly from nonprofit institutions, by assigning one point for the receipt of each of the following kinds of aid in 1985 – health care, free food, free clothes, and free shelter – and then summing these points for each resident. We used this composite to assess whether those groups of SRO residents who had little or no access to sources of informal help obtained a disproportionate share of the aid from formal sources of help.

SRO veterans and the elderly, two groups who usually possessed the fewest and smallest helping networks, used formal aid far more frequently than did the other SRO residents. Over half (53 percent) of the elderly had used some type of formal aid, compared with only 42 percent of the younger residents. Two out of three of the SRO veterans versus only one out of three (32 percent) first-timers used formal aid. Blacks, who usually possessed large helping networks, relied on formal services significantly less than did nonblacks (37 percent to 64 percent).

Thus, poor blacks, despite long-established programs designed to meet their needs, are still not being effectively reached by these social service programs. The SRO veterans and elderly used formal services to substitute for a lack of informal sources of aid. Conversely, blacks relied on aid from their informal networks instead of using formal services, a practice common among the working poor of Chicago, especially among black households.

SRO veterans do not form relations of mutual aid based on close personal ties as do black residents, especially black women. First, the SRO veterans are far less likely to have ties with kin, the social group at the core of most helping networks. In part this reflects the fact that veterans of the SRO way of life are older than first-timers and so have fewer relatives with whom mutual aid can be expected. The largely male SRO veterans also purposely avoid the sorts of social bonds like marriage that would place involuntary and perhaps restrictive obligations on them. When the veterans did report helping networks, these were composed largely of friends, not the inherited ties of kinship. Second, the SRO veterans know how to use the SRO hotel and other formal institutions in the city to meet their needs without relying on personal networks. The use of formal institutions and the weak ties of the SRO world to obtain occasional help from acquaintances and friends reflects an urban style of social life for this segment of the SRO residents.

The residents of SRO hotels do not fit the stereotype of transient and isolated social deviants avoiding work and social responsibility. The vulnerabilities from which these residents suffer are not social, but economic and physical. Their deviance has more to do with the economic weakness their class position imposes on them. If many of the residents are misfits, it is not by design or choice. What marks these single members of the urban working class as a group is residence in an SRO. But the legacy of Skid Row removal and reform — the stereotype of the Skid Row bum — continues to push these residents to the margins of acceptable, normal city life. To the uninformed outsider, residence in an SRO merits the stigma of moral corruption, the taint of illegitimacy.

This morality-play conception of SRO life does not square with the evidence. The tales of deviance and pathology used by middle-class reformers, officials, reporters, and others to repudiate the SRO way of life are little more than misleading metaphors based on exceptional cases. The residents of the SRO hotels in Chicago choose to live there for much the same reasons that the urban middle-class residents are returning to high-density luxury apartment towers near downtown: convenience and security. Unlike their wealthy neighbors, however, SRO residents can neither afford to pay to live among others who match their social standing nor avoid forming social ties that might bind them to their neighbors. The wealthy urbanites purchase security and the trappings of community; the SRO residents must make it. The hotel residents cannot insulate themselves from the dangers of the city, so they collaborate despite their differences to make their world safe.

The spatial design of the SRO hotel with its high-rise density of tiny oneroom units earned the scorn of housing reformers, planners, and public officials for decades. However, it was not until the mid-1950s that the Chicago housing code was revised, virtually outlawing the SRO hotels. Thus, when Bogue conducted a comprehensive assessment of the SRO hotels on Chicago's Skid Row in the late 1950s, although the vast majority passed inspection with respect to operational standards, most failed to meet the structural standards of the building code.

The SRO hotels lacked adequate plumbing (69 percent), sprinkler systems (86.7 percent), and enclosed stairways (54.4 percent) because these physical features were not included in the original construction of the buildings. In contrast, few hotels failed to meet the standards for such operational conditions as heat (1.3 percent), hot water (1.3 percent), pest control (6.3 percent), unblocked fire exits (7 percent), functioning fire escapes (5.1 percent), and the like. The managers and owners did for the most part meet the basic standards of physical maintenance and fire protection, as long as these did not require major structural improvements.

The deteriorating physical appearance of the SRO hotels when combined with the negative assessments of their physical quality by city inspectors, public officials, and professional reformers contributed to the public perception of the SRO hotel as a nasty and dangerous environment unfit for human habitation. The popularity of the hotels among the single poor was therefore interpreted among officials and reformers as a sign of the economic desperation of the Skid Row residents as well as these residents' deviant tolerance for substandard living conditions. Such interpretations made way for the argument that the SRO hotels actually contributed to deviant and pathological life-styles among their impoverished clientele. Few professionals came to the defense of the hotels when urban renewal programs planned and carried out their destruction.

We analyzed the social value and usefulness of the SRO hotels remaining today from the point of view of the residents rather than relying on the preconceptions of middle-class analysts, planners, and officials. The SRO residents did not consider the hotels to be dangerous or oppressive environments. They expressed considerable satisfaction with those qualities of hotel living that make luxury high-rise buildings attractive to young single professionals, that is to say, convenience and security.

The SRO hotels attract a relatively diverse clientele, thereby avoiding the stratified homogeneity created by the housing market or by the policies of public housing authorities. The structure and organization of the hotels encourage residents to collaborate in ways that produces a characteristically urban, tolerant residential community. The distribution of security, affordability, and informal aid does not depend on the social status or income of SRO residents, but on their common residence in the SRO hotel.

In contrast to homogeneous public housing projects for low-income residents or congregate housing for special populations, the SRO hotels offer a social organization that combines a generous tolerance for social differences with a strictly enforced set of house rules. The social ties among residents do not reflect a community of shared sentiment, but instead an urban sense of public responsibility. Privacy is respected, but residents need not be socially isolated unless they choose to be.

Hotels as a Place to Live

Most residents were pleased with their living arrangements. Forty-four percent claimed that they were very satisfied, and another 48 percent reported that they were somewhat satisfied. Only 16 percent expressed dissatisfaction. We analyzed the reasons residents offered for their satisfaction and dissatisfaction and discovered some dramatic patterns.

Tenant complaints concentrated on the physical deficiencies of both a single room (12.1 percent) and the quality of the hotel (7.2 percent). By far the most common complaint was the small size of the room. Among other objections, the most poignant came from residents of cubicle hotels. One fifty-five-year-old male suffering from emphyzema feared that "my children may be ashamed of me if I die in a flop." Another man of about the same age but in better health emphasized that the cages offer little privacy. "It's a flophouse – you can't bring visitors. It's not like having an apartment where you can have people over." Most others facing less unpleasant quarters mentioned specific problems they faced at the time of the interview: a leaky sink, the lack of a kitchen or a telephone, an infestation of vermin, noisy neighbors, or other such problems.

The residents of cubicle hotels have significantly lower incomes on average ($5,027) than do residents in other SRO hotels ($7,511). And although the same proportion are employed, more than three out of five cubicle residents work as unskilled operatives or laborers, compared with only 30 percent of the other SRO residents. These are tenants whose economic status places them only one step above people who were forced to sleep outside or in an emergency shelter in 1985. Socially, however, the cubicle tenants open-ended questions. Respondents frequently mentioned several items, which required multiple codings per respondent. Thus, the percentages are based on the total number of respondents for each row. "No response" is the same for both satisfaction and dissatisfaction since this refers to people who offered no opinion include people different from those who have ended up on the street.

They are mainly older white males with a history of SRO living. The few cubicle hotels that remain continue to serve as a haven for the dependent poor, but not for those who match the characteristics of today's homeless; these are the poor who match the single poor who faced the threat of homelessness in the 1950s on Skid Row. Seventy percent of the cubicle hotel residents were veterans of the SRO way of life and had learned to use these scarce hotels as an alternative to homelessness and a foothold in the bottom rung of the private housing market hierarchy.

In contrast, residents rarely mentioned the physical qualities of the SRO when describing their satisfactions. Most emphasized the convenience of the hotel's location, its affordability, and a variety of social benefits including relationships with other tenants, management, security, and privacy. One out of five tenants liked SRO living because of the location of the hotel. Most comments were like those of a white thirty-five-year-old woman who reported that "everything I need for living is near – church, grocery store, the loop, North Michigan Avenue."

Other comments were similar to those offered by a fifty-year-old unskilled operative who pointed out that his SRO hotel "is close to where I work and near good public transportation." A few emphasized the advantages of the surrounding neighborhood. "Compared to other neighborhoods that I know of, things are cheaper," claimed a Greek male in his early fifties. "I eat out a lot and there are a lot of places to eat in the neighborhood. I have epilepsy and can't cook." Thus, what makes SROs satisfactory is not just affordability and the collective facilities, but location as well. Location is important for the poor as well as the middle class and represents a crucial ingredient in the success of the SRO hotels.

Many of the tenants enjoy SRO living because of social ties to other residents (14.1 percent) and managers (11.3 percent). For instance, some respondents, like one middle-aged black woman, referred to a community in which "everyone seems to look out for each other here, and that makes me feel good." In a few cases the ties with owners and managers were quite strong, as in the case of one thirty-six-year-old female tenant who liked her female building manager because "she's real good to me. I've been here so long it feels like home." But most respondents simply referred to the "nice" people and managers who were friendly and predictable and, most important, who proved not to be aggressive or threatening.

The SRO offers many tenants a safe and secure haven in the frequently risky environments of surrounding urban neighborhoods. The social ties of the SRO contribute to the security of tenants. "I feel very secure," replied a thirty-five-year-old woman when asked about the reasons for her satisfaction with the SRO. "The people living here are very nice. They're pleasant, and if something goes wrong, they help." Another tenant, a forty-six-year old black male, summed up a common experience when he explained that "I feel safe here. There are no break-ins. We are like one happy family."

But references to a sense of community were not universal. Other residents preferred the privacy and independence of the SRO environment (9.8 percent). "No one bothers you and you have your privacy. I like that," said a thirty-eight-year-old black man recovering from surgery. "It's quiet and no one disturbs me," claimed a fifty-eight-year-old cancer victim. The response of a sixty-year-old black man perhaps best captures the essence of these remarks. "Nobody bothers me and I don't bother nobody. That's it!" Although the appreciation for privacy was strong, it did not preclude social ties. Many who mentioned multiple reasons for their satisfaction were like the elderly white male who professed the following list. "People are nice. The rent is reasonable. No one bothers you, and I like talking to the other boys that live here." Privacy and comradeship complement each other in the social world of the SRO hotel.

The affordability of the SRO units was significant mainly to those tenants with low incomes, especially those residing in the cubicle hotels. Like most tenants, residents did not express satisfaction with the rent they had to pay, but those with few resources appreciated the importance of a rent they could afford. Some offered excuses, like the twenty-two-year-old black man who claimed, "This is all I can afford right now." Others were less apologetic. "For the money, its an all-right place to live," declared a fifty-nine-year-old Hispanic male. "It's cheap. I can't afford no forty to fifty dollars a week."

The cubicle hotels offered the cheapest rents of all the hotels in the survey. Whereas the average monthly rent for the entire sample was $199, the cubicle hotel rooms rented on average for half as much, $99. When asked why they had moved to their present hotel, considerably more than half of the cubicle residents gave cheap rent as their reason, compared with barely 17 percent of those living in the better quality SROs. The cubicle hotels provide the first step of rudimentary shelter for single people on the rental housing market ladder. Furthermore, these are the only hotels in which the Illinois General Assistance (GA) grant for poor individuals – $154 a month – could actually pay a month's rent and still leave some money for other expenditures.

Cubicle residents recognize the precariousness of their perch and the serious shelter privation that awaits them should they fall from the security and privacy of their cubicle nest. In expressing his satisfaction with this otherwise dismal housing, one tenant from a cubicle hotel explained, "I like living here. There aren't too many places like this anymore, and if you don't live in a place like this you live in the street." Or as another tenant put it, in more abbreviated fashion, "It beats sitting on the street." The positive evaluations of their hotels by cubicle residents usually reflect their relief at having escaped both the insecurity of the streets and the indignity of the shelters.

Assessing Preferences and Problems

Because residents offered multiple reasons for their satisfaction, we did not know which reasons were the most important to them. Therefore, we also asked residents what they most liked about living in their present SRO hotel. Tenants most like the social benefits of SRO living (42.8 percent); location (21 percent) and affordability (17.5 percent) follow. The physical features of the single rooms and the hotel proved to be the least preferred aspect of SRO living (31.7 percent).

Perhaps the most important finding was the fact that almost two out of five of the respondents could not name or mention anything that they disliked, compared with only 7.2 percent who had similar difficulty thinking only one choice. Thus, the percentages are based on the total sample of respondents for each column and sum to a hundred of something they most liked.

Residents do not feel trapped in the hotels; rather, they appear to like and take advantage of those aspects of the hotel that make urban living easier and more efficient: convenience, social contact, and affordability. Most do not like the fact that their rooms are small and cramped, the hotel old and unattractive, but they are willing to overlook the lack of such amenities in return for other benefits. Residents know their economic limitations and have found a niche in the residential marketplace that offers them a valuable tradeoff between convenience or access and living space.

We also asked residents to report their concern with a selection of characteristics that critics depicted as uniquely associated with SRO hotels. The results strongly contradict the image of the SRO as a squalid flophouse. More than three out of every four residents praised the safety (76 percent), quiet (77 percent), privacy (78 percent), and winter warmth (76 percent) of their rooms. The only environmental problems complained about that even approached the conditions of the stereotype were summer heat (34 percent) and roaches (53 percent). In other words, with the exception of the very real problem of infestation, the quality of individual units in SROs in comparison with other forms of low-rent housing seems quite high. Comments such as "I'm comfortable in my room" or "It's my home" were not uncommon.

Residents especially recognized and appreciated the social management of the buildings. Nearly 88 percent of the residents knew the managers or desk clerks personally. These staff people take phone messages, distribute mail, screen visitors, and perform other small but important services for residents. Another 52 percent said they knew the owner, whom three out of four claim they see at least once a month. These social ties between resident and manager provide in most cases a mutually beneficial relationship. For instance, the brother of a hotel owner lives in the hotel and helps out by working there. In his own words, "I have everything at one place and I like it."

Another resident praised the desk clerks because "they screen people that come see you and if they don't like them they tell them [the visitors] they can't come in." This link between screening and security plays an important role in making these modest units livable. One respondent was proud of this arrangement and felt that her sister "who lives in an expensive building" enjoys less security than she does, given the protection from unwanted intrusions she enjoys. "No one goes upstairs unless the desk clerk okays it," she explained. Ironically, the respondent's sister pays more rent for an apartment that offers less apparent security than the SRO hotel room.

SRO hotels do not provide simply an inexpensive room for the single working poor, functioning as a sort of private-sector public housing in which affordability becomes the sole criteria of access. The hotels do provide relatively inexpensive shelter, but what is more important, they offer services that enhance the quality of life for those of modest means without requiring the sacrifice of autonomy or independence. For many of the first-time residents the SRO hotel provides a way station, a place to stay until their personal circumstances change and enable them to move to more spacious quarters. Others, for whom expectations of increased economic prosperity or social reunion are improbable, may learn to adopt the social life of veteran SRO users.

Initiation into the SRO life-style, however, does not necessarily mean a loss of economic and social resources. As Bogue found among the migrants to Skid Row in the 1950s and as we discovered in the mid-1980s, the newcomers to the SRO world usually come there initially out of necessity, a necessity imposed by a lack of economic and social resources. The SRO environment does not create these pressures, nor does it contribute to them. Instead, the SRO provides an alternative for poor single people, making it possible for them to use their residential space both as a means of recovering lost prosperity and social ties as well as creating a meaningful way of life in the midst of severe social disadvantages and economic uncertainty.

The Social Diversity of the Hotels

Most developers and owners of multifamily residential buildings seek to specialize, attracting residents similar in age, race, income, or – less frequently – sex. Discrimination in the real estate market and the rental market is not only taken as given but promoted as a marketing device to attract small middle- and upper-middle-class households back to the city from the suburbs or outlying city neighborhoods. New high-rise residential buildings, physically cordoned off from the poor who inhabit the older structures nearby, offer specialized living environments for narrow social segments of the growing professional and managerial class.

Ironically, these buildings mirror the public housing programs in Chicago, which were also organized on the basis of policies that would separate their residents from nearby neighborhoods, by confining the city's black residents in spatially segregated communities. The result today is hundreds of high-density buildings filled with an almost exclusively dependent population in which femaleheaded households predominate.

These common social and economic divisions that shape the residential organization of virtually all urban space in Chicago do not seem, however, to fragment the social order of the SRO hotels. As we point out, the social divisions that usually link the uneven distribution of income with the social characteristics of race, sex, and age among members of urban society tend to be less prevalent among SRO hotel residents. The variations that do occur cut across the social inequalities that usually define the boundaries that segregate residential neighborhoods into relatively homogeneous social enclaves.

Most of the hotels offer a residential environment that allows for social and economic diversity without the systematic imposition of hierarchical order across different social domains. Perhaps because most are poor or on the threshold of poverty, they cannot use economic strength to entice or even pressure others to do their bidding. The residents share enough different yet overlapping vulnerabilities to make mutual exploitation not only risky, but even dangerous.

The hotels provide an institutional setting that protects privacy by involving residents in the provision and maintenance of social order in the public spaces of the building. Detailed ethnographic studies of individual hotels in other cities have documented the way the social organization of SRO hotels combines a generous tolerance for social difference with a strictly enforced set of house rules. The social ties among residents do not reflect a community of shared sentiment, but an urban sense of public responsibility.

Although we lacked the resources needed to study the relationships within each hotel, we did estimate the degree of social heterogeneity of the respondents in each hotel. To compare a variety of characteristics using a single measure, we used the index of dispersion. This technique provides a straightforward and easy-to-interpret measure of heterogeneity. A value of 0 on the index means that the residents in that hotel all fall within a certain nominal category (e.g., greater than fifty-four years of age), and so for that particular score we could say that the residents of that hotel are similar in age. A value of 1 on the index would mean the opposite, that the residents are evenly distributed among the different age categories (25 percent in each of four categories), in this case, that the residents are heterogeneous in age.

We calculated index scores for three social, two economic, and two SRO characteristics. The scores are listed in appendix B. These scores have been summarized in table 8-3 and illustrate the distribution of the eighteen sample hotels according to the heterogeneity of their resident characteristics. The majority of the hotels possess residents who differ greatly in age, income, employment status (employed, unemployed, or out of the labor market), and length of stay. Despite the relatively small proportion of women overall, most were dispersed among the hotels.

Only a few hotels had no women at all. The predominantly male SRO veterans, however, were unevenly distributed. As we noted above, there were few veterans of SRO living in the South Side hotels that scored low on the heterogeneity index. A similar pattern was evident for race as well. Since virtually all residents of the South Side hotels are black, the heterogeneity scores of these hotels are quite low. However, the low scores of the South Side hotels reflect the fact that the overwhelming proportion of residents in these neighborhoods where the hotels are located are black, not that hotel management here is discriminatory. Only three of the hotels on the North Side fall into the homogeneous category (in this case, all white). The other nine exhibit some racial integration.

The unique social environment of the successful SRO depends, we think, on this mix of different kinds of tenants. The emphasis on decent collective services combined with the social bonds of trust formed among residents ties the diverse people together in a community of bounded responsibility. Residents respect the privacy of others and yet share the expectation of mutual cooperation and even aid to promote a secure living environment. Conflicts do emerge between such disparate neighbors as a young day laborer and an elderly retiree, but the established social routine of the hotel – the "house rules" – provides a framework for negotiating settlements and avoiding escalating conflicts.

At the time of our interview residents in one hotel were especially upset by changes in the admission policy for new residents. The management had begun to accept a large number of outpatients from a nearby psychiatric care facility to reduce the hotel vacancy rate and increase cash flow. The residents felt especially threatened, not necessarily by the fear that these people were dangerous (the middle-class response), but by the inexperience and in some cases inability of the former patients to collaborate in the maintenance of the fragile social order of the hotel. The old residents did not believe that these new residents could be trusted to follow the informal house rules on their own.

Half the residents in the hotel, when asked to describe anything unusual around the hotel during the past six months, complained that the crazy newcomers were "replacing the old tenants." Since the outpatients were not employed, they tended "to stand around a lot and loiter outside the hotel." Some feared that they gave the impression that there are "just a bunch of crazy folk living here now." The visible and vulnerable tenants attract trouble, and as a result, one old-timer emphasized, "the police end up coming into the hotel to handle problems with the crazy people." The newcomers were mainly dependent and hence vulnerable residents whose dependency, as their numbers increased, threatened to overwhelm the balance of reciprocal exchanges that kept the hotel secure: The old residents felt offended and resentful at the management and the newcomers for imposing the burden of the newcomers' dependency on their social world.

To more accurately assess the relationship between the social diversity of the SRO residents and the security of SRO living, we developed two measures of security for each resident. One measure indicates whether a resident mentioned security or relationships with other tenants as, one of the things he or she liked or disliked about SRO living. The other measure is an interval-level score of reported security breakdowns, including one point for each of the following problems: an influx of dependent tenants, disturbances requiring that the police be called, vandalism of the common spaces (e.g., lobby furniture broken), or arson. The security indicator measures the perception of security; the safety indicator measures the actual incidence of security breaches. We analyzed the effect of SRO resident social characteristics on variation in the size of both the safety and security indicators.

If security and safety depend on the social and economic homogeneity of residents, then we expected to find that residents of a certain type, for instance, women, would score consistently low or high on these measures. The perception and experience of security did not vary much with the social and economic characteristics of the residents. In other words, the distribution of security did not depend on particular characteristics, as it so frequently does in the residential environments of the middle class. There were two exceptions. In the case of safety, SRO veterans reported significantly fewer breaches of security in their buildings than did nonveterans.

This may reflect either the fact that in the hotels where SRO veterans live there are fewer breakdowns in security or that SRO veterans are less likely to report such breaches as a problem than are nonveterans. We believe the first explanation is consistent with the other evidence on SRO social organization, but we cannot test this inference directly. Residents with a greater burden of economic hardship, but not necessarily lower incomes, were also likely to live in hotels where security breakdowns were more frequent. Since the economic hardship score consists mainly of residents with high rent burdens who may also suffer from recent economic displacement, shelter deprivation, or hunger, the positive relation may indicate rent gouging of new and vulnerable residents by management. Breakdowns in security are frequently accompanied by short-term economic exploitation as owners prepare to abandon their property. Residents have little defense against such systematic practices, when they do occur.

Despite these exceptions, the overall security of residents remains tied to a shared vulnerability within the confines of the SRO regardless of status or means. This shared fate promotes a sense of common defense that encourages residents to follow the house rules. The social mix of the relatively strong and weak protects against the dependency of a homogeneous population of physically or mentally disadvantaged residents. We disagree with authors like Janice Smithers who argue that a shared "consciousness of kind" promotes mutual security. Smithers focused on an exclusively elderly population in a single SRO hotel and, we think mistakenly, ascribed shared vulnerability to the shared demographic characteristic of advanced age.

We do not dispute her findings, that the elderly helped contribute to their mutual security, but argue that these efforts were not based so much on similar age as on shared vulnerability to nonresident strangers in the and shared weakness does not promote security; rather, the combination of shared vulnerability and a mix of strong and weak does. In the hotel that Smithers studied the management and local public housing authority provided a twenty-four-hour security guard to discourage intruders. It was the combination of the powerful threat of the guard with the surveillance efforts of the weak residents that made for a secure hotel environment-not the fact that all the residents were old.

Unlike most other forms of residential shelter, SROs offer little private dwelling space. Furthermore, compared with differences in the size and composition among rental units in apartment buildings, the differences among single room units in SRO appear marginal. What counts, as our respondents made quite evident, is the quality of the collective services of the hotel and its location. Hence, we expected to find that rent differentials within SROs would reflect differences in the quality of the individual dwelling rooms less than the different types of rental agreements formed between tenants and landlords. Most important in this respect are the different room rates based on the payment interval. Renting by day or week costs more than renting by the month. In effect, the weekly renter usually pays more for the same amount of space a monthly renter enjoys. In addition, renters who inhabit the same building for a long time tend to avoid rent increases of the magnitude that newcomers face. Their predictability is rewarded with a lower rent.

The mix of short-term and long-term payers produces a symbiotic community within an SRO hotel. The short-term payers are predominantly wage workers, many of whom constantly confront the uncertainty of layoffs or cutbacks. The demands of the labor markets for the working poor undermine efforts to maintain the routine payment of large sums of money such as rent. Although the annual income of some of the better paid workers might allow them to rent their own apartment, renting an SRO room on a daily basis proves not only less expensive but more convenient.

The old-timers who rent on a monthly basis tend to receive income from entitlements. These residents enjoy a predictable flow of funds that makes routine rent payment desirable. The incomes of these residents usually fall below those of their employed neighbors. However, because they pay by the month, they usually pay less rent. The predictable flow of funds from the monthly renter reduces the cost of turnover for the management and provides greater social stability, all of which reduces the operating costs of the hotel. The managers return a portion of these savings to the long-term renters in the form of lower rents.

There are of course exceptions among these two types of residents, for instance, poor public-aid recipients who pay an exorbitant portion of their income for rent, or relatively wealthy eccentrics whose rent burden (the ratio of rent paid to income) may not even reach the double digit mark. In order to test for these relationships among the SRO residents in our sample, we calculated the differences in source and amount of income, length of stay, rent, age, and rent burden. The mean values are presented in table 8-4.

The weekly rate payers were younger and far more likely to earn their higher incomes from wages than were the monthly rate payers. Two out of three (68 percent) reported wage-based earnings, compared with barely one in three (32 percent) of those renting by the month. However, the weekly rent payers reported a much shorter average stay (a little more than two years) than did the monthly rate payers (an average of almost four years). The weekly rate payers also paid substantially higher rents on the average ($248) than those who paid by the month ($162). However, despite higher incomes and more reliable source of income from wages, the weekly rate payers did not enjoy a substantially lower rent burden.

The differences between the two groups of rate payers supported our expectations. The weekly renters were younger newcomers whose wage earnings provided a higher income than the entitlement income relied upon by most of the old-timers. Most important, the relatively more prosperous newcomers usually paid more rent for their rooms than did the old-timers who paid monthly. Usually, when their incomes increase, people pay a smaller proportion of their total income for rent. Thus, we needed to find out if the relatively more prosperous newcomers who paid by the week paid more for the same kinds of rooms as the old-timers who paid by the month so, this meant that newcomers who paid by the week in the same hotels with monthly rate payers actually subsidized the rents of the old-timers.

To test for a subsidy we had to control for the actual mix of rate payers (weekly and monthly) in the eighteen hotels included in our study. To control for this potential subsidy effect, we divided the hotels into two groups, those with a mix of rate payers (a minimum of three each) and those with a virtually uniform rate payment pattern (predominantly weekly or predominantly monthly). Although all the SRO hotels advertise differential rates, our sampling uncovered de facto specialization. We grouped the hotels by mix because in the uniform rate hotels, weekly rate payers' higher rents could not subsidize the rents of monthly rate payers who did not live in the same hotel.

We compared the rent burden of residents in hotels where tenants reported a mix of weekly and monthly rate payers. Although the rent difference was significant between weekly

($247) and monthly ($155) rate payers, the difference in rent burdens was not. Thus, the weekly ratepayers not only receive a significantly larger income than monthly rate payers, but they pay a higher rent on average as well, regardless of hotel type. However, the weekly rate payers in the mixed-rate hotels carry a greater rent burden than they otherwise would in a hotel where all the residents pay by the week. The higher rents paid by these weekly rate payers in hotels with both weekly and monthly rate payers indirectly contribute to lower rents for the monthly rate payers – if the rooms are not substantially different in quality.

We suspected that much of the difference in rents and even rent burden might hinge on difference in the quality of the individual rooms within the hotels with a mix of payment rates. About 50 percent of the residents in the mixed-rate hotels rented rooms with a private bath. After analyzing our exhaustive inventory of room characteristics, we found that the presence of a private bath was the characteristic that most clearly defined a large difference in room quality meriting more rent.

We knew that tenants renting rooms with baths paid significantly more rent than those renting only a room. However, when we calculated the difference between the average rent burdens carried by weekly and monthly rate payers, we found that their burden did not vary significantly when controlling for the presence of a bath. In other words, the difference between the rent burden carried by weekly and monthly rent payers was not statistically significant regardless of whether both rented a room with a bath or not. Despite their having higher average incomes, the weekly rate payers did not enjoy a lower rent burden. In effect, the weekly rate payers in hotels with a mix of rate payers appear to pay more than monthly rate payers for the same quality of units.

This difference in rent level combined with no difference in rent burden signifies that the short-term payers subsidize the incomes of the long-term payers by enabling the owners to charge lower rents to monthly rate payers. The arrangement works to the benefit of all parties, including the owners of the hotels. Without the mix of tenants, the symbiotic link that helps ensure the quality of collective services might be undermined. If the hotel becomes inhabited exclusively by old-timers, the rent might drop precipitously, necessitating cutbacks in services and perhaps major rehabilitation or conversion. If the hotel becomes exclusively dedicated to short-timers, then the costs of maintaining the predictability and security of the collective services might rise enormously. The economic viability of many SRO hotels is tied, we believe, to successful management of this social balance.

Sharing referrals and other information represents a relatively low-risk form of aid available to virtually anyone who lives in an SRO hotel, regardless of social vulnerabilities and characteristics or the extent of economic hardship. Because the more substantial forms of help provided within personal helping networks rely on bonds of trust established in close relationships to ensure that reciprocity will be respected, aid within personal helping networks will follow the social and economic characteristics of residents, just as it does in such networks elsewhere. However, aid within the SRO networks does not follow the segmented pathways of shared social characteristics, but rather knits together a diverse SRO clientele.

The frequency of SRO helping episodes that residents reported for the year prior to the interview did not vary with resident needs and resources, as did the size of personal helping networks. Using regression models to test for the statistical effects of SRO resident characteristics on the size of the SRO helping episode index, we found that the needs and resources of SRO residents, whether social or economic, predict little of the variation in the size of the SRO helping episode index, regardless of who provides the help. Thus, the distribution of informal aid in the SRO helping network is not organized according to a social and economic hierarchy, but on the basis of shared residence in a hotel.

The SRO helping network matches the diverse needs and resources of the residents because it is based on weak ties requiring only very modest contributions. The information and occasional money distributed in the SRO social world forms a latticework of weak ties that help residents take advantage of opportunities or anticipate and avoid privations. The management of the hotel plays a crucial role in maintaining the hotel community, not only by enforcing security measures or controlling the number of vulnerable tenants but by actively supporting and encouraging the provision of informal aid. The withdrawal of such support is usually a prelude to the demise of the hotel.

SRO residents enjoy the benefits of social ties in ways common to other working-class individuals. However, the tenants of the SRO hotel live in a more socially diverse residential environment than do their class peers and in most cases benefit from this diversity. The perceptions of insecurity and reports of social disorder in SRO hotels did not come from any particular strata of the residents. The vulnerable did not feel more threatened, nor did the more prosperous enjoy greater safety. Security was a common good to which each contributed and from which all benefited, although the extent of mutual benefit is not evident.

The mix of rate payers in many hotels put the economic diversity of the residents to good use in a different fashion. The management charges higher rents for weekly renters, anticipating the costs of frequent turnover. This premium is quite substantial, even when controlling for differences in room quality. The owner makes more revenue from the weekly tenants, giving less cause to raise the rent for long-term monthly ratepayers. The weekly rate payers with higher average incomes modestly subsidize the rents of the lower income monthly rate payers. Diversity in this case produces unintended redistribution.

Taken together with the findings, the data in this chapter, we believe, provide substantial evidence of an active and useful community life shared both by residents within the hotels and between individual residents and others outside. Furthermore, this community builds upon and complements the privacy, security, accessibility, and affordability of the SRO hotel units. All of this occurs despite the fact that most of the SRO residents are poor, suffering from a wide variety of physical, social, and economic hardships, and must make do with a tiny room. When contrasted with the standards of middle-class residential standards and social life, the SRO world may appear terribly deficient. However, when compared with living in an overcrowded household, an emergency shelter, or the street, the SRO hotel appears quite attractive.

The residents of SRO hotels offer real-life examples of the social prototype of what urban life has frequently promised but seldom delivered, for those of modest means: trading off space for the convenience, security, and affordability of high-density living. The tenants, drawn mainly from the ranks of the working poor, utilize the convenience, security, and affordability of the SRO hotels to maintain their independence and social standing in the midst of the serious economic obstacles they encounter at the bottom of the occupational hierarchy. Yet, SRO residents live in a socially and economically diverse environment enabling tenants and their hotel managers to maintain a symbiotic relationship of mutual support. SRO hotels not only provide affordable shelter but also make a unique contribution to the diversity of social life in Chicago. In a city infamous for its residential segregation, the remaining SROs stand as outposts of civilization in a city landscape increasingly fragmented into bunkers of uniform prosperity or vulnerable pockets of poverty.

Chapter 5

Compensation Trends in Hotels

SURVEY HIGHLIGHTS

There is a general impression that salaries in the hospitality industry are low, and that hotel managers are paid a salary lower than in some other attractive sectors, such as call centres. While there may be some truth in this at face value, there are many factors of the subject to be considered to gain a proper perspective. The HCE Survey is based on the compensation data for the financial year 2002/03 from 106 branded hotel properties across India, ranging from the three-star category to the five star deluxe categories. More than 700 senior executives within the industry have participated in the survey. Information was compiled from responses to a detailed questionnaire framed for the purpose and sent to the corporate offices of the hotel groups.

Compensation details have been presented for thirteen senior management positions in the HCE report; this data has been further classified into a variety of categories for the purpose of comparison.

It may be noted that the salary, bonus and retirement remuneration of expatriates has been excluded from our calculations for all the positions. For each of the positions, the minimum and maximum base salary earned has been presented, as well as the base salary at the 25, 50 and 75 percentile levels. The 25 percentile can be defined as the lowest value (in this case, base salary) that is greater than 25% of the values; similarly, the 50 percentile is the lowest value that is greater than 50% of the values and the 75 percentile is the lowest value that is greater than 75% of the values.

The term base salary includes basic pay, house rent allowance, conveyance allowance, education allowance and special/ dearness allowance. It does not include annual bonus, which has been presented as a separate item. 'Average Retrials' indicates provident fund and/or gratuity and/or superannuating, as applicable across individual hotel properties, while 'Average Benefits'

Implies medical and leave travel allowance entitlements. While most hotels provide car/transportation facility to their senior executives as part of the total compensation due to them, we have not included this in our calculation of average benefits, as different hotel groups follow different policies with regard to this particular entitlement.

The data reflected confirm that compensation in the hotel industry continues to be connected to the hierarchy of a traditional organisation chart. The General Manager (GM) is the highest paid executive, followed by the Resident Manager (RM). As per our survey results for 2002/03, the head of Food Production is the highest paid department head, followed by the Sales and Marketing head.

Taking into account all-India figures, the median (50 percentile) of the annual base salary of a GM was Rs 720,000 in 2002/03. For GMs of hotels with rooms greater than 200, the median of his/her annual base salary was Rs 1,280,000. In other words, the median basic pay of GMs of hotels with rooms greater than 200 were about 77.7% higher than the nationwide average.

Significant variations were also noticed in other designations: for example, the median basic pay of the Sales and Marketing head at hotels with rooms greater than 200 was 55.8% greater than the nation-wide average basic pay of Sales and Marketing heads. By the same comparison, the head of Human Resources at hotels with rooms greater than 200 earned

52.3% higher. The largest variation was observed in the case of Housekeeping: the median basic pay of the Housekeeping head at hotels with rooms greater than 200 was 94.8% greater than the nationwide median basic pay for this position.

The average bonus of a GM was about 18.4% of his/her average base salary. This is more or less in line with bonus pays for GMs in the hotel industry in the United States, where bonus as a percentage of average base salary is 20-22%. The RM's bonus was 7.3% of his/her average base salary - lower than the bonus as-percentage-of-average basic of both India-based GMs as well as RMs in the US (13%).

Benefits worked out to 12.2% of the GM's average base salary and 14.6% of the RM's average base salary. Retrials as a percentage of average base salary were 10.7% and 10.8%, respectively, for the GM and the RM.

For the Sales and Marketing head, average bonus as a percentage of average base salary worked out to 15.0%, while benefits worked out to 12.6%. For the Finance head, bonus and benefits as a percentage of average base salary were calculated to be 15.3% and 18.4%, respectively.

Survey Highlights - Expatriates

As part of the main survey, we conducted a study on the compensation package of expatriates in two positions - the GM and the Executive Chef (head of Food Production), details of which are presented. Although compensation data was obtained for other senior management expatriate positions as well, these could not be presented, as the sample size in all such cases was inadequate to merit a reasonable analysis.

As is generally the case worldwide, in India as well, different hotel groups provide different types of benefits to their expatriate employees. Therefore, for the purpose of our analysis, we have taken in account a sum total figure - cost to company.

Hospitality and tourism are certainly two of the most widely used words in the fields of hotels, restaurants, travel and related areas. They are used independently or in combination with other words, such as hospitality industry or tourism industry. As prevalent as these words are in conversations and in literature, they are used broadly, loosely, interchangeably and erroneously, according to Keiser (1998). In a study of four-year educational programme titles in the United States, Bloomquist and Morero (1997) refer to the lack of clarity among titles in tourism/hospitality programmes. A wide variety of programme titles with different words representing purposes of schools was noted. Some use "hospitality" and others use "hotel and restaurant" to identify similar programmes. Meanwhile, some departments commonly use "tourism" and others "travel" to identify similar programmes. During a survey by the authors, schools were asked to indicate words that would be preferred if the field were to adopt a common title for all the programmes. According to the survey, the titles that were popular among academics are (listed in order of popularity):

1. Hospitality
2. Management
3. Tourism
4. Hotel
5. Restaurant
6. Institution
7. Travel

Growth of Hospitality Management Degrees

In the United States alone there are over 150 institutions offering fouryear hospitality management degrees, with an annual enrolment of approximately 30,000. Considering that in 1960 there were only 15 institutions offering such degrees, this is seen as phenomenal growth. The hospitality industry and hospitality institutions are experiencing tremendous growth. Will this result in a trend towards professional schools with four-year programmes that combine the best of technical skills with management and business education?

If they can create a curriculum that fuses the technical skills of a good culinary programme with the management and business skills of a good hospitality management programme, then their graduates may become more attractive to prospective employers. The traditional focus of hospitality education is being challenged by the rapidly changing needs of the hospitality industry for more general managerial skills and interpersonal competencies. This may represent a fundamental shift in the hospitality industry's definition of the optimal balance between what is generally applicable and what constitutes specific training.

Joint ventures in international business training can offer educational institutions many possibilities for expanding their programmes. Such linkages can provide particular benefits (International Trade Forum, 1987). Joint degrees between traditional universities with a good reputation in management and social science studies and institutions with a good reputation for technical education can be seen as a good answer to some of the education offerings–industry expectations gaps. Joint degrees can offer universities and colleges, in both developed and developing countries, mutual benefits in such partnerships. Some of the more common benefits are:

- Expansion of markets
- Exporting of programmes
- Expanding subject knowledge base

Joint Degree Programmes in Developing Countries

Developing countries at times can provide partnerships that are extremely interesting and beneficial to their partners in developed countries. As an example, the popularity of the Caribbean for numerous joint degrees initiated by universities in the United States and the United Kingdom can be indicated.

It is evident that joint degrees between traditional universities and other educational institutions (colleges, polytechnics and new universities) focused on technological education are becoming common. As an example, the University of the West Indies (UWI) has developed a number of joint degrees with technical universities and colleges in Jamaica, Barbados, the Bahamas, Antigua, St Lucia and Trinidad and Tobago during recent years. It is also noted that many universities in developed countries seek educational partnerships with reputed educational institutions in developing countries. Some universities now seek franchises, affiliations, formation of consortia for mutual benefit, as well as virtual university linkages. In a changing horizon in developing countries such strategies often prove to be useful in networking and rapid expansions. Credentialling and accreditation also seem to be useful tools for educational institutions in developing countries to gain recognition and improve the marketability of their programmes.

The host population must also be educated in the requirements of their target market to sustain a thriving tourism industry. As stated by Caothup:

The more aware our target market becomes, the more necessary it is for the destination to match this component of international travel. It can be seen that education, both at the market source and at the destination, must be included as one of the major players in international tourism. Without an educated international population, the desire to travel diminishes and, without an educated host population, the ability to satisfy the visitor declines.

In keeping with the growing importance of leadership skills and the changing developmental needs of middle managers, a change in hospitality education is imperative.

According to Umbreit (1992, 71):

Hospitality educators must understand that these changes are permanent and that graduates from their schools will need a different set of skills to succeed in a restructured business environment. Hotel and restaurant firms are already learning that their survival is predicated on taking a fundamentally different approach to the way they manage their operations.

"Understanding of the latest trends and problems faced by the industry is extremely relevant to the universities offering tourism and hospitality degree programmes. More and more managers are required to assume more diverse responsibilities" (Williams and Demicco, 1998). The evolution of multidepartmental management is due mainly to organizational downsizing and consolidation of support service management.

Academic Challenges in Developing Countries

Some educational institutes in developing countries attempt to create and design educational programmes simply by copying popular programmes from developed countries. In doing so, most of these institutions aim to take shortcuts in introducing academically accepted programmes, but as a consequence they lack industry and market orientation. In creating tourism and hospitality management degrees in developing countries, it is important to learn from the experience of the developed countries, benchmark and maintain high academic standards.

It is equally important, though, to identify and analyse current and anticipated future needs of the tourism and hospitality industry of the respective developing countries or region.

A number of important issues have been discussed by tourism and hospitality educators in recent years. The value of hands-on, industrial experience has now been generally recognised, and few hospitality management schools would dare not to include it in their curriculum. A matter which is still the subject of considerable controversy is: should we teach industry specific skills or general management competencies?

Lower Skill Levels

In a paper on "Skills Improvement in Hotels: The Case of Sri Lanka", Jayawardena and Edrisinha (1993) report that only 13% of the work force of about 17,500 in Sri Lankan hotels has had vocational training. Similar situations are noted in many other developing countries. Surprisingly the hotel skills situation is not extremely positive in some of the developed countries either. The general business journals and trade press report that "the current work force in the United States is not adequately skilled or educated to meet the technological needs of the next decade.

If those findings are valid in the hospitality industry, there is reason to question hospitality education as it is being provided today". In educating hospitality managers of the future, it is important that sufficient operational skills and trainer skills are developed. These skills will be very useful especially during the early years of management careers when on- and off-thejob training of junior employees are seen as important routine tasks of supervisors and middle managers.

Expectations and Needs

Meeting both industry and student expectations of hospitality/tourism education is an ongoing challenge, which may best be met by further stakeholder involvement in the design and improvement of course curricula. In addition, hospitality/tourism education needs in the Asia Pacific region provide both challenges and opportunities for education and training providers. Hospitality/tourism curricula are also implicit in a framework developed by Ritchie (1995) for designing and developing tourism/hospitality management programmes.

Criteria emphasized include sensitivity to industry needs, balance between economic development and environmental protection, building on and developing skills of faculty members, location where tourism is a significant component of the local economy, and a balance of conceptual material and practical experience. Echtner (1995) examined the challenges facing developing nations when designing tourism programmes. She concluded by advocating a three-pronged approach: professional education, vocational training and entrepreneurial development.

Lack of Funds

To raise the standards of both hotel management and operations within the hotel industry in China, there is a great need for better hospitality education. However, given the lack of funds available to build quality educational institutions and staff them, it is necessary to explore alternative ways of achieving the same end (Huyton and Ingold, 1999). Owing to lack of funds, often the facilities such as training kitchens, training restaurants, libraries and computer laboratories of hospitality schools in developing countries are inferior to their competitors in developed countries. Developed nations such as the United States, Canada, Japan and some of the European Union countries often assist developing countries with generous funding.

Charles (2001) argues that the challenge is to forge and sustain the collaboration, cooperation, partnership and participation of all the major stakeholders of Caribbean tourism - the public and private sectors, the education and training institutions, the representative organizations and associations, the trade unions, the media, the people of the region - in the development of the industry and the people in it. Imagination and creativity are essential ingredients in developing new educational programmes in developing countries. This is so, as often developing countries are handicapped in terms of technical expertise and equipment.

Changes in Student Demographics

In implementing tourism and hospitality management degrees, one should be aware of changes in of demographic trends of the target student population. According to Pavesic (1993), in the United States, the average age of the hospitality student is rising, and women will soon outnumber men in programme enrolment by a 2 to 1 ratio. This demographic change will have an impact on teaching specific courses, the level of content of the courses and teaching methods.

Too much is taught from the front of the class now, and lectures will be replaced by student-directed learning. The female perspective will replace the male perspective in the way the material is presented. In the Caribbean, female dominance over males in student numbers has been quite common for many years in tourism and hospitality, as well as most other disciplines. Education has been identified as the factor which, in the framework of existing social structures, will be most influential in determining the achievement of most of the other objectives identified for women's development. Many women recognize that they have been using education to facilitate their more active participation in the workforce and this has had, and continues to have, an impact on society in a number of ways. In September 1999, when UWI commenced the Caribbean region's first master's degree in tourism and hospitality management, 77% of the students who enrolled in this new programme were women.

Negative Attitudes

Owing to unpleasant memories from the colonial past, negative attitudes towards service still linger in some developing countries. In the Caribbean, where the forefathers of many citizens were captured and forcibly shipped as slaves across oceans to unknown lands, the problem of negative attitudes towards service is quite common. Service to "white" tourists sometimes is seen as going back to the plantation era in the Caribbean. The result of this is difficulty in attracting higher quality staff to tourism and hospitality jobs and students to tourism and hospitality management programmes in the Caribbean. This situation is different in most other developing countries where the slave trade never took place. Notably, in most Asian countries, hospitality and service seem far more culturally deep-rooted compared to the Caribbean.

This means that tourism and hospitality educators operating in the Caribbean have to be sensitive to this common feeling. Certain adjustments have to be made to curricula and delivery methods. Even terms common in the global hospitality business such as "bus boy", "bell boy", or "room maid" are considered bad words in most Caribbean countries. A hotel general manager was once told by a union leader in Jamaica that the staff refused to wear certain types of uniforms. These were designed by a top French designer for employees of Le Meridien hotels worldwide to maintain uniformity and general standards.

The reason given by the union leader and employees for this refusal was "these uniforms remind us of the colonial past". Instead of considering this as an act of insubordination by the staff, this general manager changed the uniform design in order to maintain industrial harmony. sector-funded Caribbean Hotel Association (CHA), national tourism organizations, national tourism and hotel associations and other academic institutions. A regional consulting firm was commissioned by CTO to conduct a study of tourism training needs in twenty-five Caribbean countries. The study was carried out in 1998. A total of 1,112 private and public sector organizations participated in the study.

The Hotel Kracauer

S ince the recent rediscovery of Siegfried Kracauer as a theorist of visual culture, and the subsequent English language publication of a sampling of his Weimar-era feuilletons, the broad outlines of his biography are finally coming into focus for American readers: the long friendship with Walter Benjamin, labor in the outer orbit of the Frankfurt school, exile in Paris and New York, and so on. What is less well known is the fact that Kracauer spent a brief but very significant period as a practicing architect. After finishing a design degree in Munich in 1909, he found work at various firms in Frankfurt where he was put to work drafting small-scale commercial and residential structures. He gave up this career in 1919, when he felt it had become too desultory, and he took a position as feuilletonist at the *Frankfurter Zeitung*.

Yet his fascination with architecture remained with him, not only as a frequent focus of his reportage but as a source of spatial images [*Raumbilder*], which he elaborated across a broad range of topics. In fact, it was only as a critic and social theorist that Kracauer's architectural imagination could be said to have come into its own. The various employment agencies and department stores that turn up in his writings are not just formalistically "rendered," because he never regards space as ideologically neutral: "Every typical space is created by typical social relations which are expressed in such a space without the disturbing intervention of consciousness. Everything that consciousness ignores, everything that it overlooks, is involved in the construction of such spaces" (Kracauer, *Schriften* 5.2.185). "Typical space" is the operative term here, because he examines architecture in tandem with leisure, entertainment, and domesticity, the broad spectrum of nonspecialized activity that has frequently been theorized in the postwar years under the rubric of "everyday life." As Kracauer recognizes, architecture in an everyday context constitutes a particularly double-edged medium: because buildings embody unresolved social contradictions in proximate form, they serve as a locus of potentially radical transformative power.

And yet because buildings are appropriated by habit as we live in and through them, these contradictions tend to go unremarked. Ideology lies, Kracauer says, like Poe's purloined letter, out of sight in plain view. This is the starting point for what would prove to be his decades-long critical encounter with the built structures of metropolitan modernity. If the easily overlooked locales that reproduce social relations acquire a mythic dimension through the naturalizing force of repetition, then he works against this process by reading them as so many ciphered communications.

Among Kracauer's preferred sites for such culture-critical detective work, the one he returns to repeatedly, like the scene of a particularly opaque crime, is the hotel lobby. The typical metropolitan grand hotel is remarkably well-suited to his project, since it houses a full range of everyday practices by transposing them to a controlled environment. It is the quintessential heterotopic setting, where one can, under a single roof, attend a wedding of five hundred people, buy a pair of pants, and shower.

Kracauer essay "The Hotel Lobby" serves as the pivotal chapter of *The Detective Novel* (1922), his first sustained theoretical treatise on urban mass culture. Lobbies subsequently turn up as a consistent topos in his Berlin feuilletons for the *Frankfurter Zeitung* of the 20s and early 30s, including (among others) "Parisian Hotel," "In a Luxury Hotel," "Chemistry in the Hotel," and "Evening in the Hotel." My point here is that we should regard Kracauer as something of a "hotel flâneur," since to a great extent he learns to read the modern city out of the hotel's interior topography, with corridors serving as his avenues, and function rooms and front desks as his plazas and police bureaus.

The hotel lobby serves Kracauer as a particularly flexible structuring principle, since like an architectural rebus, it allows him to conflate discussions of diverse urban practices, much the way Benjamin does in using the nineteenth-century glass-and-iron arcade for explorations of modernity in Paris and Berlin. But unlike Benjamin, Kracauer never lays out this spatial paradigm in a systematic or even quasi-systematic fashion. Kracauer's lobby has, instead, to be "excavated" from his various notes and essays; and in doing so here, it is my aim to draw together some of the seemingly disparate strands of his writing, in particular the connection between his work as a film theorist and architectural observer.

As Sergei Eisenstein (another former architect) remarks in his essay on montage, architecture and film are "preeminently" spatial, in that both prime the viewer to track a series of "carefully disposed" visual phenomena (59). It is perhaps one of the most piquant features of Kracauer's output that he works the intersection between the two media by producing a scenographic form of cultural critique, one which employs filmic methods of cross-cutting to suggest movement through the built environment of the city.

For Kracauer, lobbies would seem to invite such discursive overlap. They function, after all, as mediating structures, whether one is employing them figuratively or passing through them as units of space. The lobby of the big city hotel orients the guest or visitor as they enter from the street: it marks what is exterior and interior and, accordingly, what practices are to be sanctioned. As a spatial paradigm of metropolitan modernity Kracauer's hotel lobby does bear a resemblance to Benjamin's glass-and-iron arcade.

Each in its own way is an example of "ambiguous structure" in which the strict (and illusory) bourgeois dichotomy between public and private is both undermined and reaffirmed. Not surprisingly, critics have tended to read the broad range of Kracauer's city writings with an eye to Benjamin (and through him, to Georg Simmel's metropolis of "shock and speed"). Yet more than formal differences remain between the two. Benjamin examines the collapse of this public/private dichotomy through what Susan Buck-Morss calls "industrialized" phantasmagoria (81); but because Kracauer was more keenly attuned to mass culture than his more reticent Frankfurt School colleagues, he was able to take the trope of the lobby places Benjamin never could in comprehending changes in the way space is socially produced.

The metropolitan hotel functions for Kracauer as the paradigmatic local instance of an emerging global culture in which space serves as an object of consumption through highly differentiated forms of tourism, mass media, and urban spectacle. As a result, we can recognize in Kracauer's lobby the code for those formations of civic life that we use to map our contemporary late-modern economy,. including the private-public broadcast spectrum, total-living enclaves, and resurrected urban cores where the metropolitan is replayed as a series of consumable stock images (sites which serve as the starting point for many of our now all too familiar narratives of urban decline).

What is interesting about Kracauer is the fact that he traces out these developments within the context of the "classic metropolitanism" of 1920s Berlin. This is useful not so much because he offers a proleptic view or prefigurement of the contemporary, but because he opens the contemporary up for reevaluation: his work forces us to look at the recent spatial turn in cultural theory and our own increasingly conventional ways of topographizing history, and to consider why it is that so many of these "mappings" and "sites" are themselves infused with a kind of nostalgia. For if it is the case, as Kracauer suggests, that architecture is subject to occult forces, then we ought also to ask: to what degree is this true of our own architecturally informed critique?

A fascination with the urban hotel belonged to Weimar Germany's moment, and was by no means unique to Kracauer. Indeed, by the time he began writing his Berlin feuilletons in the mid-20s, the grand hotel had already become a standard trope across popular and high cultural lines, from the "transcendental homelessness" of Georg Lukács's "Hotel Abyss" to Vicki Baum's relentlessly spinning *Drehtür*. Beginning at the turn of the century and lasting well into the 20s, hotel construction had undergone a tremendous proliferation across Europe and the U.S.

Hotels came to resemble cities in microcosm, vertical cities housing laundries, valet services, barbers, gymnasiums, travel offices, drug stores, libraries, music rooms, baggage rooms, automobile fleets, libraries, swimming pools, clothing stores, banks, florists, gift shops, screening rooms, medical services, convention halls, newsstands, mail services, roof gardens, and ballrooms — to name only the respectable services that hotels provided. Like the self-contained superblock, the privatized space of the metropolitan hotel could be said to have turned its back on the city. And yet at the same time, the hotel recuperated urban life on terms that extended its own ability to manufacture desire. The hotel was not just an airbrushed city within the city; it also sold the city outside, the dirty city, a distinctly cosmopolitan self-image. "In the middle of our quotidian view," the Weimar-era journalist Hans Kafka writes, "stands the hotel, a miniature model of a great international metropolis".

The glamour that suffused these structures was derived from the fact that their patrons consumed a modern or "smart" view of a metropolitan environment both disconnected and linked to the city the hotel served. Construction was in this fashion tied to local boosterism: grand hotels were often conceived as civic showcases meant to put the city on the larger map as economically and culturally viable. This was as true for the Adlon in Berlin, which was partly financed by prewar government tax breaks, as it would later be for the Palace Hotel in East Berlin, which served as a "show window" to the world (today we might find yet another metropolitan equivalent in Dubai, where the Chicago Beach Tower Hotel, taller than the Eiffel Tower, is being pitched as an instant global trademark).

As part of the social imaginary of postwar urban life, the socalled *Großstadthotel* was subject to a complex process of mediatization. Hotel ballrooms regularly furnished broadcast sites for radio (for example, New Year's concerts live from Berlin's Fürstenhof, or the five o'clock tea dance from the palm court of the Esplanade). Lobbies and offices were used as settings for mass-market potboiler fiction. And the German movie studios, most notably UFA, began turning out numerous examples of the so-called "Hotelfilm," a relatively short-lived genre that includes Murnau's "The Last Laugh," as well as now more obscure titles like "The Green Monocle," "The Fabulous Countess," and "Hotel Secrets."

It was characteristic of these films that they were set on a delirious, American-style scale and exuded a horror-tinged fascination with repeating and expanding urban spaces. Soundstages accommodated the construction of improbably capacious hotel suites, hallways, and function rooms – so that a film like "Grand Hotel," the 1932 adaptation of the Vicki Baum novel, is able to push microcosmic logic to the extreme by playing itself out entirely within the parameters of the building. Berlin is glimpsed as a mere backdrop through the window of Grusinskaya's rooms, while the camera keeps its back to the street even when it approaches the exterior of the hotel.

In reviewing the film's Berlin premier, Kracauer alludes to the fact that Weimar audiences were acquainted with a highly recombinatory set of hotel types ("Berliner Nebeneinander"). There was the dowager with an unmarried daughter, the Russian paper-aristocrat, the Roman waiter with the debutante, the shipping magnate and the film star, and so on. Hotel lobbies are notoriously charged with narrative possibility. The hotel, as microcity, is a site of exchanges of all sorts — information, money, services, goods. And among these we might include identity as well, since as sites of displacement, hotels tend to magnify that sense of the performative that is concomitant with urban anonymity. This is what gives the lobby its particularly promiscuous energy. Open to dispersal, the lobby invites guests into the scrambling of identity codes and deterritorialization of desire that Deleuze, for one, associates with the euphoria of capital.

Popular narratives of the 20s played off the grand hotel as a site for identity exchange (potboilers plotted the movements of parvenus, gigolos, and other dissimulators who guaranteed "respectable guests" — like the audience itself — the bourgeois frisson of not knowing with whom they were sharing a roof). For its part, hotel management contributed to the widespread perception of the lobby as a site of mobility and desire by actually marketing narrative possibility: the hotel was frequently promoted as a place where "things happen." Public relations departments were first established during this period to produce metropolitan "scenes" — a practice that constituted an interiorized form of big city boosterism (a typical ad campaign of the time was "Seen at the *Fürstenhof,*" which proffered scenarios such as: "Why certainly that was Charles Spencer Chaplin you saw.

Did you think he would brush the dust from his big shoes without mulling over the culinary delights here?"). House publicity directors were responsible for formulating press releases detailing on-site events and sightings of celebrated guests. And it was not unusual for the larger metropolitan hotels to put out their own newspaper: the Esplanade in Berlin, for example, published an in-house daily gazette that detailed arrivals and items of local interest.[4] Such information would often later turn up in the soft news of the city papers' social notes and photogravure sections, and was occasionally recirculated through the wire services and, later, picture syndicates of international venues like Condé Nast, which specialized in a kind of high-gloss pictorial tourism.

The kind of metropolitan hotels Kracauer was familiar with were, in the teens and 20s, just beginning to be consolidated into panEuropean chains organized under the hospitality industry's newly developed management ethos.[6] These large-scale machines for living were structured according to principles of integrated services and standardization of materials; the latter extending from linen and decor to portion control in the restaurants. Hotel space was instrumentalized by being made calculable, generic, and thus potentially exportable.

According to the gauge method of industrial management, skill was located in the organizational system itself, so that departments were divided and subdivided according to an ever finer Taylorist specification of function. Escoffier, head chef at Berlin's Hotel Adlon, was the first to arrange kitchen labor into stations – *Chefkoch, Fischkoch, Saucier,* etc. – each marked by a particular headgear. In general, efficiency and quality control depended on the establishment of routine reinforced through the regular ergonomic drilling of the *Kaltmasells,* porters, waiters, and bellboys. Not just staff, but guests as well were subject to these kinds of "spatial narratives." The Berlin architect Karlwilhelm Just, for example, developed "room sequencing" as a management tool meant to preclude backtracking and bottlenecking on the part of hotel guests (Just 12).

But of course buildings never entirely predetermine the scenarios they house. As de Certeau reminds us in his essay on the flaneur (99-100), even walking is itself a process of spatial appropriation, or "displacement." Merely crossing the threshold of the hotel carries with it, intentionally or not, ways of resisting the hotel's manufactured sense regime. Such breaks or ruptures may be minor (i.e., the bellhop smoking in the pantry) or momentous (as when Sparticists occupied the lobby of the Berlin Kaiserhof in 1919, or when Rosa Luxembourg and Karl Liebknecht were murdered in the basement of the Hotel Eden).

Public relations departments were aware of the particularly unstable nature of the hotel environment in which guests generally pass through in a matter of days, thereby heightening the level of metropolitan anonymity. As the 1920s hotelier Lucius Boomer observes, it is incumbent on management not only to take eventualities into account, but also to develop strategies to play down any rupturing events like crime or domestic violence that may take place on the premises. "If a guest chooses to take leave of his life," he writes, "suppression is as good as expression" (253). Retaining control of the hotel narrative was a form of moral hygienc mcant to protect the good name and commercial viability of the house.

To this end, the hotel was transformed into a huge, private information-gathering apparatus. Through electronic "room-boards" the staff had immediate access to information about the location, capacity, price, and decor of all rooms, along with knowledge about the status and personal habits of their occupants. The front desk, a quasi city gate, managed interior pedestrian traffic and served as a kind of policing unit under legal obligation to check for unregistered aliens, and under a selfimposed moral and aesthetic imperative to bar access to indigents and undesirables.

Time stamps, tabulating devices, and telautographic machines were introduced to manage the volume of detail. The information on staff and personnel was of particular concern, since the hotel industry was (and is today) so service intensive. With a guest to staff ratio sometimes as low as two to one, there was an enormous working population to manage, many of whom lived on the premises in unseen subterranean or otherwise secluded dormitories constituting, in effect, one-building versions of a company town in which labor was meant to be seamlessly self-effacing.

An elaborate, self-regulating, and mutually reinforcing system of information gathering extended throughout the staff, from plate checkers responsible for so-called "garnish control" to assistant housekeepers who were required to make written reports ("room checks") on the work of the cleaning personnel.

A staff of plainclothes house detectives circulated through the building, noting suspicious conduct and collecting evidence of property damage under guidelines set by the insurance companies. Whether stationed in the lobby or on call, they were required to keep the desk captain apprised of their own whereabouts.

Kracauer traces the movements of such house investigators in "The Hotel Lobby," an essay that was crucial in helping him lay out the terms of his own culture-critical detective work.[7] It is not so much a genre study as a speculative treatise, and is therefore less concerned with detailing particular settings than with establishing generalized "spheres" of quotidian life (as opposed to spheres of sacred or specialized activity). But before considering Kracauer's work, it is helpful to turn to his friend and colleague Walter Benjamin as a point of comparison, since he also focuses on the detective and his habitus in unraveling the expressive dream images of the city. Benjamin locates the prototypical "scene of the crime" in the apartments of Eugene Atget's "Intérieurs parisiens." "Noticeably almost all these pictures," he writes, "are empty . . . they are not lonely but voiceless . . . swept clean like a house which has not found its new tenant".

Given the fact that these rooms are not only deserted but physically undisturbed, the apparently groundless terror Benjamin notes can only be explained through the layout of the rooms themselves, where fear revolves not around evidence of a criminal act but in its anticipation, as if it were encrypted in the structure itself. Far from being destabilizing, imagined threats of criminality – or of urban contagion or the masses – play a constitutive role in the formation of both the domestic environment and the subject who occupies it. "Living space," Benjamin writes, "constituted itself as the interior. The office was its complement.

The private citizen who in the office took reality into account, required of the home that it should support him in his illusions". Decor bears the mark of domestic anxiety: the highboy or cabinet outfitted with pediments – the interior equivalent of exterior facade — betrays, Benjamin says, a "rampart mentality".

Through mementos, displays of photographs, and the strategic placement of mirrors, the parlor functions as the archival or "deep space" of bourgeois memory — memory that is reified by the layout of home furnishings in a kind of topography of habitual, everyday life. This encapsulated space is confronted by perceived threats it both resists and needs in order to maintain itself, and is therefore animated by a form of repetition compulsion through which it is replicated, in discrete subunits, as casing: "The nineteenth century," Benjamin writes, "had a covering for everything: slippers and pocket watches, thermometers and egg-cups, cutlery and umbrellas — preferring velvet and plush covers which preserve the impression of every touch". Since legibility, or the promise of legibility, guarantees the integrity of both structure and subject, the bourgeois interior is mobilized as an apparatus for reading the self though the trace of events.

Classic detective fiction shares in this interiority effect: through a logic of perpetual masking and unmasking, the reading of the crime scene posits a depth it presumes to reveal. Gathering forensic evidence, the detective proves to be a model subject, since such reading ensures the boundaries of self and the integrity of domestic space through the securing of property. What is striking about the sequence of events that follows the initial discovery of a crime is that it is narrated retrospectively.

The detective renders domestic space a legible scene, and in reconstructing the crime narrative "after the fact," opens the interior up as locus of potentially limitless clues. There is nothing that cannot be made legible, because the detective's search is haunted by an originary event that, as far as narrative logic is concerned, remains offstage, or "extra-mural."[8] Such detective space is ritually reconstituted by the reader at home.

Benjamin, for one, recognized a connection between early sensationalist fiction and the development of a particularly bourgeois spatial perspective. He writes: "Colportage as a phenomenon of space is the foundational experience of the flâneur, the city-walker. Space draws the flâneur on by asking: what has taken place *within me?*". The domestic interior is, he notes, both the setting for detective fiction and the site of its consumption.

This is an observation we may take a bit further by recognizing that this "reading room" traveled, that it extended into other nineteenth-century sites, for instance, into ships' cabins and Pullman railroad compartments, with their flocked wallpaper, carpets, lamps, and heavily tufted armchairs. These were not only favorite places to enjoy sensationalist murder stories (detective narratives enjoyed their early success in the form of Reiseliteratur, literature suitable for traveling), but a common fictional setting for them as well — a fact that should not only give us some idea of the ability of domestic ideology to replicate itself architectonically, but also indicate something of its geographic reach.

Kracauer, like Benjamin, begins his investigation of detective fiction by tracing the practices of traditional detective figures such as Dupin and Holmes. Yet in doing so, he circumscribes a very different kind of crime scene than that found in the classic, long nineteenth-century model. Kracauer relocates the prototypical detective to the lobby of a generic metropolitan hotel, a space that at least at first glance is reminiscent of the *Roman noir.*

Although Kracauer was unfamiliar with the school of so-called "hard-boiled" fiction at the time he wrote his essay, his choice and treatment of the hotel as crime scene suggests *noir's* idiom, in which the crime scene no longer fits the paradigm of the bounded room, but rather gives the impression of being diffused and unlocalizable, turning on conspiracy plots because criminality is regarded as systemic. Far from maintaining a cleanly detached subject position, the noir detective is often drawn into his field of inquiry as victim or suspect.

Critical distance remains, but it is inevitably undermined or challenged as part of the narrative's motive force, so that as the sovereign domain of the bourgeois subject is demystified, it mutates into the various forms of transit space -underpasses, cafeterias, garages – in which *noir* is traditionally situated. Kracauer shares in this typologization: the retrospective and therefore self-sustaining reading of the crime scene as found in Çonan Doyle or Leblanc is, he says, a "mere legality," or an exercise in formalism. The bloated autonomy personified by the detective figures is an operative ruse. Police roam the hallways where they traverse a space of unrelatedness, spreading themselves out in what he calls "a spatial desert" – desert being the quintessential nomadic space: i.e., trackless and therefore "depthless."

In contrast to bourgeois domestic space, which is occupied, broken up, textured, and hence dimensionalized, the nomadic space of the lobby is "smooth" and open to cross traffic. Kracauer's lobby suggests, then, both a mode of spatialization and a manner of being in space marked by this kind of depthlessness. He writes of the visitors in the hotel lobby that "they correspond to the empty terms that draw differences out of uniformity. Faces vanish behind newspapers and the artificial light illuminates only phantasms. . . . If they possessed an interior, it would have no windows". The hotel lobby traversed by Kracauer's prototypical detective is "a herbarium of pure externality". As a thoroughly policed, traversed "open environment," it represents both a depletion and an excess of readability, that is, a space of pure publicity.

In Kracauer's major work of the 20s, *The "White Collar Workers* (subtitled a "report from the newest Germany"), he brings the traditional practice of the flaneur up to date by helping readers navigate an increasingly unfamiliar metropolitan environment. By establishing new terms of legibility, he attempts to domesticate, or bring home, the new Berlin of white-collar mass culture to his bourgeois public (the task of the flaneur, Benjamin says, is "to make the city livable" – i.e., legible). Kracauer's hotel lobby can be seen as a microcosmic version of the Weimar-era Berlin described in his journalism as a city determined by "hinfließende Zeit," a city of disjunctive memory "difficult to map" because, he says, you would have to use discreet "points," not "lines". As a *Grofistadt* Berlin in miniature, the lobby is a spatial intermezzo of a piece with other transit sites in his work such as the Linden-arcade or Potsdamerplatz or the underpasses at the Tiergarten.

This is Berlin as perennial Grand Concourse, long treated by Kracauer's critics according to modernist categories of discontinuity and homogeneous time.[9] To be sure, Kracauer's city images draw on what Anthony Vidler identifies as shock, speed, and transport, but they contain other spatial and temporal orders as well, since Kracauer's urban nomadism often hits a register no longer determined primarily by mechanical velocity. During his years in Berlin, Kracauer came to focus both his feuilletons as well as his more sustained theoretical work on various forms of manufactured design environments.

These constituted his Berlin insofar as he used them to map what he considered to be an emerging, ostensibly post-bourgeois cultural landscape: they included the UFA studios at Babelsberg, the protocinematic display spaces and experience-scapes of show windows, theme restaurants, the newly reopened Lunapark, and the Haus Vaterland on the Potsdamerplatz. The latter, an 8000-person-capacity domed amusement hall and cinema complex, was promoted as containing "the world under a single roof." Patrons were offered the promise of "traveling in place" through a series of rooms coded as foreign locales (i.e., Bavarian and Hungarian lounges, a Wild West bar with "jazz and Negro dancers"). Writing on the Haus Vaterland, Kracauer compares it with the transit space of the metropolitan hotel, thereby acknowledging a structural homology between total design and the tourist industry: "At the heart of this pleasure barracks," he observes, "lies a sort of enormous hotel lobby, over whose carpets the guests of the Adlon can walk without in any way feeling compromised".

This disjunctive use of spatial images is typical for Kracauer. He uses a rapid cross-cutting of *Raumbilder* (space-images) to lay out a synergy of cultural practices. Where Benjamin employs discrete, snapshot-like pictures of Berlin and Paris, Kracauer offers critical *mise en scènes,* brief narrative sequences both filmic and architectural in which movement is evoked through the splicing of built environments. Indeed, Kracauer makes use of his lobby paradigm in an explicitly cinematic context in his essay "The Cult of Distraction" by comparing the contours of the metropolitan hotel with those of the Berlin movie palace, the implication being that the roving eye of the cinema spectator and the tourist share a similar cultural logic. According to him, the *Lichtspielhaus* finds its aesthetic principle in the flat "surface effect" of the film mediumwith such effects extending well beyond the screen to the theater's play of internal and external lights and its wraparound ad space (*Reklameflächens*), to photo spreads in UFA-owned periodicals, all the way to the metropolitan hotel itself. "The hotel and the film palace," he writes, "are optical fairylands shaping the face of Berlin. They are landmarks of pleasure – whose glamour aims at edification."[10]

Kracauer traces a double-sided logic here: as the architectonics of the city are increasingly spectacularized, image spaces become the sites where civic life is most convincingly enacted. He examines urban experience within the bounds of technological space and time, and by conflating the discourse of architecture with that of visual media, he offers an anticipatory blueprint of key developments in the built environment. The most obvious late-twentieth-century example of this is thirdgeneration Las Vegas, which has literally transformed the hotel lobby into cinematic space: guests "check into" film as they enter the themed lobbies of the Mirage, Luxor, or MGM Grand, with their narrative sequences of sinking galleons and exploding volcanoes. Architects and planners have "learned from Las Vegas" in the way they have always learned from hotels, namely, as laboratories for urban technology.

The principles of entertainment architecture are, of course, now widely dispersed, with the international hotel often serving as one nodal point in a wider system of commercial, "storied" environments. Indeed, this conflation of information and space has been given its most recent twist in so-called "hypersurface" construction, permutations of which include animated pedestrian arcades, glass video screen galleries, and smart houses with graphic touch-screen walls (structures that serve as the *built* equivalents of the televisual agora or the digital museum). As Paul Virilio writes: "From the new perspective devoid of horizon, the city is entered not through a gate . . . but through an electronic audience system. . . . Telematics replaces the doorway" (11-13).

Kracauer, too, construes the hotel lobby, his gateway to the metropolitan, as a form of mediatized space. If he characterizes the nomadic environment of the lobby as "flat," it is the flatness of a screen. As a hotel flaneur, he is repeatedly confronted with discrete scenes of metropolitan life where, sitting in the lobby he assumes the subject position of the flaneur as moviegoer. In the essay "The Palace Hotel," he observes the comings and goings of an international clientele in a lobby which, he says, has the auratic "distance-effect" of a film set. It seems to have been built, he says, "with a film comedy in mind: any second one expects Willi Fritsch to step out from behind the green curtain."

In his piece titled "At the Luxury Hotel," he asks whether the guests have not derived their entire existence through "the grace of an imaginary director." We see him actually entering the filmic scene in the case of "Evening in the Hotel" when, after checking into an unnamed Berlin hotel, he decides to take a walk outside and is immediately bombarded by the "surface effects" of the city's leisure economy, including department store displays, marquees, automats, and klieg lights illuminating the front of a train station in a cinematic day-for-night effect. He returns to the lobby to seek sanctuary, takes a seat in a club chair, only to find the street distractions reconstituted inside. "Walking into the hotel in the afternoon," he reports, "I sat in the corner of the lobby.

Suddenly I heard the sound of a saxophone a group of partygoers entered a film wound itself out before my eyes the group deported itself *flüchenhaft* -as if flat" (*Schriften* 5.201). Miriam Hansen is right in characterizing Kracauer as a "participant-observer" in the popular culture of Weimar (73). But we ought to take a close look at the terms — the spatial terms -of this posture. For far from abandoning "the domain of philosophical idealism and bourgeois culture," as Hansen would have it, it is precisely in Kracauer's role as a habituè of mass culture that he attempts to preserve this domain. His effort to use the spatial categories of idealist critique to map the contours of white-collar leisure is inevitably frustrated. In "Evening in the Hotel," for example, a glass door separating him from the main lobby momentarily affords him a minimum of specular distance.

But once the door is opened, "surface effects" overwhelm him and he therefore finds himself incapable of establishing the kind of detachment or epistemological privilege conventionally acted out by the detective and flaneur. In documenting an emergent Berlin, Kracauer is indeed forced to adjust his habits of critical perception. Unlike Benjamin, however, who effects a radical renegotiation of critical distance through a form of imminent dialectic, Kracauer still construes critique in terms of the "deep space" of bourgeois autonomy. When he characterizes white-collar workers circulating through the lobby as "homeless," this allows him to invoke — albeit negatively, by way of absence — a *phantom* interiority with its now deferred but still compelling promise of bourgeois readability (his version of the modernist "waiting room"). Kracauer's exercise in cognitive mapping leaves him without familiar spatial coordinates.

This is an aporia, or conceptual wall, he frequently runs up against, yet it by no means exhausts his suggestiveness as a critic, since there are other moments in his work where, however tentatively, he suggests alternate models by positing the possibility of dimensionality — i.e., the possibility of critique — beyond bourgeois categories of sense perception:

"Certain cultural values have become unreal," he writes, "by the careless misuse of concepts such as interiority . . . [a term] which refers to lofty ideals, but due to social change, is one that has lost its meaning as well as its supporting foundation".

Kracauer was himself well aware of the power of architectural forms like the bourgeois interior to haunt both the terms of cultural critique and the shape of the built environment. In the essay titled "Parisian Hotel" he enters the "depthless" transit area of the hotel lobby to find domestic interiority returning with the force of myth spatially realized. "The vestibule of the hotel is of unexpected scale," he writes, "a lobby opens itself up as a spacious, modern place with club chairs and a chimney in English style. Scarcely have I entered, than I shiver – not because the lobby is filled with dusk and there is no person in sight. But rather, this discomfort comes from my sense that all life has been drained from this place. I turn around and see only a still life that confirms my supposition". In other words, in the middle of the lobby's "flat" transit space we find the bourgeois interior reconstituted as a semblance of a semblance, a recapitulation of a coded set of depth effects. The 20s metropolitan hotel, typically selling itself to the world as "a home away from home for those who travel," strategically employed domestic signs to mask its functionalist apparatus. Furniture suites were customarily presented in hallways, at elevators, in lobbies, and at other points where the bare traffic space of the hotel was thought to be too unnerving for guests.

These generic groupings, consisting of some version of high-back plush or classic club chairs, a coffee table, and vase or mirror, offered no more than was necessary to connote the lineaments of a venue for secrets and intimate exchange. These were interiors resistant to the impress and trace of the subject that motivate the detective. On the contrary, a specific delegation of pages – the so-called *Hallendienst* – was charged with the task of keeping the lobby in a pristine state with the disposition of its furnishings intact. (It remains the same today: the only allowable trace of the subject in the lobby is the hotel logo, the "signature" of the corporate citizen left branded in sand-filled ashtrays – the very opposite of the classic scene of the crime in which a *cordon sanitaire* is established precisely in order to maintain traces.)

"What the hotel is expert at providing," Kracauer writes, "is the effect of lived-in rooms". Domestic phantasmagoria haunt the grand hotel. And as Benjamin reminds us, like all phantasmagoria, they are dominated by the force of mythifying repetition through which they are stabilized and replicated. Throughout his career, Kracauer figures the hotel lobby as a site of heightened exchange value, subject to nomadic, deterritorializing flows of information and desire.

In taking the measure of the lobby as a paradigm and gauging its relevance for social theory, we might want to keep in mind what Deleuze suggests about how the rules of exchange and internalization relate: capital cannot acknowledge the full extent of its own power to radically deterritorialize, so it brackets out this external (i.e., absolute) limit by setting up an interior (i.e., relative) limit which it then perpetually reproduces as a form of ideological alibi (alibis always turn on the question of location). Because this limit inevitably remains internal, it is "superseded" only by being more broadly reconstituted. As a cultural paradigm for metropolitan modernity, then, Kracauer's hotel lobby embodies a complex logic by which the nomadic, smooth space of advanced capital continues to call up nostalgic depth effects through various forms of place-making. "Anything can serve as a reterritorialization," Deleuze writes, "anything can stand for the fantasized lost territory; one can reterritorialize on a being, an object, a system. . . .

The State apparatus performs a deterritorialization, but one that is immediately overlaid with reterritorializations through property, work and money" (Deleuze and Guattari 266). In this sense, Kracauer's hotel lobby, with its own version of spectacularized interiority, limns those cultural paradoxes that have their model in a tourist industry where the authentic is posited and sought as a sign of itself: invented traditions, heritage manufacture, or the nostalgic evocation of metropolitan cores that want to convince us that contiguity and density of settlement are tantamount to epistemological centeredness – assumptions that govern not simply the work of neourbanist planners, but also many of their critics in their narratives of public-cultural decline.

Given the repetition compulsion that informs Kracauer's hotel paradigm, there is one recent project that would not have surprised him: the Helmut Jahn Sony Center complex at the Potsdamerplatz, incorporating, as it does, the bombed-out remnants of the Grand Hotel Esplanade within its steel skeleton and glass curtain walls.

In this soon-to-be-completed centerpiece of twenty-first-century Berlin boosterism, one enters through what remains of the hotel's Wilhelminian limestone façade and passes through its reconstructed palm court before emerging into The Forum, a vast, tented super-lobby housing an 18,000-square-meter urban entertainment complex. A "local" Berlin is thereby conjured under the aegis of global capital.

This private-public space – enframed, climatized, furnished – offers a consumable, indeed, inhabitable, image of civic life, with the encased and interiorized hotelshard serving as a kind of overscale souvenir, a metonymic relic meant to summon up Berliny as a mythic metropolis. The project is part of a process the city's official advertising team has termed the "rebranding" of the city; but, considered from the perspective of Kracauer's hotel lobby, it seems more akin to an uncanny revisitation.

It is not just certain developments in late- twentieth-century built space that would have seemed familiar to Kracauer, but their theorization as well. After all, since the 1980s, the trope of the hotel lobby has had something of an unacknowledged comeback, most notably through the work of Fredric Jameson, who has made the atrium of Los Angeles's Hotel Bonaventure a key site in mapping the nowhere and everywhere of global hyperspace. With numerous theorists coming in his wake, the Bonaventure lobby has acquired virtual landmark status in criticismalong with an inevitable degree of reification. At least in Jameson's case, a certain revolving door effect is at work here, insofar as he unwittingly retraces certain anxious steps from Kracauer's hotel walks:

> *I am more or less at a loss when it comes to conveying the thing itself, the experience of space you undergo when you step into the lobby or atrium. . . . I am tempted to say that such space makes it impossible for us to use the language of volume or volumes any longer, since these are impossible to seize. . . . It is an element within which you yourself are immersed, without any of the distance that formerly enabled the perception of perspective.*

As the terms of idealist readability are implicitly equated with readability per se, the lobby frustrates Jameson's efforts at cognitive mapping, sending him into a crisis of interiority (he too is haunted by architecture). Yet even among theorists less anxious than Jameson, these long-standing habits of critical perception are still in play whenever the Bonaventure is used to posit "striking lessons in the originality of space" or a "revolutionary spatiality," rather than both a shift and a return. For what such claims of radical rupture actually do is reconstitute modernist historicism (and its rhetoric of breakthrough) via the back door, by spatializing it.

Instead of a historical master narrative, we are given a master itinerary, with Los Angeles as its epoch-making capital. The thing about such mappings is that they are inevitably laid out in contrast to a nostalgically evoked, early-twentieth-century "classic" metropolitan moment of the kind frequently represented by Weimar-era Berlin.

But this is where Kracauer may get the last word, because, viewed through the optic of his hotel lobby, such "classic metropolitanism" can be seen as having already partly spooled itself out as a series of stock, commercial images. Kracauer's lobby invites us to cast a backward glance at the present. And in so doing, it frustrates the very logic of nostalgia – nostalgia that informs not only the stories our spaces tell us, but also the stories we so often tell about space.

MARC KATZ is on the faculty of the Claremont College where he is a member of the Program in German and a participant in inte-disciplinary studies in the humanities. He has published on Benjamin, Wim Wenders, and Kierkegaard. He is currently writing a book on taste and cultural theory.

Chapter 6

Guidelines for Foreign Investment

THE SELECTIVE PROMOTION

In February of 1984, the National Foreign Investment Commission of Mexico surprised the investment community by announcing that it would apply the Foreign Investment Law of 1973 (FIL) with flexibility and would consider permitting foreign capital investment of up to 100 percent in a significant number of activities. Actually, Mexico had been expected to increase its restriction of foreign investment in view of the Government's efforts to decrease its economic dependence upon other countries.

For more than a decade, Mexico had limited foreign equity participation to 49 percent. Since the FIL allows for exceptions, the 49 percent limitation on foreign ownership is in essence a general principle. The policy, however, had been to enforce strictly the 49 percent limitation with few exceptions, which prompted the erroneous belief that this policy was in fact the law.

The initial reaction of foreign and Mexican investors to the recent shift in policy has been mixed. Some investors are concerned that businesses that incorporate with 100 percent foreign equity under the 1984 Guidelines will later be subjected to governmental decrees limiting future activities. These investors would favor fixed statutory rules in the form of a legislative amendment rather than flexible application of the current law.

Other investors have assumed a more positive and rational attitude toward the change. They take the position that, even if Mexico were to return to the 51-49 percent concept, businesses incorporated under the 1984 Guidelines would retain their 100 percent foreign equity. This position finds support in the fact that businesses that had 100 percent foreign equity prior to enactment of the FIL in 1973 retained their 100 percent equity afterwards. Indeed, United States investors currently hold approximately two-thirds of the $11.5 billion in foreign investment in Mexico.

A second question that appears to have been overshadowed by the release of the Guidelines is whether 100 percent foreign ownership is preferable to 49 percent foreign ownership with investment incentives. At present, Mexico offers a variety of attractive investment incentives to businesses that incorporate with at least 51 percent Mexican equity. Consequently, there are distinct advantages to both majority and minority foreign equity. In the final analysis, the needs of the particular enterprise will dictate the decision.

Since the Guidelines were announced rather recently, and in view of the state of the world economy, it is too soon to determine their actual impact. It appears, however, that the pendulum of Mexico's attitude toward foreign investment has finally reached that central balance essential for rational economic development: the selective promotion of industries necessary for positive economic growth.

This article provides an overview of the Mexican legislative process and discusses the various restrictions on foreign investment. The current implementation of the 1973 FIL is also examined, including the ramifications of minority and majority foreign ownership. The substance of the 1984 Guidelines is presented, and the perceptions of bankers, corporations, the Foreign Investment Commission and the foreign investment legal community are explored.

Finally, the article analyzes the advantages and disadvantages of regulating Mexico's foreign investments through legislative amendments rather than administrative policy, Mexico's changing position on foreign investment and the benefits of 100 percent foreign ownership under the 1984 Guidelines in view of the investment incentives offered to businesses with 51 percent Mexican equity.

Foreign Investment Legislation

To a large extent, Mexico's regulations on foreign investment are the result of administrative policy rather than the legislative process. In many cases, these policies have been adopted or changed with little or no publicity, and they frequently have been enforced under laws designed for unrelated purposes. Consequently, the policies are often difficult to define and must be deduced by their application to specific cases.

A prospective foreign investor must examine not only Mexico's foreign investment laws, but also the policies and practices of the executive branch of the federal Government to ascertain if, and to what extent, a business may be established in the country, the conditions under which the business will be received and whether the regulations to which the business will be subject are consistent with its interests.

Throughout the past century, foreign investment in Mexico was affected by divergent trends. During the period spanned by the regime of Porfirio Díaz (1876-1911), it was believed that substantial investments in mining, utilities and basic industries would bring Mexico into a position commensurate with that of industrialized countries. As a result, foreign investment was allowed to such an extent that it dominated the economy. In fact, much of the nationalistic sentiment evoked today in Mexico over foreign investment derives from the prominence attained by foreign enterprises during the lengthy Díaz regime.

In the absence of domestic investment sufficient to build a foundation for further development, extensive infusions of foreign capital were necessary, but they inspired a growing fear of increasing foreign influence. Moreover, Mexico's natural resources and labor were being exploited in the process. By the early 20th century, "the economic penetration of the country by foreign enterprises resulted in almost complete loss of control of the country's destiny to foreigners and foreign interests."

Recovery of Mexico's "economic destiny" was one of the primary ideals to emerge during the country's Revolution of 1910-1920 and has remained an essential tenet of every subsequent administration. The Mexican Constitution, promulgated in 1917, placed restraints on foreign economic activities and foreign ownership of land, which indicated the direction that limitations on the role of foreign capital would take in the future.

The Legislative Process

Although Mexico is a federal republic with both federal and state levels of legislative jurisdiction, the overwhelming majority of the statutes affecting its foreign investors are either federal or modeled after federal laws. Federal legislation is enacted by Congress; however, Congress rarely does more than give approval to statutory drafts submitted by the Executive. To become effective, the legislation must be promulgated by the President and published in the *Diario Oficial de la Federación*.

In addition to indirect control over the legislative process, the President has authority to enact general rules in the form of regulations, which explain and supply detailed precepts for the application of specific laws; to legislate directly in foreign trade; and to exercise other legislative powers pursuant to congressional statutory delegation. Indeed, a significant amount of existing legislation was enacted under the President's "extraordinary legislative power."

In 1938, however, the Constitution was amended to provide that such "authority to legislate could be granted only in connection with a suspension of individual guarantees in times of grave national emergency under article 29." Constitutional guarantees have been suspended only once since that time, in 1944, and, although most of the presidential decrees issued during that period were later repealed, the decree establishing the basis for quantitative restrictions on direct foreign investment remained intact.

Restrictions on Foreign Investment

The Emergency Decree of 1944 granted extensive discretionary control over foreign capital to the Ministry of Foreign Relations and was intended to avert disruption of the economy by temporary investments of flight capital. The decree introduced restraints on the "creation, modification, liquidation and transfer of stock" of Mexican companies that might have foreign shareholders and were organized subsequent to its enactment. While it originally affected few and relatively insignificant activities, the Emergency Decree was nonetheless the precursor of present legal restraints on foreign investment in Mexico.

Two years later, the Interministerial Committee was created to coordinate national and foreign investment. Composed of representatives of the President and several ministries, it was established to make "a systematic and continuing study" of foreign investment in Mexico so that "a proper balance" between foreign and domestic capital could be maintained. The committee, however, "largely ratified the practices already adopted by the Ministry of Foreign Relations under its discretionary powers." Since 1953, the committee has functioned haphazardly, and its significance has depended upon the conduct of the incumbent administration.

Nevertheless, the committee's inaction did not deter enforcement of the Emergency Decree, which the Ministry of Foreign Relations in fact expanded beyond its literal provisions. Even though the Emergency Decree applied only to specifically delineated activities, the Ministry instructed notaries and public registry officials that licenses were required for the incorporation or amendment of the articles of any company, regardless of the purpose or nature of the business.

At the same time, beginning in the early part of World War II, Mexico's attitude toward foreign capital shifted in an effort to improve the economy. Between 1940 and 1965, direct foreign investment almost quadrupled, and by 1969, it exceeded two billion dollars. This increase, however, was accompanied by pressure from Mexican industrialists to limit the inflow of foreign capital. Extensive foreign investment was noted to result in decapitalization and to increase the country's balance-of-payments problems. Government economists also were concerned and recommended that "the pattern of investment in assembly and processing operations, characteristic of the 1940's . . . be broken and greater use of domestically produced intermediate materials encouraged to stimulate import substitution."

Efforts were increasingly made to displace foreign investment. Joint ventures of Mexican and foreign capital were promoted, as were industrial integration programs, and foreign participation was excluded from certain industries and severely limited in others. In 1966 the Ministry adopted another significant policy: to deny licenses for the acquisition of majority interests in existing Mexican companies.

The mélange of restricted industries suggests that there was no overall planning or general policy concerning foreign participation in the Mexican economy. Some of the restrictions related to national security and the public welfare, while others seem to have been imposed in response to pressure from ad hoc private groups fearful about foreign competition. Furthermore, although special laws were enacted that expressly limited foreign investment in certain industries, other industries were added to the restricted list "solely on the basis of policy decisions by the Ministry of Foreign Relations, acting either on its own initiative or, more likely, on the initiative of, or at least with the concurrence of, other governmental agencies."

By 1970, the only legal restrictions on the amount of foreign participation in industrial activities were those resulting from the application of the Emergency Decree of 1944 and the exclusion of private participation, both domestic and foreign, in nationalized industries. The Government used other techniques, however, to divest foreigners of control and ownership, including tax incentives and the selective application of import controls. As one author has noted, the administration "seemed to prefer the flexibility in shaping its policies to individual investment projects that was allowed by the absence of a general law on foreign investments," and it adopted "specific statutory restraints in selected industries as it felt the need or desirability [to arise]."

The resultant overall attitude toward foreign investment was "one of cautious acceptance," although many perceived it to be excessively protective and nationalistic. Foreign investment was encouraged as a complement to domestic investment, and the Ministry of Commerce and Industrial Promotion increasingly insisted on Mexicanization and industrial integration.

Businesses dependent upon imports of raw or intermediate products or materials, or of machinery or equipment learned that procurement of the necessary import licenses might depend on whether they had become Mexicanized. The Ministry of Commerce and Industrial Promotion supervised not only the issuance of such licenses, but also industrial integration programs. In return for a guarantee by the Ministry that the necessary licenses would be granted, that imports of competing products would be excluded or that Mexican competitors would need to meet the same conditions, new and existing companies agreed to increase the Mexican content of their products, limit prices and payments abroad, observe quality control standards and divert 51 percent of their capital stock to Mexicans over a specified period of time. Furthermore, foreign investors learned that the availability of tax concessions depended upon Mexicanization. As a result, an informal process of clearing investment projects with the Ministry of Commerce and Industrial Promotion developed, as prospective foreign investors sounded out the administration for assurances that their projects would be favorably received.

The position of the foreign investor also changed. Tax and other concessions were offered to concerns with majority Mexican ownership under the 1972 Law for the Promotion of New and Necessary Industries, to manufacturing businesses in the border zones and areas outside Mexico City, and to enterprises exporting Mexican manufactured products; but the administration was no longer receptive to the establishment of firms for the final processing or mere assembly of imported parts or intermediate products. Also, enterprises that were heavily dependent on imports were subjected to strong pressure to develop domestic production. The informal process of clearing proposed new investments and important expansions of existing facilities was "virtually institutionalized," and although still not required by law, the Ministry usually insisted that the projects be underwritten with a majority of Mexican capital.

Between 1972 and 1976, Mexico extended the controls over foreign investment. Of utmost importance was the Law for the Promotion of Mexican Investment and for the Regulation of Foreign Investment (the Foreign Investment Law or FIL), enacted in 1973. Its purpose was to codify existing laws, regulations and policies, and it established the National Foreign Investment Commission (FIC) to exercise significant discretionary powers created by law, and the National Registry of Foreign Investment (FIR).

The Foreign Investment law and the Foreign Investment Commission

Since 1973, the FIL has been the principal source of foreign investment restrictions. It applies to capital investments in Mexican businesses, to investments in the acquisition of Mexican real or personal property, and to other specified transactions, including the pledging of Mexican corporate shares to foreigners and foreign participation in a real property trust. It is restrictive, however, only with regard to direct investment; it does not explicitly regulate indirect investment such as loans.

Actually, the FIL set forth only two major changes in the restriction of foreign investment. It limited foreign participation in the management of a corporation to the proportion of foreign capitalization and established the 49-51 percent concept as a general rule. This was the first time legislation required majority Mexican participation in a broad spectrum of activities and not in just a single activity. Although the FIL does not explicitly define either foreign investment or foreign investors, it does provide a list of activities and individuals that will be considered as such.

It stipulates those economic activities exclusively reserved to the Government, those reserved to Mexican individuals or corporations without foreign participation and those in which foreign participation is specifically limited to less than 49 percent. It also contains a general provision limiting foreign participation in new businesses whose activities are otherwise not regulated to a maximum of 49 percent. Furthermore, the FIL requires governmental authorization for investments acquiring more than 25 percent of the equity or more than 49 percent of the fixed assets of an existing Mexican company, and for any transaction resulting in the transfer of management to a foreign investor.

Unless a foreign investor is interested in establishing a business with more than 49 percent foreign equity, the business may simply be registered with the FIR. However, the final decision on whether a foreign investor may hold a majority of foreign capital and control rests with the FIC.

Since the 1973 law vested the FIC with broad discretionary powers, the commission could increase the "maximum" 49 percent foreign equity whenever it deemed the project beneficial to the Mexican economy. The burden, though, now fell on the foreign investor to show that majority foreign equity and control would "stimulate a balanced and equitable development" and "consolidate the economic independence of the country."

The FIC consists of representatives of the President and seven ministries, and meets on a monthly basis. Pursuant to its statutory powers, it may:

1. Increase or reduce the percentage of foreign participation in geographical areas or economic activities when there are no required definite percentages and establish the terms and conditions under which the investment will be received;
2. Resolve on specific percentages and conditions for those projects which "may justify special treatment";
3. Resolve on projected foreign investment in companies established or to be established in Mexico;
4. Resolve on the participation of existing foreign investors in new areas of economic activities or in new product lines; and
5. Establish "requirements and criteria" for the application of foreign investment laws and regulations. Pursuant to the FIL, the FIC issues General Resolutions setting forth standards and requirements for applying the law, although there are no "regulations" per se.

Applications submitted to the FIC for approval of majority foreign equity are first analyzed by a technical committee and then submitted to the FIC for formal acceptance. Invariably, applications undergo a process of negotiation, ranging from 4 to 16 months in duration.

Investment with majority foreign equity has had several disadvantages: the length of time required to obtain approval for either the formation or expansion of a company, and the restricted sources of tax and other investment incentives. In contrast, an investment of 49 percent or less foreign equity can be organized immediately, may be expanded into different areas or used for new product lines, qualifies automatically for tax and other incentives, and usually will provide easier access to administrative agencies and the various licenses required for imports. Furthermore, Mexican laws protect minority shareholders, whether Mexican or foreign, against decisions by a majority group of shareholders, and additional protection may be secured by provisions inserted into the bylaws or articles of incorporation.

Since the enactment of the 1973 FIL, exceptions to the 49-51 percent concept have been granted rarely and only under special circumstances. Foreign equity in excess of 49 percent has tended to be approved in such sectors as tourism, priority industries, advanced technology, capitalization and investments preserving employment, and for priority activities of Mexican corporations with severe economic problems. Furthermore, the overwhelming majority of these exceptions have been contingent upon agreement eventually to Mexicanize.

The FIC bases its decisions on the criteria set forth in the National Industrial Development Plan (NIDP) and the FIL. The foreign investment allowed should always be complementary to the Mexican economy; there should not be substitution of fields covered; the company should be ready to export; it should commit itself to a precise plan to train Mexican personnel; a high percentage of the financing should come from abroad; there should be diversification of the sources of investment; the company should have a significant positive effect on local employment; the project should preserve the cultural and social values of Mexico; it should be located in an underdeveloped geographical area; and it should contribute to the technological development of the country.

Two of the most significant criteria considered by the FIC in determining exceptions under the FIL are whether the proposed activity is an industry or is in a geographical area encouraged under the NIDP. Although each presidential administration adopts its own NIDP, the underlying premise remains constant. Accordingly, the 1983-1988 NIDP incorporates criteria set forth in the FIL. Moreover, the 1983 NIDP contains detailed political and economic policies governing "the Mexican State, the diagnosis of the national problems, the purposes and strategies of solutions in a national and international context, and the bases for implementation of those strategies."

Each NIDP, therefore, provides indicators of the attitude and direction to be taken by the incumbent administration toward foreign investment.

In February 1983, the Constitution was amended, enabling "the federal government to adopt measures of great scope in economic matters, and reorienting the principles governing the actions of the state and private individuals." The amendments embody principles consistent with the present administration's philosophy of *la Rectoría del Estado* (the state as sovereign and the sole conductor of the economy). The amendments identify activities reserved exclusively to the Government, but they also provide for the development of the private sector.

In view of the increasing restrictions on the amount of allowable foreign equity in various activities, the formidable effort required to obtain an exception to the 49-51 percent "rule" and the few exceptions granted, the FIC's announcement in February 1984 that it would consider up to 100 percent foreign capital investment in a significant number of activities ran completely counter to the expectations of the investment community.

Mexico's present policy on foreign investment is in the process of evolution and finds support in the FIL, the NIDP, resolutions of the FIC, and declarations by the Executive Secretary of the FIC and the Secretary of Commerce and Industrial Promotion. It focuses primarily on the selective promotion of new or necessary industries. No longer amenable to the acceptance of foreign investment in an indiscriminate manner, it does, however, encourage activities that will further the economic development of the country.

The primary objective of the 1984 Guidelines for Foreign Investment is the active, systematic and selective promotion of foreign investment in specific activities considered the most important for "a fair and balanced growth of the Mexican economy." That promotion is to focus on those areas which will generate a positive foreign exchange balance, produce competitive exports and import substitution, contribute to national scientific and technological development, advance Mexico's further integration into the international community, involve large investments, and create employment and geographical decentralization of industry.

In analyzing the basis of foreign investment policy, the FIC acknowledges that, "[a]lthough an adequate Law exists for direct foreign investments, a systematic policy has not always been followed for an effective utilization of its potential for the country's development." The FIC has found that, in reality, "the effective use of investments to promote national technological development, to efficiently replace imports or generate exports for a positive trade surplus" has been hindered by multinational corporations that "frequently tend to seek benefits through equipment and technologies already obsolete in their own countries, protectively, and obtain excessive gains at the expense of national consumers."

Similarly, the FIC concedes that, while past practices have quantitatively limited foreign investment, such practices have not induced a "favorable direction." Instead, foreign investment policy "has been limited to a simple check of investment propositions, set forth in accordance with international production strategies, or marketing of foreign companies' products, not always adequate to local, or national priorities or those of certain sectors." The FIC also recognizes that negotiations regarding foreign investments have been "limited to imposing local integration requirements or filling export quotas," with "the latter in many cases hav[ing] been difficult or impossible to follow."

The Guidelines represent the FIC's attempt to correct these deficiencies by adjusting Mexico's policies on foreign investment and its regulation. While foreign investment will remain a "complement" to domestic investment, the "policy will cease to be merely defensive and [will] turn active and systematic, promoting the formation of foreign investment alternatives, according to needs derived from national development priorities."

The Guidelines list priority activities that may receive up to 100 percent direct foreign investment. Priority undertakings, as delineated in the Guidelines, include the production of nonelectric equipment and machinery, electric machinery and appliances, electronic equipment and devices, and equipment and material for transportation; metal mechanics; the chemical industry; other manufacturing industries; advanced technology services; and the hotel industry. The Guidelines state, however, that the enumerated activities are of an "indicative character" and that the list may be expanded by the Ministry of Commerce and Industrial Promotion "as a result of specific proposals or through the various groups of the national productive sectors."

Certainly, one of the most important goals of the Guidelines is to encourage national technological development. As the FIC recognizes, however, preference will need to be given to "coinvestment" in order to "guarantee a *real* transference of technology." Nevertheless, compared to large firms, small and medium-sized foreign companies are to receive "more flexible treatment" since it is presumed that their "investments and transference of technology carry lesser risks of dependency and may be valuable in agricultural and livestock sectors and certain branches of capital equipment and consumers' items."

Increases in the percentage of foreign equity in Mexican companies by capitalization of debt, sale of stock or waiver of stock subscription rights of first refusal by Mexican shareholders may be granted for financially troubled industries on the list of national priorities. Alternative measures, however, must first prove unworkable, and the increase of capital must be indispensable to the survival of the company. Furthermore, provision is made for the expansion of existing foreign companies in priority areas where such expansion will lead to the "modernization of the plants, the commitment of greater volumes of exports and increase the level of national integration in the production process."

Another significant aspect of the Guidelines is the absence of a requirement to Mexicanize within a specified time period. Although the FIL does not deal with this issue, almost every exceptional allowance of majority foreign equity that was granted before the Guidelines were issued required Mexicanization, usually within 10 years. The FIC has acknowledged, however, that "the process of Mexicanizing companies in which foreigners participate has in many cases resulted [in] an illusion with undesirable effects on industrial concentration, pricing policies and available investment resources."

Some reports announcing the Guidelines have viewed them as an open invitation to any and all foreign investment. The Guidelines very clearly state, however, that only certain activities will be promoted. Although other activities are generally welcome, the requirement of minority foreign equity will continue to apply. The activities promoted under the Guidelines are strategic in nature, in conformity with the goals of the NIDP, and even those activities will be analyzed by the FIC in terms of the criteria set forth in both the NIDP and the FIL. On August 30, 1984, the FIC published five new resolutions pursuant to the Guidelines.

Their purposes are twofold: to update the FIC's General Resolutions in accordance with the economic priorities of the NIDP and the Guidelines, and to improve and expedite the application process for majority foreign investments. For example, the resolutions eliminate the need for FIC authorization for certain foreign investment activities in in-bond companies; for the substitution of foreign directors, provided the ratio of domestic and foreign capital is not changed; and, under certain circumstances, for the opening or relocation of specified establishments. Additionally, the resolutions enlarge the powers of the Executive Secretary of the FIC, and he may authorize certain actions without prior FIC approval.

The resolutions also include provisions that are expected to decrease significantly the amount of time required to complete an application for majority foreign capitalization. Pursuant to the resolutions, applications to the FIC are to be negotiated through the Executive Secretary, who is then to submit them to the FIC for its formal acceptance within 30 business days of completion of the file.

Announcement of the Guidelines has resulted in much speculation and misunderstanding. Research for this article included interviews that were graciously extended by bankers, corporations, the FIC and foreign investment legal practitioners. Their perceptions of the Guidelines assisted invaluably in the following analysis of Mexico's changing position on foreign investment.

Mexico's Changing Position

Contrary to past practice, the Guidelines were not published in the *Diario Oficial*, although they were announced in all the major newspapers and distributed in the form of a pamphlet. Because the *Diario Oficial* is the official repository of all federal legislation, the failure to publish the Guidelines in it signified a definite effort to make clear that the change was one of policy. Even though the FIL allows for exceptions and the 49 percent limitation on foreign ownership is in essence only a general principle, the fact that the FIC had strictly enforced that limitation with few exceptions for the past 11 years had prompted the erroneous belief that this policy was the law.

When newspapers misleadingly interpreted the change as a new attitude "welcoming" foreign investment, some investors responded with guarded cynicism. Since they had been led to believe that 49 percent was the legal maximum, some foreign investors would have preferred fixed rules in the form of a legislative revision. Fearful that this policy could just as quickly be replaced by past practices, these investors have been critical and have adopted a wait-and-see attitude. Additionally, foreign investors are concerned that the Government will later issue decrees restricting their future activities. The perception of both the newspapers and the critics is limited and faulty in many aspects.

Businesses incorporated under the 1984 Guidelines would retain their 100 percent foreign equity even if Mexico were to return to the 49-51 percent concept. It is extremely unlikely that a future decree could be applied retroactively. It is generally believed that the 1973 FIL cannot be so construed. Moreover, although corporations could not expand by establishing new plants or adding new product lines without Mexicanizing under the FIL, additional protection has been available through the incorporation of an enterprise as a variable capital company since approval of neither the FIC nor the Ministry of Foreign Relations is required to increase or decrease the variable portion of the capital. Consequently, corporations organized as variable capital companies have been able to expand and avoid pressure to Mexicanize when challenged to do so in the past.

Second, Mexico has always "welcomed" foreign investment. It is the manner in which it has structured its foreign investment policies that has led some to believe otherwise. Even after enactment of the FIL in 1973, the amount of foreign investment increased significantly, particularly in the years 1976 and 1980.

Also, the Guidelines do not signify an open door "welcome mat." The Guidelines explicitly state that certain listed activities are being promoted. Certainly, it is not unreasonable for Mexico to refuse to accept indiscriminate foreign investment. A careful examination of Mexican policies and practices over the past century discloses a process that at times has had its divergences, but always with a purpose. An unrestrained open door policy was extended when foreign investment was viewed as beneficial and necessary for industrial growth. When the resultant foreign dominance of the economy became painfully apparent, however, measures were taken to alleviate the detrimental effects. Nonetheless, the character, rather than the magnitude, of foreign investment was affected by the changing regulations.

As was uniformly noted by the bankers, lawyers and government officials interviewed, except for outright exclusions, laws really do not affect the magnitude of foreign investment in a country; other circumstances do, including political and economic views, labor rates and export possibilities. Regardless of the exclusion of foreign investment from certain activities, Mexico generally has been viewed as offering political stability, financial reliability in meeting its debt payments and a safe climate for investment.

Those interviewed were asked why, in their opinion, Mexico did not revise the FIL, and two responses predominated. First, the FIL already allows the FIC to grant exceptions when deemed beneficial to the national economy; there is therefore no need for a legislative revision. Second, although Mexico is politically stable, there is a nationalistic sentiment remaining from the periods in which foreign investment was allowed to dominate the economy. The enactment of a legislative revision would likely create apprehension that Mexico was once again indiscriminately allowing foreign investment to meet a short-term economic problem, and the political cost of such a reaction would be high. As it stands, the Guidelines have not been seen as a threat to Mexican industrialists, but rather as a progressive step toward increased technology.

Furthermore, not only is such a revision unnecessary, it is also not in keeping with the goals of the FIC. The development of a rational economic plan that selectively promotes those industries deemed beneficial to the national economy requires flexibility sufficient to allow continuous reassessment of the country's needs. To lock the administration into further rigidity would preclude the very growth Mexico is striving to achieve.

Views differed over whether Mexico will press for Mexicanization in the future. One of' the corporate officials interviewed believes that the Government is likely to promote Mexicanization in specific areas in which it has an interest. An attorney with extensive experience in dealing with the FIC, however, disagrees on the basis that the Government has nothing to gain from Mexicanization at this time. In the past, nationalistic political motives prompted the policy, or the Mexicanization or nationalization was directed to strategic areas of the economy such as oil, mining and petrochemicals. Additionally, as was noted in the preceding section, Mexicanization in itself is no longer viewed by the FIC as a desirable goal. In fact, one of the elements of the new policy will be to examine the effectiveness of Mexicanization operations.

Even if Mexico does later restrict the availability of investment incentives or press for Mexicanization, the fact remains that it is still an excellent investment choice. Almost every state offers a variety of investment incentives in addition to those provided by the federal Government, such as land, physical facilities and access to utilities; labor is still less costly than in most developing countries; and Mexico's marine, land and air transportation services and its geographical position as a neighbor of the United States help make it an attractive location. There are, of course, advantages to incorporating with majority Mexican capital.

An investment of 49 percent or less foreign equity may be organized immediately by simply registering with the FIR. Although the new resolutions should significantly decrease the length of time required to obtain approval of majority foreign equity by the FIC, common sense suggests that the process will still take considerably longer than incorporating with 49 percent or less. More important, an investment with majority Mexican capital qualifies automatically for tax and other investment incentives pursuant to the 1972 Law for the Promotion of New and Necessary Industries and other decrees. Although an investor may negotiate for incentives with both the FIC and the government of the state in which it will be operating even if majority foreign capitalization is planned, certain advantageous incentives are available only to companies with majority Mexican equity. Also, a company with majority Mexican equity will probably have easier access to administrative agencies and the various licenses required for imports.

Nonetheless, definite benefits may be gained by an investment of 100 percent foreign equity. One foreign banking official noted that there are both accounting and reporting advantages. In addition, a facility constructed by an investor entirely with foreign capital will have an asset worth more than the original investment after completion. If 51 percent is later sold to Mexican investors, the company would then be eligible for tax incentives.

Majority foreign equity has other positive ramifications. From a lending point of view, the risk may be different. A bank is more likely to extend credit to a subsidiary of a company that is well known or with which the bank has had a prior working relationship. Experience has proven that a parent company is much more likely to stand behind and support a wholly owned subsidiary, and any creditor is more comfortable lending to a party with which it is familiar, in contrast to a company newly formed with unknown management or shareholders.

Last, 100 percent foreign equity is unavoidable in certain industries. A company that has developed expensive, unique technology will not share that asset with anyone else. Such an attitude does not spring from a fear of Mexicanization; the intangibility of technology precludes nationalization, as was aptly noted by the chief legal adviser of an industrial conglomerate.

The particular needs of the enterprise dictate the decision whether to invest with majority foreign equity. For investors in Mexico, the fact that the Guidelines promote specific industries and that the new resolutions should expedite approval by the FIC are obviously factors to be considered. Regulations, however, do not necessarily affect the economic and political situation of a company, which is usually the main factor taken into account in such a decision.

Yet regulations can provide an indication of the governing country's attitude and probable treatment. Mexico has decided that the activities delineated in the Guidelines are the ones that most benefit its economy, and it issued the Guidelines to notify the international community that in these areas it will be most accommodating in meeting the needs of the foreign investor.

It is still too soon to detect the impact of the Guidelines, especially when one remembers that there are many other factors that need to be considered in speculating on Mexico's short-term investment growth. At present, Mexican assets have been frozen as banks wait out the financial crisis and debt restructurings. Even if a company decided to locate in Mexico, the freeze alone could inhibit such a move since most prefer to invest with borrowed money. Also, many plants that had expanded in the early 1980s found themselves idle with the recession and are now trying to orient themselves for exports.

Nonetheless, the overwhelming majority of persons interviewed are optimistic in believing that the Guidelines signify an important change in attitude by the Mexican Government. Since 1973, its attitude had been defensive, shaped by an acute awareness of the detrimental effects of unrestrained foreign investment and dominance. The new attitude of selective promotion of specific industries must be viewed not in terms of the percentage of foreign participation alone but, more importantly, as an identification of the administration's goals for foreign investment, including more sophisticated technology, higher employment, substitution of imports and increased exports.

Mexico appears to have finally taken a macroeconomic approach toward foreign investment. It is an instrument that must be used rationally, for only by selectively promoting those industries beneficial to the nation will Mexico achieve the international standards of competitive technology and exports necessary for continued positive economic growth.

Mexico's approach toward foreign investment is in a process of evolution. After veering from completely unrestrained reception to excessively protective and nationalistic restriction of foreign capital, the country appears to have reached an equilibrium. By announcing that it would actively promote foreign investment in specified industries, Mexico has placed the international community on notice of its intention to progress rationally toward further economic growth.

Because its foreign investment regulations are largely the result of policy established by an administrative body with broad discretionary powers, it has been difficult in the past to predict how favorably a prospective enterprise might be received. According to FIC officials, however, one can now look to the criteria set forth in the NIDP and FIL and to the list of activities to be promoted under the 1984 Guidelines and obtain a clearer indication of the conditions to which a company will be subject and whether they are consistent with its interests.

The Guidelines, together with the resolutions of the FIC, signify a changing attitude. Up to 100 percent direct foreign investment will be considered in specified activities; increases in the percentage of foreign equity in Mexican companies may also be arranged; and foreign companies in priority industries will be permitted to expand under certain circumstances. Although the FIL had allowed for these exceptions, prior to the announcement of the 1984 Guidelines they had rarely been granted.

Foreign investments that are subject to these exceptions, however, will not be approved automatically. They will still need to be analyzed by the FIC in terms of the criteria set forth in the NIDP and FIL.

Whether to invest with 100 percent or 49 percent foreign capital is a decision dictated by the needs of the particular company; but the availability of a choice makes Mexico an even more attractive country in which to invest. Fear of future restrictions, such as requirements to Mexicanize, is unreasonable in view of the overall profit potential and should not be a determining factor in whether to select Mexico as an investment choice.

Although persons involved in the field are optimistic about this change in attitude, they are also aware that regulations do not substantially affect the magnitude of foreign investment in a country.

Other circumstances have much greater significance, and owing to the current recession, it will take time to evaluate with accuracy the impact of these policies on Mexico's shortand long-term economic growth. The development of a rational plan that selectively promotes industries deemed beneficial to the national economy, however, should greatly assist Mexico in achieving competitive international standards.

Foreign Investment Code and Decree

In about only twenty lines of text, the Code announces its prohibition on nationalization, the areas in which it permits investment, and the privileges it will extend to investors in enumerated areas. Investments are to be in the form of contractual business cooperations, joint ventures, or private ventures. Although sparse in text, the declaration is one which international investors interested in the Southeast Asian trade arena have impatiently awaited. The Code declares that investment is now allowed in the areas of agriculture, forestry, industry, communications, transport, service, and tourism.

This provision is so all-encompassing that the rhetoric of "allowing" investors seems one last vestige of the socialist government's eternally close supervision. In reality, the 1986 reforms gave provinces unprecedented autonomy to pursue foreign trade with neighboring Thailand. Not only is foreign trade encouraged, but the reforms have also vested factory managers with capitalist-like powers as they switch to "socialist business accounting." This new management policy gives managers more freedom to run their factories by allowing them to pursue raw materials, resources, and trade ties with other South-east Asian nations, such as Vietnam and neighboring Thailand. Technical knowledge imported to Laos must be "appropriate," not yet in use in Laos, advanced, and have high socio-technical efficiency.

In addition, the Decree lists other requirements to which imported technology must "answer to." The language implies that this is a list of desired standards and not of actual requirements. Imported technology should be capable of improving the quantity and quality of products for domestic consumption or international exportation using less labor, power, and natural resources while ensuring worker safety and environmental protection. The Decree requires importers to be in possession of documents and legal certificates to the technology or technical know-how imported.

When machinery is granted entrance, it must be accompanied by the "means of production" (i.e., directions for use thereof). Additionally, support services, which include technical advisors, installation, experimentation, worker training, and distribution of information concerning the imported technology, must also be provided. Moreover, technology grantees must be given authorization to use an industrial model or other technical knowledge that may be contained in the industrial patent. Granted technical know-how may include designs, formulas, or other items with "technical characteristics."

The Lao Peoples' Democratic Republic (LPDR) guarantees protection of the industrial patents of technology donors. However, to make use of this protection, grantors must first enter an agreement with grantees, and then apply to the Foreign Investment Management Committee (FIMC) for a license. The agreement must contain:

1. The name of the donor and the recipient, as well as the content and analysis of "technological characteristics";
2. A schedule of the grant;
3. The price;
4. The terms of the grant;
5. The donor's restrictions on the recipient;
6. Conditions on the industrial patent;
7. The donor's guarantee of the technology;

8. Detailed conditions for worker training for subsequent technology transfer; and
9. Dispute resolution procedures.

A potential problem is that the Decree does not define "technological characteristics," a phrase that might be interpreted in at least three different ways. The most extreme reading of this requirement renders an industrial patent guarantee ineffectual because "technological characteristics" must be divulged to grantees. The FIMC could require that grantors reveal technological characteristics that amount to trade secrets. In the American common law, the protection that guarantees which industrial patents will be recognized does not extend to trade secret protection.

The Decree does not address trade secrets; consequently, trade secret violations that do not rise to the level of an infringement on industrial patents would remain unprotected. A less extreme reading of this provision would require that grantors simply list the superficial "characteristics" of imported technology. Yet a third reading, reductio ad absurdum, would require only a description of imported technology (e.g., "word processing unit"). It is unlikely that this provision would be construed so as to limit the LPDR's control of imported technology. Therefore, until clarification, the broader reading of this requirement appears to be the most likely interpretation, a possibility that may frighten potential investors.

Another definitional problem having to do with liability for damage gives rise to the possibility that contributions of machinery may be subject to further regulation. The Decree requires that such contributions be necessary to the joint venture's commercial production, not yet made in Laos, or too expensive to import based on the world market price. Also, the machinery's quality must be ensured. Anyone responsible for damaging imported machinery before the term of the joint venture ends must "assume the responsibility." The Code states that losses or "damage ... due to the machines, parts of equipment, technical expertise and technologies, contributed by one side to the joint venture ..." must be the responsibility of the contributing side.

Responsibility for losses is a problematic concept. Would a properly trained employee who injures himself be liable for contributory negligence or would his employer be liable under strict liability? The Code declares that whoever provides the machinery, components, technical know-how, or technology will be held responsible. At first blush, this provision inheres fault in the foreign investor, since the investor is the party most likely to contribute technology. The Code's analysis appears to be that "but for" the contribution of the machinery, the injury would not have happened. This looks like a strict liability standard.

The protection afforded by this provision seems to anticipate unscrupulous, exploitative investors who, while taking advantage of the abundant, low-cost labor pool, may also abandon their responsibilities to create safe workplaces for their Laotian employees. However, since Laos remains fairly underdeveloped, most contributions made by foreign investors are likely to be in the form of technology, machinery, and components. It is unlikely that the Lao government would attempt to attract investors with promises of privileged status, only to impose strict liability once their capital is invested in the country. Investors, however, may be hard-pressed to reach this optimistic conclusion, since there are no legal assurances as to a structure of fault allocation. Thus, further regulation is necessary here.

The new laws permit investment in agriculture; forestry; industries using indigenous raw materials and natural resources of Laos; industries that use "modern techniques" to produce goods for export or to produce domestically consumed goods; and the building of major infrastructure. Neither the Code nor the Decree enumerates the privileges that the LPDR may confer upon investors in these areas.

The Decree details the permitted sectors of foreign investment that were outlined within the Code. The Decree appears to delimit permitted areas of planting and processing within the field of agro-forestry by naming various indigenously cultivated crops. However, clauses such as "planting, processing of different varieties of vegetables," "integrated forestry business (planting, exploitation, finished processing)," and "seeds and livestock producing centers," appear to be all-encompassing, allowing almost any conceivable commercial pursuit within the field of agro-forestry.

The Decree delineates other permitted areas in the field of industry, such as electricity, mining and, oddly enough, toys. Unlike the provision for agro-forestry, this provision does not pretend to limit or restrict industry in any way. To the contrary, the provision reveals that Laos intends to open itself up to massive development of its infrastructure and exploitation of its rich store of natural resources.

Another provision encourages construction of hotels, tourist sites, and various other entertainment centers. The Decree's only restriction regarding construction is that it must be in conformity with the programs outlined by the LPDR government. The concern relates to uniformity of quality and scale because the permitted areas of construction are designated specifically to improve the country's infrastructure.

The LPDR clearly articulates that it will not authorize foreign investment in areas that affect the sovereignty, order, and security of society, or which do not conform to requirements for the economic and social development of Laos. The Decree, for instance, prohibits environmentally damaging investment. Recent ecological problems beset Laos' plans for a $500 million dam, the Xeset Dam in southern Laos, which was scheduled to become operational in 1991.

Investors with overwhelming debt are also prohibited from investing in Laos. However, the Decree does not indicate the level of unacceptable debt or point at which leveraging would make a foreign investor unattractive. The government desires to attract capital investors in a world where leveraging is perfectly acceptable as a means of expanding businesses. Thus, the LPDR may have to accept a certain amount of high debt load among its investors.

The Decree also forbids long-term projects that make great use of imported materials, the products of which are locally consumed, but which cannot qualify as import substitutes. Not only does the spectre of socialist austerity rear its head in this provision, but free and rigorous competition is also discouraged.

The provision protects against runaway consumerism by inhibiting the production of goods that otherwise would have been imported as "necessary" items. Practically, however, this provision indicates that the LPDR discourages enterprises that would compete with local entrepreneurs who already meet the local demand. The Decree provides no guidelines to aid in the determination of what qualifies as such a product. Without guidelines, the worst-case scenario becomes possible, one in which a foreign project, after its inception, closes down for violating this provision.

The LPDR also reserves the right to forbid certain projects. Again, this presents problems because it gives the LPDR arbitrary power. Given the developmental circumstances of Laos, however, the LPDR would most likely temper any urge to act arbitrarily. Such action would surely toll the death knell for a country still struggling in the birth of economic reforms. Nevertheless, investors balk at such broad unilateral reservations, and the LPDR would be wise to reevaluate this provision and specify all types of prohibited projects.

The investment managing organ of the Council of Ministers alluded to in the Code is named in the Decree as the Foreign Investment Management Committee (FIMC) and is headed by the Chair of the Council of Ministers. The Ministry of Commerce and the Office of Foreign Economic Relations constitute its standing members. The Decree grants to FIMC the power to interpret the Code and to authorize and approve investment, although implementation of the Decree is shared with ministers, heads of state organs, and chairs of provincial and municipal administrative bodies.

The Decree specifies certain ministers--such as the Minister of Commerce and Foreign Economic Relations, the Minister of Economy, Planning and Finance, the Minister of Science and Technology, the Minister of Foreign Affairs, the Minister of the Interior, the State Bank and other concerned ministries that are responsible--to issue and recommend detailed implementation of this Decree within the limits of their roles and rights. Ultimately, however, the FIMC appears to be the only governmental body actually empowered to interpret and amend the Code and Decree.

Furthermore, although the Decree explicitly invests the FIMC with power to interpret the Code, it only implicitly vests the Board with power to amend the Decree, declaring that only sectors and localities authorizing foreign investments "in the Lao PDR are to control and amend their authorization to conform with this present Decree." Because only the FIMC authorizes foreign investments, by default it becomes the ultimate arbiter of the Code and Decree, unless it delegates its powers to administrative agencies that it, or the government, might create.

The Council of Ministers may override the FIMC by virtue of the Code's elastic clause allowing the Council to "issue the detailed provisions for the implementation of [the Code]." However, a literal reading would indicate that the Council's power is to "enforce" detailed regulations and not to promulgate them. Hence, the FIMC appears to remain the final arbiter of both the Code and Decree.

The FIMC's supervisory powers over business ventures, be they contractual business with Lao investors, joint ventures, or foreign enterprises, are extremely broad. Thus, the Decree declares that the FIMC shall follow and control the business operations of foreign investors. For instance, the FIMC is required to create a professional auditing organ to control the accounting reports filed by enterprises with foreign shares. In its report to the FIMC, the auditor must assess its own system of auditing enterprises, the system of regulations on general accounting, the state of implementation of an enterprise's accounting system, and the precision of figures and data used in the accounting reports of audited enterprises. The FIMC is also given authority to initiate legal action against persons who deviate from their investment licenses.

Although these provisions seem to indicate a suspicion of foreign investors, the FIMC will not function oppressively because, along with its function as a protectorate of Laotian interests, it acts as a public relations organ with respect to foreign investors. For instance, FIMC advises and holds discussions with foreign investors willing to establish wholly foreign-owned enterprises in Laos.

Further, the Decree requires FIMC to provide facilities so that foreign investors can "discuss and sign agreements on the establishment of joint ventures ...." Additionally, the FIMC must consider and solve issues "as requested by foreign investors," and advise them about investment areas promoted by the LPDR. It would be unwise for the FIMC to provide a strong disincentive to investment by applying overly rigorous standards in scrutinizing company charters and joint venture regulations.

Under the Code, foreign investors must submit four documents to the FIMC: an application for a wholly foreign-owned enterprise or joint venture, a draft contract, draft rules and regulations for the enterprise, and an economic and technical analysis statement. The FIMC may require more documentation, and it has the power to designate fees for business authorization requests. The FIMC will consider the application and notify the parties no later than ninety days after submission. Once approved by the FIMC, investors must report the progress of their investment implementation activities within ninety days.

"Projects for which investment will be promoted ..." must meet five additional standards. First, projects must import advanced technology capable of processing products in a large quantity and of such quality as to possibly compete in the world market, but with the least resource depletion possible. Secondly, projects must develop infrastructure; and third, produce export merchandise or establish services earning mainly hard currencies and using domestic raw materials. Fourth, they should offer training of managers and technicians. Finally, projects must be those deemed especially important by the LPDR.

Contractual business consists of cooperation between foreign investors and either the state collective, state-private economic organizations, individuals, or private sector companies. The Decree defines contractual business as a mutual sharing of responsibilities for business purposes that results in commercial production without the creation of a joint venture bearing the juridical person status. To be valid, all contracts for business in Laos must obtain approval and licensing from the FIMC. Upon receiving a request for contractual business authorization, the FIMC must respond within thirty days.

Contracts must include: (1) the names of the parties to the agreement; (2) nationality; (3) address; (4) objectives of commercial production; (5) rights, interests, and obligations of the parties; (6) conditions for the transfer of interests and obligations; (7) terms of the agreement; (8) dispute resolution regulations; and (9) necessary "main programs," which include a listing of resources, products, and markets, as well as projected earnings in foreign currency and kip, the currency of Laos. A potential problem here is that although the Decree specifies that these necessary "main programs" be included in a contractual business arrangement, it does not issue complementary sanctions for non-adherence to them.

There is some evidence that contractual business can succeed under current conditions in Laos, due to the fact that many state collective enterprises that were operating at a loss have either been privatized, hence the term "state-private," or their managers have been given more autonomy in making business decisions. For instance, in Pakse, Laos' third largest city, a recently converted state enterprise, the Champassak Wood Processing Co., has increased its turnover from kip 95 million in 1985 to kip 266 million in 1988. The manager of Champassak attributes this increase to the company's conversion into an "autonomous enterprise" that allows him to find his own resources and pursue his own trade ties with Thailand.

Partners to a contractual agreement can either transfer their interests and obligations to or invest a third party. The provision allowing partners to invest for third parties is not clear, but it appears to allow partners to contractual agreements to act as an investment liaison. Such a provision could be viewed as meaningless since there are no prohibitions in the Code or Decree that would prevent someone from acting as an investment liaison in the first place.

However, upon closer inspection, this provision might allow third parties using partners to contractual agreements as investment conduits to bypass the FIMC's business authorization requirement, for there are no business authorization regulations governing such third party investors. It is highly unlikely that the LPDR intended this result, but the possibility indicates a need for a clarifying provision.

For transfers to succeed under the Code and Decree, transferrers must reach an agreement with their partners. The Decree mandates that transferees send the enterprise's regulations and the certificate of juridical and financial status to the FIMC. Here, again, the FIMC must approve the transfer in writing. Transfers are not valid unless so approved.

No requirement exists that parties seek FIMC approval for termination of a successfully completed contract before its stipulated termination date. However, if a contract's time term has expired and its terms have not been fully realized, and if the parties desire an extension, they must make a request to the FIMC. The parties must make the request at least one month before the agreement terminates, and the FIMC must then notify the investors of its decision within fifteen days from the receipt of such request.

However, parties might breach a contract by allowing it to expire with outstanding obligations remaining. The Decree anticipates this scenario, declaring that any claims "as mentioned in a lawsuit" are valid even after contract termination and that rights to pursue these claims also continue. The clause "as mentioned in a lawsuit" is vague. The context of the provision implies that claims from the contractual agreement remain valid.

Another reading of the clause requires that one look to Laotian law to ascertain the validity of any ensuing claims or liabilities arising out of contract termination. The better reading is the former. The LPDR provides that purely contractual agreements will be regulated by mutual agreement between the parties, whether they are foreign investors and the Lao business community or Laotians themselves. In light of this, the first reading reflects the full reign granted to contractual agreements by the Code and Decree.

In its request to the FIMC for authorization to conduct business in Laos, a joint venture must provide: 1) a request, signed by both partners; 2) a joint business agreement; 3) a financial, economic, and technical analysis; 4) information on each partner, company regulations, the juridical status of persons to the agreement, and the financial status of each partner; and 5) any other documents that the FIMC deems necessary.

The Decree requires that joint venture business agreements contain the name, nationality and address of parties; location; office; "sector" of commercial production; size of the venture as well as total capital to be invested; licensed capital; and capital as defined in the joint venture agreement. Additionally, agreements must include the percentage of shares, forms of shares, beginning and ending dates for capital contributions, conditions and regulations for the transfer of capital, and profit and loss sharing between partners to the joint venture.

Regarding "organic structure,"the agreement must comprise the number of members appointed by each partner to the management council, duties and rights of the management council, the chairman, the director, and the deputy director. Agreements must state principles of management regarding the venture's financing, accounting, statistics, control of its own accounting, and the percentage of shares attributed to the different funds within the enterprise.

An insurance license should also appear in a joint venture agreement, showing that the assets and property are insured with a reputable insurance company. There is no mention here of any requirement that a wholly foreign-owned enterprise also be duly insured. This suggests the government's emphasis is on protection of the Lao partner to the joint venture. The agreement must also delineate principles of labor management, salaries, and welfare and labor insurance. In addition, the life term of the joint venture, conditions to prolong and terminate it, and methods of paying accounts after the venture's termination must be included.

With respect to methods of resolving disagreements, the Decree states that agreements should contain dispute resolution regulations, which must indicate the language of choice if it is other than Lao. Within the agreement establishing the joint venture, the partners may consent to arbitration or submission of the dispute to any law enforcement body, or they may submit their dispute to the Council of Ministers, which is the economic arbitration body of the Lao government.

Lastly, agreements must declare their own validity as well as the validity of any ensuing addenda. After receipt of the required documentation requesting authorization for the establishment of a joint venture, the FIMC must respond within ninety days.

The Decree requires that joint venture produce documents to show that an agreement was reached as to technical and technological supplies for the venture. This requirement fails to specify which parties are required to come to an agreement on technological supplies. Since the requirement is one of "agreement" and not of "approval," it is possible to read the provision as exclusive of the FIMC.

However, the licensing requirement for importing technology that requires agreement to be reached between the donor and the recipient points to the conclusion that the FIMC is integral to the joint venture agreement on technological supplies. In fact, this provision in the joint venture context appears to be redundant.

Chapter 7

Process and Personalities

PERSONAL AMBITION

Tendering is not just a formalized process. People are involved too. And with people, come their personalities. The influence of key people can, and should, drive the whole process forward. Invariably, most people are working towards the best outcome possible; in their eyes. This creates a difficulty. What one person sees as a good way forward, another may consider to be disastrous.

Conflict between people can often be explained by the fact that any two individuals are driven by different circumstances. Sometimes the tension between individuals can be very creative and lead to excellent results. At other times, the tension just produces a negative atmosphere.

This offers an excellent example of negative management. Events and people combined to produce a harrowing result. No one could rise above the melee. Everything everyone did just made matters worse. There was no magnanimity. Unfortunately this type of experience has been all too common for those involved in CCT contracts. Sad, destructive, damaging, yet very real. People can get in the way.

Let's admit it, we all have our own agendas and career paths. We all seek opportunities to exploit new avenues, whether it be at work, at home, or perhaps in sport. All too often, however, we are not open with our hidden agendas. Thus the scene is set for conflict.

A major change like competitive tendering, or a new contract, presents endless opportunities for a wide range of people to exploit their own hidden agendas.

The case study in this chapter derives from a number of actual contract experiences. Because it is about a contract that went badly, and derives from a number of contracts, all names are fictitious. It is an amalgamation of stories given to the editor. For any reader who may take personal umbrage at the case study, please let it be understood that this case study is not about you or your work situation.

Everyone involved in contracts is bound to identify with the situations shown in this case study. The chapter is about real life CCT contract situations. It highlights how people work together to address external threats. Initially they all worked well. Their methods of preparing for the contract was a model to follow. It was only under pressure that everything fell apart.

The Tendering Set Up

Before CCT, the town of Workingham spent just over £1 million per year on maintaining all the parks, playing fields, open spaces and verges within the borough boundary. Fifty gardeners were employed. A few more were employed on a casual basis during the peak months of May and June. The population of the town was 100 000. There was a substantial industrial area in the town which provided about 50% of the jobs within the borough.

Perhaps because of the hard indoor manufacturing industry, the town's people took great pride in their parks and open spaces. The roundabouts always had very colourful, seasonal flower displays. The gardens were always well trimmed. To provide this service, the council employed four office-based staff. They were:

- John Saunders, parks manager;
- Anthea Turnbull, deputy parks manager;
- Andrew Staithe, technical assistant;
- Evelyn Hew, clerical assistant.

John had been with the council many years and was now in his 40s. He dealt with the councillors on policy issues, and day to day matters which involved their constituents. John always attended council committee meetings. He always made it known that he never took holiday between Easter and the beginning of August. Thus he was always present during the busy peak months. The council could, and did, rely on John to maintain standards.

Anthea was in her 20s, very keen to progress her career, and saw the council as a stepping stone. She resented the slow, yet sure, management style adopted by John. She was unaware that this very steady style was what councillors expected from John. That would have irritated her even more.

Andrew had only left college a year previously, and was still learning the ways of management. He designed all the flower beds. He arranged for plants to be grown in the municipal nursery each year. He also ensured that there was sufficient work during the winter months to keep the men outside employed and so improve the town at the same time. Evelyn was the clerical assistant who took all the bookings for the parks, and saw to all the time sheets and bonus sheets, invoices and all the other paperwork.

A Team Effort

They worked well together as a team. Realizing the implications of CCT, they purchased contract documents from the Institute of Leisure and Amenity Management, and set about tailoring them to their own requirements. John looked after all the conditions of contract, the tendering arrangements and formalities associated with the tender process. This involved him working in close liaison with the council's solicitor. Anthea adapted the specifications. She used her own experience, and enlisted the help of all the parks foremen. This not only involved the foremen in the CCT process, but also gave Anthea valuable local information. Andrew measured every single shrub bed and piece of grass in the borough with the help of out-side surveyors. Evelyn worked overtime to cope with all the extra typing. They thus adopted a classic division of labour:

- The manger looked after the overall process and the formalities;
- The technical specifications were prepared by the deputy;
- The technical assistant produced the bills of quantity.

Meanwhile, on the advice of the Chief Executive, the council formally agreed on a contractor and client division of responsibilities. The client side of the operation continued to report to the parks sub-committee. John, Andrew and Evelyn retained their jobs and titles, but they lost direct control of the labour force. This made John somewhat uneasy. He liked direct control.

Commercial Practices

As a matter of policy, the council appointed a direct service organization (DSO) board to oversee all contracts from a contractor's point of view. Anthea was appointed contracts manager (parks and grounds maintenance).

Anthea was very keen on her new job and set about it with vigour. She started by training the foreman and charge hands about commercial practices. She felt well placed to do this. Her father had been a grocer. She had therefore grown up with an inside knowledge of cash flow, and the need to make profit at the end of each working day and each working week. New paperwork systems were introduced which linked the rate of work exactly to the quantity of work. But it was uphill work with the foremen.

Yet Anthea was quite clear about the necessity for the new systems. It was absolutely essential to determine the actual costs incurred in undertaking the existing work. This would then allow accurate prices to be included within the tender in due course.

Competition

There was competition. The in-house team had to bid against three out-side contractors. One company was a Dutch company just commencing work in grounds maintenance contracts but with a long horticultural pedigree. The next company was a national grounds maintenance contractor who was getting bigger by the month. The third contractor was more regional, having commenced grounds maintenance contracts in a nearby town some ten years previously. All tenderers, including the DSO, were intent on winning.

The Tender Process

The tenderers kept the client officers busy. At the pre-tender meetings, all the tenderers asked many questions. Without Anthea now to help, John and Andrew had to work doubly hard to reply fully to all enquiries. They copied all replies to all the other tenderers. The many questions asked by the tenderers unsettled John to a certain extent. He began to feel a little unsure about the quality of his contract documents. He had nagging doubts that the specifications did not include everything.

On the day of the tender opening, four plain envelopes were received by the council before the closing time of noon. At a quarter past noon the Mayor opened all four envelopes. The Assistant Chief Executive logged all the prices tendered.

The DSO had submitted the lowest tender. John was relieved. With the DSO winning, he felt easy that the work would be carried out as in the past. However, he was concerned at the very low DSO tendered price.

Redundancies

Anthea was also pleased to learn that she had won the contract. In fact she was delighted. All the staff joined her in a small champagne celebration. Some had a beer. Everyone wanted to share in the success.

Anthea was quite satisfied with the low price. She had to be. After all, it was her price. She knew exactly what she was doing. She intended to reduce the number of casual staff employed during the summer. She was also relying on natural wastage to reduce the number of permanent staff. Nevertheless, in the two months between the tender opening and the start of the contract, Anthea made herself very unpopular. She asked the DSO board to agree to four early retirements. The board members thought that they should have been involved earlier. They resented being told after the event.

The contract commenced on the 1 January-an odd date to start a grounds maintenance in the northern hemisphere. However, that was the date which was stipulated in the Act of Parliament.

The first three months went well. Client, contractor and council were all satisfied. The financial year ended in March. Thus the contractor had a short three-month financial year. A profit of £15 000 was declared. Anthea was ecstatic. She threw a small party for all the staff after work on a Friday evening. John, now as client, was slightly peeved by this profit. He felt he had somehow been ripped off. Because the party was purely for contractor staff, he was not invited.

The next three months, up to July, were not so easy. They were the peak months of maintenance. It was also a very wet spring that year. The grass grew quick and lush. With reduced staff, it was proving difficult to meet all targets. Grass was not cut as often. It grew ever longer. Of more concern to Anthea, however, was the fact that the working teams continued in their old ways. They did the work they had always done. They did not work according to the contract documents. They carried out some work for which the contractor would never receive payment. Instead of waiting for a variation order, the teams would carry out the work as in the old days.

Non-Performance

Meanwhile, John was getting complaints about the grass not being cut. Large swathes of grass were being left behind.

This was because the grass had been left to grow too long before cutting. Children were making haystacks out of this grass. Worse, they were then tramping clumps of long, wet grass it into their homes. Complaints increased. In his time-honoured fashion, John spoke kindly to Anthea about the difficulties and the need to improve.

Defaults in Theory

Anthea tried cutting the bonus payments to force everyone to work according to the contract. The unions complained. Councillors got involved. At the same time councillors were receiving complaints from residents about lack of performance. They then complained to both Anthea and John. The mayor demanded action. John realized he would have to use the default system provided for within the contract. He looked up the documents.

The Default Clause Stated

Where works have not been carried out according to the contract documents, a rectification notice will be issued to the contractor. The contractor will be required by the rectification notice, to rectify the defect or deficiency within 48 hours. Failure to do so will leave the contractor liable to the issue of a default notice. If the works subject to a default notice are not undertaken to the entire satisfaction of the supervising officer within five working days, then the supervising officer will be at liberty to employ another contractor at the expense of the first contractor to undertake the works. Furthermore, the accumulation of twenty-five default points in any one month period, will lead to the termination of the contract.

John reread the paragraph. It seemed quite clear. It also seemed relatively easy to action. He then thought of the hundreds of bits of grass around the borough which may or may not have been cut according to the contract documents. It would be quite legitimate to issue twenty-five rectification notices tomorrow. He pondered on the issue overnight.

He had to be seen taking decisive action. The councillors expected nothing less. Furthermore, he was annoyed. When he was in charge, this poor state of affairs would never have happened. Yet, he wanted to be fair. So, next day, he served five rectification notices.

Defaults in Practice

Anthea was inflamed. She maintained that the service delivery was little worse than in previous years. The work programme had only slipped by three weeks. It was just unfortunate that it was a wet spring. Moreover, the grass cutting was being carried out much more cheaply than previously. In addition, she felt bitter. After all, it was the contractor who had to do all the work. John and his colleagues could sit in the office.

Anthea went to see John immediately. There was a very bitter dispute. Evelyn left for an early lunch. She could not stand the upset. Andrew was not in the office. He thus did not know of this row until later in the day.

On that morning, Andrew was visiting sites where grass had not been cut according to the contract. He also had being reading the default procedures. As the technical assistant now, he felt that it was his job to maintain standards on behalf of the residents of the town. Just before lunch, at the same time that Anthea and John were having their set to, Andrew called into the grounds maintenance depot and issued his first five rectification notices.

John cancelled the notices after Anthea's remonstrations. John also rebuked Andrew. In future, Andrew was to report to John before issuing defaults. He told Andrew that the issue of defaults was confrontational. That was not his management style.

Although Andrew learnt from Evelyn about the row, he did not know what the row had been about. In view of his humiliating rebuke, he did not care to ask anyone.

Resentment

Tempers cooled over the following weeks. Work output improved. Anthea, shaken by events, took on more casual staff.

By the autumn the contract was working relatively smoothly. There was now, however, an underlying resentment between the client and the contractor. The formal monthly meetings between the client and contractor were packed with everybody watching everybody else. Instead of there just being Anthea and John at the meetings there were more than half a dozen people. Andrew now attended, and Evelyn took minutes. The senior supervisors from Anthea's team attended. They were all making sure that no one was making a move which would be detrimental to their own interests.

By December, Anthea was just about breaking even. She threw a small party for her own staff. She did not invite the client officers to the party. They joked about contractors inviting the client out to slap up Christmas dinners. Anthea did not even rise to the bait. She still had a further three months of this financial year to try and turn in a profit.

Bureaucracy

In January, a council policy decision infuriated Anthea. Due to cash limitations imposed by central government, the council was put into a financial straightjacket. The council responded by placing a freeze on all vacancies and all uncommitted expenditure. No posts were filled. No new machines were purchased.

But Anthea had allowed many vacancies to accrue to save cash. She intended to advertise in January and appoint in February and thus have a full complement of staff. This would allow her to complete the winter schedule of work and make a flying start into the new grass-cutting season which started in March.

Anthea complained that this new policy was not fair. This would not happen to a private contractor. How could she manage a contract if she did not have the resources? Her complaints got her nowhere. The freeze remained.

It was a warm, wet spring that year. By April it was not possible to maintain the grass and grounds to the stated frequencies. The work was not being undertaken due to the freeze on staff. Complaints flowed. John still tried to hold the line. He refrained from issuing rectification notices.

Annual DSO Profits

Then, in early May, Anthea announced the provisional trading results for her first full financial year. To everybody's amazement it showed a £50 000 profit. John was aghast. Here was a contractor making a profit out of a service which that contractor manifestly was failing to deliver. His attitude hardened.

The simple truth was, however, that the large profit was due entirely to the freeze on recruitment in the last two months of the financial year, and the lack of expenditure on new machines.

Matters got much worse, as spring turned into early, warm, wet summer. Without sufficient staff and no new machinery, it was impossible to cut the grass frequently enough. Anthea concentrated her staff on the high profile sports facilities like the bowling greens and the cricket wickets. General grass cutting was abandoned to a much reduced cutting frequency As more staff left, Anthea gave up any pretence of keeping to any schedule.

Control Mechanisms

Meanwhile John was preparing his explanations for the external auditor. He knew that there was to be a special study this year on the first year's CCT contracts. With the profit which the contractor had accrued, and the known inadequate delivery, John felt very unsure of his approach to the external auditor.

And now, the contractor was not performing. John had no alternative. He used the default procedure. First he issued rectification notices. The contractor could not, and did not, rectify the deficiencies. Default notices followed. Then alternative contractors were employed to do some of the work. The work undertaken by this new contractor eased the pressure on the in-house contractor.

Punitive defaults

Regrettably, due to a lack of communication, the second contractor sometimes doubled up on works undertaken by the in-house contractor. A piece of grass would be cut twice within one week, where the specification required it to be cut once in two weeks. Local residents who had complained that their grass had not been cut in weeks, found their grass cut in the morning by one contractor and in the afternoon by another contractor.

Not only did this infuriate Anthea, but to rub salt into the wound, the in-house contractor had to pay for all the other contractors. The cost was punitive. John thought that Anthea could afford it. More important he believed that she should pay. It was her fault. But the use of outside contractors clearly hurt both parties. Anthea and her team lost financially. John lost credibility due to the lack of control over the two sets of contractors.

Weekly, there were blazing rows between Anthea and John. But John continued playing it entirely according to the book. Rectification notices were issued, followed by default notices, followed by bringing other contractors in to do the works. The number of complaints mushroomed. He spent at least half his week just responding to residents' complaints attempting to get works done.

Personal injury

Not only was John maddened by all the difficulties, he was also deeply upset. Everything he had held important in his working life, was being trampled underfoot. He was working 70 to 80 hours every week. Yet he remained appalled by the mess which lay around him. His pride in his career was in tatters. By August, John was off work on sick leave suffering from stress. At the same time, Anthea's accounts were radically in the red. Residents were totally dissatisfied with the service, and councillors were continually criticizing. And yet, council policy in relation to the freeze on posts remained.

Anthea summarized the principal difficulties in a candid report to the Direct Services Management Board:

- The in-house contractor was still considered part of a local government set-up.
- There was no autonomy.
- The contractor was bound up in red tape.
- There was no chance to act commercially.
- The staff freeze had led directly to standards of work not being maintained.
- It was ludicrous to employ outside contractors when in-house contractor could do the work more cheaply.
- There was an essential need for the in-house contractor to be treated like a private contractor.

The direct services management board took umbrage at the tone of the report. They considered that they were running the contract, not Anthea. Furthermore, they had to take account of all the government's many requirements. Grounds maintenance was only a small part of a larger picture.

Anthea, now defeated, gave in and let the inevitable happen.

At the end of that financial year the grounds maintenance contract declared a substantial financial deficit. There was a possibility of the DSO being closed down after being audited by the government. The full financial impact of the client's actions only now became totally apparent for all to see. Councillors on both the DSO board and the client parks subcommittee were appalled by the actions of John and Anthea. The councillors saw the rows and lack of cooperation. The absurdity of the financial situation was hidden by the constant smoke from the client and contractor officers. 'A curse on both your houses' was the view of the councillors. They only had one course of action open to them.

A consultant was employed to check through the mess. First the consultant was require to assess the financial consequences of the actions of the client and whether these actions had been justified. The consultant was also asked to verify if all works performed by Anthea had been paid for. Some works had been clearly undertaken by the DSO team which had not been specified.

If the works were required to maintain previous standards (the stated aim of the contract), then additional payments were justified to the contractor. The consultants and the council's Finance Department became closely involved with the contract that second summer. There was no other option. There had been some dramatic staff changes. John retired early on grounds of ill health. Anthea moved to the private sector. She became the contract manager for three nearby towns. Andrew was placed in Anthea's position. He rapidly changed his tune.

Managing specifications

All contracts change as they grow and mature. Childhood is similar. Growing up is all about adapting to constant physical and mental change, and in an ever-changing environment. So it is with contracts. For success, changes and alterations to a contract need to be accommodated easily and smoothly.

To a certain extent, change can be easily accommodated in a maintenance contract by issuing variation orders. These are quite literally an order to vary the works being undertaken. For example, following residents' requests, a variation order may be issued to cut the grass more frequently in one area of the town. In a grounds maintenance contract, there is an endless stream of variation orders. The contract needs to be varied to take account of the ever-changing growth patterns of nature.

In this chapter, we examine the growth and change of contracts. The development of sports is the example chosen to illustrate the key issues. By looking at sports, we also see the interactions within a management contract.

A management contract is different from a maintenance contract. For example, if casual swimming is reducing in popularity over the years, perhaps increased fun sessions are needed. But is the reduction in popularity due to the inefficiency of the contractor, or some national pattern? Managing a leisure centre, sports hall, swimming pool and the like requires careful and constant assessment of customer requirements. People's use of leisure time changes continually. Each year brings its own particular fashion or craze. This affects the environment in which the contract is operating, and in turn affects both client and contractor.

There is too, the need everywhere to develop and promote sport and the benefits of physical activity. As we all know, activity makes the heart grow stronger. In a contract situation, both client and contractor need to agree the change.

The theory

For a leisure centre or sports hall; development of sports is a key requirement. A structured approach to the development of sport:

- Helps the customer;
- Increases attendance;
- Increases income.

More importantly, a proper approach to sports development obviously fulfils the purpose of providing the sports hall in the first place. Central to the process of sports development is the belief that everyone should have the opportunity to reach their potential, with the only constraints being their interest and ability. This means ensuring that sporting opportunities exist for everybody, regardless of age, gender, ethnicity or ability.

Within CCT, local authorities were allowed to keep sports development on the client side of the authority. Simultaneously with the introduction of CCT, many authorities were undergoing spending cuts. Not only does this chapter highlight sports development, it also provides a graphic example of the division between:

- The client, or purchaser;
- The contractor, or provider.

This division of responsibility is the basis of all contracts. There is a further interplay in respect of sports development. Developing interest in a sport is hard work. Initially there may be few participants. However, the pump-priming nature of sports development will (if successful, which most programmes are) lead to increased use. And of course, increased income. Therefore a sports session of no particular interest to the contractor initially may later become of key financial interest.

So given these many varying aspects of sports development, given the pressures of producing CCT specifications and tenders, and given the sheer gamesmanship employed in the whole process, the scene is set for widely differing interpretations and applications of sports development.

In this first part of the chapter, Geoff Nichols surveys the methods adopted for the introduction of sports development within a CCT environment. He has made specific studies on the impact of CCT on sports development within leisure contracts.

There follows an example of good practice. The case study relates to the implementation of a sports development specification into a leisure management contract at East Hampshire District Council in southern England. Example specifications, the method of pricing, and the tendering background is given. The tendering environment or backcloth is all important in determining the nature of each and every contract.

Building Sports Development into CCT

The following account of the methods by which the needs of sports development have been built into CCT is based on the experiences of 12 leisure departments. All employ sports development officers. It shows the strengths and weaknesses of the two major approaches and draws conclusions for the next round of contracting. Client-side initiatives for new sports sessions are most likely to come from the sports development sections. Through these the client side was able to develop the service and achieve flexibility within the constraints of a contract.

However, the lessons learnt from the first wave of tendering are also relevant to authorities with no specialist sports development officers (SDOs) in which new initiatives will have to come directly from the client officer. The needs of sports development had to be adequately protected in the contract specification in the event of the contract being won by either the DSO or a private company. In doing this a balance had to be struck between protecting existing sessions and allowing for flexibility. There was a need to protect existing and potential sessions that contributed to all stages of the sports development continuum. The sports development continuum moves:

- from foundation;
- to participation;
- to performance;
- and then excellence.

There was also a need to ensure sports development could offer a flexible service. The key problems, as perceived by one SDO, were:

- How do you put a philosophy into a specification?
- The emphasis of our work changes all the time.

In other words, sports development has certain objectives to meet. The best way of meeting them will continually change over the period of the contract.

Preparing for CCT

The degree of involvement of client sports development sections in the preparation for CCT varied. It was difficult in authorities where the sports development section had only recently been established. Here, the political profile of the sports development section within the department was low. So, too, was the section's contribution to contract preparation.

Involvement was also made difficult by the haste with which some of the first contracts were prepared.

In some authorities complacency and inexperience were also contributing factors. Some authorities were concerned not to let commercially sensitive information escape to potential bidders. Here preparations for tendering were conducted in relative secrecy by a few officers. In these instances involvement of the sports development team might only occur near the end of preparations for contracting. By then, there was little opportunity for them to make a significant contribution. The sports development sections were more likely to be consulted if they were large and well established, had a strong political profile in the department, and if the client and chief officer were supportive.

Different Approaches

There were two major ways of meeting the needs of sports development within CCT. First, the required sports sessions could be specified in detail by the client at the outset of tendering. Thus the contractor would be then required to deliver. Second, a client sports section could be given a budget with which to buy its way into facilities. There are strengths and weaknesses of both approaches and the most satisfactory contracts involved a combination of both.

A comprehensive specification of sports sessions was usually based on what was being done before CCT. A thorough specification would include details of the:

- time;
- venue;
- facilities;
- payment arrangements.

It would include a clear specification of responsibilities between client and contractor including details such as who was responsible for collecting charges, for promotion and for providing instruction.

In practice the thoroughness of the specification varied. There were bound to be considerable lessons learnt from this first experience of contracting. And there were. For example, the Sports Council found that most contracts did not specify the minimum number of people that should be attending certain sports sessions. They argue that you might specify that sessions should be put on but unless this is supported by specifications of target attendances there is no guarantee the client will achieve what it wants.

And what is wanted is ever-increasing participation in sports and physical activity by an increasing proportion of the population. Increased use by young, fit people is only a small part of the picture. An increase in physical activity, whatever the nature of the activity, is beneficial to the large majority of the population.

However, the first round of contracting revealed that a lot of authorities did not have detailed information about their users. The Sports Council's National Information Survey specifically identified this lack of information which local authorities had about their users. This meant that tightly specified targets for use might be unrealistic in the first round of contracting but that it might be possible to build them in next time.

Client officers felt that a thorough specification was a strength. A thorough specification was more likely to protect the service if the contract was won by a private contractor. This depends on the extent to which the objectives of the contractor, whether the DSO or a private company, differ from those of the client. This will be discussed later, but the conflict of objectives was not as great as was perceived before CCT.

A separate client budget...

The second method was to allocate the sports development team a budget within the client section with which to negotiate use of facilities.

This gave the sports development teams a great deal of flexibility. Individual arrangements could be negotiated with facility managers for different types of session. For example, if a session was being set up that was likely to become a regular part of a facility programme and contribute to the facility's income the costs of setting it up might be shared between the sports development team and the contractor. The sports development team would not pay for the facility, but the centre manager would keep the income.

If a session was being introduced to fill a particular gap in the sports development continuum, for example a specialist coaching course, then this might not be expected to contribute to the facility's income.

In these cases, the sports development team might negotiate a hire charge for the facility, meet the cost of putting on the session and keep any income.

If a session was to become a regular part of the facility's programme it was important that the facility manager was fully involved in its planning because he or she would be the person who would be responsible for it in the long term. In this case the facility manager would want to agree a price for participants that would at least match the revenue that might be obtained from alternative programming.

On the other hand, if the sports development team was hiring the facility and keeping the income they would set the prices. For one-off special events, for example a summer coaching scheme, the sports development team and contractor would plan the event together, sharing costs and sharing the income. The range of permutations of sharing costs and income was a practical way of dealing with the varied needs of sports development work.

While the flexibility of this approach was its major strength it required each new session to be negotiated individually between SDO and facility manager. It required a sports development's budget to be adequate to allow it to provide the required service. It also stressed the importance of a good working relationship between SDOs and facility managers.

A Mixture of Both

Naturally there is a third way. Some contracts used a combination of both approaches and this was a good way of balancing the need to protect existing sessions and allowing for development.

A basic specification of regular sessions would be combined with a variation budget that enabled the sports development team to negotiate access to facilities. Some contracts used aspects of one approach or the other but did not adequately develop the specification to protect the interests of sports development. For example, some contracts specified times and venues for sessions but left the price paid by participants to be negotiated.

In some cases there was an imprecise attempt to specify prices. For example, one authority specified that rates should be 'at a price that is not prohibitive to disadvantaged groups'. In practice the greatest difficulty the SDO had was in negotiating a price he felt was acceptable to the people in his target groups. Because sports development is continually starting new and different sports sessions, it was difficult to specify all prices in the contract. In some cases the sessions might fall within general categories for which prices had been specified in the contract. Often this was not the case, and a price had to be negotiated.

If this was so client officers could still influence prices if they wished by stipulating in the contract that prices of any new sessions should be agreed by them. The most inadequate contracts were those where the requirements of sports development had not been built into the specification or those where a private sector bid winning the contract had exposed how poorly it had protected sports development needs.

Conflicting Interests

Even in the most comprehensive of contracts the major sources of difficulty were where the interests of client and contractor conflicted. However, there were also many instances where they converged, although these were not always fully exploited.

Within CCT the contractor is now primarily concerned with his financial performance. As one client officer described his DSO manager:

- His attitude has changed completely...
- His idealism has gone out of the window...
- He is now looking for pounds and pence.

The conflict of interests in sports development is most apparent when the SDO is trying to establish new sessions at peak times. The contractor is interested in the opportunity cost, the revenue that he loses as a consequence of accommodating the new sports development session. This has made it virtually impossible for sports development sections to introduce sessions using facilities at times of peak demand, such as weekday evenings. At these times the facilities can be filled by the contractor much more profitably. Examples include keep fit sessions and five-a-side football.

If sports development use of these facilities at these peak times has not been specified in the contract it will not be possible to negotiate access because it will be too expensive to compensate the facility manager for the loss in revenue.

One SDO reported, 'we don't even try to book the centre on Wednesday nights as it is full of aerobics classes'.

This has been a problem for sessions towards the top end of the sports development continuum that require specialist facilities. These sessions may use voluntary instructors who work in the day. Thus evening sessions are the only time that they have available for coaching. The essential need for evening use of a facility is intensified when, say, the course is aimed at school-age participants. National coaching foundation courses have been adversely affected in this way

Another example was a proposed swimming session for Asian women, which would have required exclusive use of the pool. This would either have required existing users to be excluded, with the consequent loss of income, or that the pool be opened at an additional time, with the extra costs this involved.

A further area of conflict has been over pricing. This is especially true of sessions which have not been tightly specified and are a matter for negotiation between SDO and facility manager. The facility manager will be keeping the income from the session. Here a sports development objective of equality of access for all income groups could conflict with a facility manager's objective of profit maximization. A sports development officer reported that there had been some drop out from his sessions in which he had to raise prices after negotiation with facility managers.

In general there is no strong evidence to show that prices for local authority leisure facilities represent a significant barrier to participation. However, this may be more important to low income groups who are frequently the target of sports development activities.

Converging Interests

On the other hand there are many instances where the objectives of sports development and facility managers converge. The most significant of these is where a sports development session will raise extra income for a facility by encouraging use at a time of slack demand.

Some sports development officers reported that before CCT the facility manager regarded an approach from the sports development team as more hassle. Now they regarded it as extra income. Therefore the managers were much more enthusiastic about becoming involved. In an authority where an SDO had only been appointed after the introduction of CCT the facility managers primarily saw him as a way of marketing their centres, and approached him to do so. This may be completely compatible with sports development objectives.

In Sheffield the sports development promotion of diving and tennis programmes brings in considerable income to the related specialist facilities. The participants in these activities can afford to pay a price that is compatible with the facility managers' objectives.

There were other ways in which the interests of sports development and facility managers converge, although these were not always recognized in practice. Extra income could be gained from catering and other aspects of secondary spending. New users of the facility would increase its profile in the local area and possibly lead to additional use at other times.

For example, in one authority the sports development team had introduced an ante-natal swimming session in a pool. This did not contribute to the manager's costs. The pool was already open and staffed. It did, however, introduce new people to the facility. Specific sports development sessions could lead to extra income through sponsorship. In one authority events for disabled participants and a drugs awareness day were financed by sponsorship. These events could also enhance the facility's image.

Sometimes facility managers seemed unwilling to be swayed by consideration of these extra benefits. Sometimes sports development officers did not emphasize them sufficiently in negotiations. In the first round of contracting the potential conflicts between client and contractor were often overemphasized. The convergence of interests was often not fully recognized.

Social Objectives

The degree to which the authority has social objectives of leisure provision that conflict with those of a market-led service will vary with political control. In one authority the social policy objectives were limited to promoting use of its facilities by the rural population. A sports development officer was appointed to thus promote the use of facilities. He had a budget to subsidize the travel costs of rural participants.

However, there was no subsidy for other sports development sessions that he set up. At these sessions participants paid a rate negotiated between the SDO and the facility manager. The contract made no reference to this. On the other hand an authority with broader social objectives did tightly specify sessions for particular target groups. This prevented the facility managers from developing more commercially oriented sessions.

Where a leisure department had experienced financial cuts during the course of the contract these might affect sports development directly and indirectly.

If sports development budgets were cut, there would be less money to buy into facility time. In this case a sports development unit with a large proportion of its facility usage built into the specification was less exposed than one that relied on negotiation and paying for the bulk of its time on an *ad hoc* basis. An indirect impact of financial constraint was that if facility managers were under greater financial pressure they might attempt to charge more for the use of their facilities and ask for higher prices from customers.

For example, two of the SDOs interviewed said that negotiations with facility managers were harder when the managers had been given tighter financial targets.

Financial constraint has encouraged facility managers to be more active in exploring market opportunities and this means that the opportunity cost of giving up time to a sports development session might be perceived as greater. For example, a sports centre which formerly had spare capacity in the morning might now have it filled with aerobics classes. Thus whereas before a sports development session would have meant extra revenue, now it would displace more lucrative use.

On the other hand, where sports development sessions would increase revenue, financial constraint would encourage the facility managers to cooperate to develop them. Thus there is greater impetus to set up sessions that the facility manager can take charge of once they are established. This has improved the work of SDOs to the extent that they are now more prepared to leave an established session and move on to set up a new one.

As a consequence of financial constraints some sports development units have altered their programmes to include some that raise extra revenue. For example, some authorities have exploited the growing market for children's swimming lessons as the implications of local management of schools reduces the amount of swimming offered in schools.

Some sports development sections have now targeted sessions at more wealthy areas of the community to generate income. This need not necessarily conflict with sports development objectives. In response to higher charges from leisure centres some sports development sections have moved programmes to where they can hire cheaper facilities, such as schools. This may enhance their work through networking with other organizations.

Thus the impact of financial constraint has not always been negative. Sometimes it has encouraged positive changes in sports development work. The impact has been less on sports development sections who rely least on use of leisure centres. These sections have been least affected by CCT.

The preparations for CCT in many authorities have strained the relationships between the client side and the DSO. The DSO may have had to accept changed conditions of service or job losses to become competitive. They have resented the loss of job security, especially compared to the client. Sports development, in the large majority of authorities, has been retained on the client side. Thus where there have been poor relations between client and contractor these have impeded sports development officers' ability to negotiate with facility managers. In one such authority the SDO summed up the relationship as 'one of mistrust'.

The problem is greatest in authorities where preparations for CCT have left the most antagonistic relationships. These have been in authorities where the approach to CCT could be described as extremely reluctant compliance rather than in those that had taken a positive approach. The clear conflict of interests and the need to negotiate individual sessions has put greater emphasis on the need to establish good working relationships.

'Ease of booking depends on the working relationship with that particular duty manager or officer', said one SDO. 'We don't use the spec. We depend more on our working relationship', he explained.

Several steps need to be taken by sports development officers in preparing for the next round of contracting.

1. They should get involved in preparing for the next round of contracting at the earliest stage possible to ensure that their interests are represented.
2. The present arrangements for building the needs of sports development into the contract should be reviewed, especially to identify areas where sports development needs are not adequately met.
3. If the needs of sports development are inadequately met because there is a conflict of objectives with the contractor, then the sports development team should calculate how much revenue the contractor would lose if the contract was altered.

   For example, if the sports development team wanted access to a facility at a peak time how much revenue would the contractor lose from the displacement of existing sessions? This would be the amount by which the management fee would have to be increased if the sports development session was tightly specified. Alternatively, it would equal the amount that the sports development team's budget would have to be increased to enable them to buy into the use of the facility.

   In either case the cost of meeting a sports development objective is now defined in terms of the sacrifice to the contractor's objective of profit maximization. This is the 'opportunity cost' of putting on the sports development session.

4. Having calculated the cost of meeting the social objectives of sports development that conflict with market-led objectives of the contractor, the sports development team should then work out if there is a cheaper way of achieving the same objective.

   For example, could a session be run at an alternative facility, such as a school? Could sponsorship be found to compensate the facility manager for loss of income? Sports development should also go back to its objectives and decide exactly how important this one is in relation to the cost of achieving it.

   Another example is where a sports development section was considering putting on an archery session at a leisure facility on a weekend morning. This was part of a strategy to develop certain focus sports. This would have displaced activities that would generate more revenue. The sports development team had to ask themselves whether this session was the best way of achieving their objectives. Furthermore, if it was, were these objectives worth it?

5. The sports development team should then decide the best combination of specified sessions and variation budget to meet their objectives. This will vary in each instance. Whichever methods are chosen they need to be justified with reference to the sports development team objectives. This is especially important when these conflict with market-led objectives and the cost of achieving them has been identified. This means that the sports development team is clear about:
   - What it wants out of the contract.
   - Why it wants it.
   - How it wants to achieve it.

6. Whichever method of specification is selected it needs to be detailed enough to ensure that the agreed objectives of sports development will be met whoever wins the contract. Again, this is most import ant in

areas where social and market-led objectives conflict. Several DSOs expressed reservations about how well their interests would have been protected if a private company had won the contract. At present they relied partly on the goodwill of DSO managers and the support of senior officers.

7. In negotiating with the client officer for the new contract arrangements the sports development unit will need to respect the contractor's position and be prepared to compromise. The sports development team should be clear about where the areas of perceived conflict are and consider jointly ways of reconciling them. They should also stress, wherever relevant, the benefits to the contractor through increased income, sponsorship and enhanced public profile.
8. Whatever is specified in the contract there will need to be subsequent negotiations with the contractor. These may be to alter specified sessions or to negotiate access for new ones. The relationship with the contractor and individual facility managers will be very important. The process of preparing for the next round of contracting should be handled in a way that minimizes the inevitable tension between client and contractor and lays the foundation for a good working relationship in the future.

Both of the major ways of incorporating sports development into the contract have their advantages.

- A tight specification of sports development sessions will protect them best where there is a conflict with market forces. Also sports development may be less vulnerable to financial cuts during the period of the contract. Even within a tight contract anything can be renegotiated. However, the time and effort of doing this will still reduce the sports development team's flexibility.

- On the other hand a system that relies on individual negotiations for sessions, supported by a variation budget, is the most flexible. This system will allow sports development to shift resources around different facilities.

A key influence on deciding the approach to specifying the needs of sports development is the degree to which the objectives of sports development and facility managers conflict. This will reflect the degree to which the authority has social objectives of provision that conflict with a market-led service. While the conflicts do exist and need to be addressed, there are many areas in which the interests of sports development and contractors converge.

One SDO pointed out that by focusing on the conflicts, 'there is a real danger that due to CCT, sports development can be seen as just a welfare service. This is not so as it covers a wide range of levels and types of activity.'

Index

A

Absolute 119, 211, 253

Accessibility 147, 181

Adoption 49, 132

Advertising 33, 52, 53, 213

Airline 85, 108

Alternatives 53, 59, 228

Analysis 8, 11, 13, 15, 43, 58, 59, 66, 68, 71, 80, 82, 83, 88, 89, 96, 98, 99, 114, 123, 124, 126, 128, 133, 140, 149, 185, 216, 230, 239, 240, 245, 248

Associations 78, 191, 193

Attacks 134

Attitudes 7, 87, 97, 100, 192

Average 15, 22, 28, 31, 32, 35, 36, 37, 38, 39, 40, 41, 42, 43, 48, 65, 72, 73, 85, 107, 146, 150, 153, 155, 164, 167, 177, 178, 179, 181, 184, 185, 191

B

Benefits 1, 46, 47, 50, 52, 55, 56, 74, 77, 88, 109, 139, 141, 148, 149, 150, 151, 165, 168, 180, 184, 185, 187, 217, 227, 234, 263, 272

Brand 39, 46

Budget 28, 266, 268, 269, 273, 276

Business 2, 4, 28, 34, 35, 37, 39, 41, 42, 45, 50, 104, 107, 108, 109, 111, 186, 187, 188, 189, 192, 217, 219, 223, 230, 237, 238, 241, 244, 245, 246, 247, 248

C

Communication 49, 104, 131, 260

Comparative 31, 89, 93, 94, 95, 96, 97, 98, 100

Competition 44, 45, 55, 56, 57, 64, 65, 72, 73, 74, 143, 220, 242, 254

Complaints 101, 145, 164, 255, 256, 258, 260

Components 43, 44, 45, 46, 48, 50, 51, 53, 54, 55, 56, 59, 60, 61, 62, 63, 65, 68, 69, 71, 73, 74, 75, 76, 77, 78, 79, 80, 82, 119, 240

Convention 38, 197, 113, 130

Criteria 170, 224, 225, 229, 236

D

Decline 32, 33, 34, 38, 40, 42, 43, 196, 212

Defensive 101, 228, 235

Defined 7, 45, 58, 61, 65, 66, 101, 116, 125, 126, 136, 147, 158, 178, 183, 248, 276

Delivery 192, 257, 259

Demand 35, 38, 39, 41, 42, 66, 82, 84, 85, 86, 107, 108, 109, 111, 113, 115, 132, 242, 270, 271

Diffusion 63

Discretionary 219, 222, 223, 236

Distribution 11, 18, 44, 74, 92, 151, 152, 158, 160, 163, 171, 172, 174, 180, 238

Diversification 225

E

Economic 2, 3, 6, 9, 26, 27, 47, 53, 79, 86, 87, 107, 141, 144, 145, 146, 148, 149, 150, 151, 152, 153, 154, 156, 161, 163, 164, 168, 170, 171, 172, 174, 175, 179, 180, 181, 182, 190, 215, 216, 217, 218, 223, 224, 225, 226, 229, 232, 235, 236, 237, 242, 243, 245, 248, 249

Effective 16, 33, 54, 98, 99, 100, 107, 120, 218, 227

Electronic 102, 201, 208, 228

Employees 3, 4, 5, 6, 7, 8, 10, 11, 12, 13, 14, 15, 16, 17, 18, 19, 20, 21, 22, 25, 26, 30, 87, 88, 90, 91, 92, 93, 94, 95, 96, 97, 98, 99, 100, 101, 104, 107, 150, 185, 190, 192, 240

Empty 202, 205

Entertainment 194, 208, 212, 241

Equipment 49, 52, 191, 221, 227, 228, 240

Evaluating 14, 101

Exclusive 66, 249, 271

F

Feedback 99

Financial 28, 49, 84, 183, 232, 235, 247, 248, 255, 258, 259, 261, 262, 264, 270, 273, 274

Focus 43, 57, 74, 132, 135, 139, 186, 193, 206, 227, 276

Franchising 46, 47

Frequency 12, 15, 60, 155, 180, 259

Functions 105, 196, 203

G

Goals 228, 229, 232, 235

Government 2, 30, 41, 42, 47, 86, 108, 198, 226, 232, 234, 240, 241, 242, 243, 249, 258, 261

Growth 18, 26, 27, 36, 38, 39, 40, 41, 42, 43, 46, 57, 60, 66, 78, 84, 107, 108, 186, 216, 227, 232, 235, 236, 237, 262

H

Hospitality 1, 8, 11, 13, 14, 15, 19, 45, 46, 47, 54, 77, 78, 79, 85, 107, 122, 183, 185, 186, 187, 188, 189, 190, 191, 192, 200

Human Resources 85, 184

I

Image 112, 148, 168, 197, 207, 212, 272

Implication 4, 68, 207

Independent 1, 4, 14, 36, 37, 44, 45, 47, 48, 50, 51, 52, 53, 54, 55, 56, 60, 64, 66, 67, 70, 71, 72, 73, 76, 77, 78, 79, 80, 82, 96, 138, 149

Industry 1, 10, 12, 18, 36, 38, 40, 42, 43, 44, 45, 46, 47, 48, 49, 54, 57, 58, 60, 64, 65, 66, 73, 74, 77, 78, 81, 82, 85, 99, 107, 108, 109, 183, 184, 185, 186, 187, 138, 189, 190, 191, 201, 207, 212, 225, 227, 228, 237, 241, 251

Intensive 201

Introduction 30, 107, 263, 264, 272

J

Justice 87, 88, 89, 90, 91, 92, 93, 94, 95, 96, 97, 98, 99, 100, 134

K

Knowledge 43, 47, 48, 49, 50, 53, 55, 60, 61, 62, 68, 74, 75, 76, 81, 87, 88, 106, 155, 159, 187, 201, 238, 253

L

Leadership 113, 130, 188

Limitations 168, 218, 258

Loyalty 33

M

Managers 2, 3, 4, 5, 6, 7, 8, 10, 13, 22, 31, 46, 49, 50, 54, 76, 79, 80, 87, 88, 89, 91, 92, 94, 95, 96, 97, 98, 99, 100, 103, 149, 163, 166, 169, 176,

182, 183, 188, 190, 238, 245, 246, 268, 269, 271, 272, 273, 274, 275

Marketing 33, 44, 46, 59, 170, 199, 227, 272

Meeting 101, 232, 235, 265, 266, 276

Motives 233

N

Negotiation 224, 271, 273

Networks 138, 153, 154, 156, 158, 160, 161, 179, 180

Neutral 7, 10, 112, 193

Newspaper 43, 101, 199

O

Objectives 85, 191, 245, 265, 267, 271, 272, 273, 274, 275, 276

Operations 39, 58, 76, 78, 87, 109, 188, 190, 220, 233, 244

Opinion 78, 79, 84, 136, 165, 232

Organizational 3, 43, 45, 48, 51, 55, 57, 61, 67, 78, 80, 81, 82, 87, 188, 200

P

Package 185

Patterns 1, 16, 49, 155, 164, 262

Perceptions 112, 114, 117, 138, 180, 216, 230

Performance 3, 7, 28, 29, 30, 38, 39, 43, 51, 54, 85, 87, 89, 91, 93, 94, 95, 96, 97, 98, 100, 256, 265, 270

Peripheral 121, 140

Planning 84, 220, 268

Population 40, 45, 51, 56, 80, 81, 82, 141, 142, 143, 145, 171, 175, 188, 191, 201, 251, 267, 273

Pricing 229, 264, 271

Probability 7, 14

Products 51, 55, 221, 222, 227, 238, 242, 245, 246

Promotions 33

Property 100, 101, 106, 175, 202, 203, 212, 222, 248

Psychological 3, 10

Purchasing 54, 160

Q

Qualitative 12

Questionnaires 12, 16, 92

Questions 12, 86, 113, 129, 132, 133, 165, 254

R

Recommended 104, 105, 220

Reference 1, 3, 9, 273, 276

Relationship 2, 4, 5, 6, 8, 9, 15, 43, 44, 50, 57, 62, 69, 70, 72, 76, 78, 80, 88, 116, 119, 124,

131, 151, 156, 157, 169, 174, 182, 234, 269, 275

Reliability 51, 55, 93, 232

Reporting 27, 28, 49, 234

Research 3, 38, 46, 55, 74, 77, 80, 81, 82, 92, 100, 139, 140, 153

Response 7, 12, 42, 110, 125, 157, 165, 166, 173, 220, 274

Restaurant 51, 186, 188

Revenue 32, 33, 36, 37, 45, 47, 181, 268, 270, 274, 275, 276

S

Situation 6, 99, 147, 157, 189, 192, 235, 251, 261, 263

Socioeconomic 143

Strategy 47, 50, 51, 52, 53, 56, 61, 65, 75, 76, 77, 276

Surveys 28, 264

T

Target 188, 191, 267, 269, 271, 273

Technology 30, 81, 86, 107, 124, 208, 225, 228, 232, 234, 235, 236, 238, 239, 240, 245, 249

Tendering 250, 252, 264, 265, 266

Tourist 34, 41, 42, 48, 86, 107, 207, 212, 241

Turnover 2, 28, 98, 176, 181, 246

U

Unique 44, 48, 173, 182, 197, 234

Universities 48, 187, 188

V

Validity 247, 249

Variance 47, 60, 77, 94, 97

W

Waiting 108, 210, 255

Wider 2, 134, 208

Y

Younger 109, 127, 152, 160, 177

Z

Zeitung 193, 195

Zero 62, 63, 65, 69